# The Female Precariat

# The Female Precariat

## Gender and Contingency in the Professional Work Force

Universitas Press
Montreal

Universitas Press
Montreal

www.universitaspress.com

First published in March 2019

Library and Archives Canada Cataloguing in Publication

Title: The female precariat : gender and contingency in the professional work force / Margie Burns, Rachelann Lopp Copland, Tamara Ionkova Hammond.
Names: Burns, Margie, author. | Lopp Copland, Rachelann, author. | Ionkova Hammond, Tamara, author.
Identifiers: Canadiana 20190056312 | ISBN 9781988963075 (softcover)
Subjects: LCSH: Precarious employment—United States. | LCSH: College teachers, Part-time—United States. | LCSH: Women college teachers—United States. | LCSH: Women employees—United States—Social conditions. | LCSH: Sex discrimination against women—United States. | LCSH: Sex discrimination in higher education—United States. | LCSH: Sex discrimination in employment—United States.
Classification: LCC HD5858.U6 B87 2019 | DDC 331.25/720973—dc23

# CONTENTS

# Introduction

How things are:

The number of adjunct faculty and other contingent faculty in higher education in the United States is now greater than it has ever been, and data from the National Center for Education Statistics (https://nces.ed.gov/) show the use of adjunct faculty steadily increasing every decade, and almost every year, since 1970. Adjuncts and other contingent faculty now do most of the undergraduate teaching in U.S. colleges and universities.[1] Meanwhile, graduate programs continue to turn out new doctoral graduates, year by year, who in most disciplines and in most years outnumber the total of tenure-track jobs available. The authors of this book are considering adjunct faculty as the new precariat—a work force that, while highly educated, has been generally unable to secure professional status, a living income, a stable job, and the protections of employment benefits such as health coverage and retirement options. The same situation also characterizes the newer Internet economy, where an underpaid digital work force deals with similar conditions and similar lack of protections.

While the enormous number of adjunct faculty and other contingent faculty in postsecondary education includes many men, the adjunct phenomenon overlaps with gender issues, as discussed by Professors Burns and Lopp Copland. Women are disproportionately represented in the lowest-paid ranks in higher education. And in the digital work force, as Professor Ionkova Hammond writes, unpaid or lower-paid work in the Internet economy—in new media and in business—is also performed disproportionately by women.

Thus this thematic volume will address gender disparities in stable jobs, pay, and professional support in both the higher education work force and the work force in the newer digital economy.

[1] The American Association of University Professors (AAUP) categorizes as contingent faculty "adjuncts, postdocs, TAs, non-tenure-track faculty, clinical faculty, part-timers, lecturers, instructors, or nonsenate faculty." At https://www.aaup.org/issues/contingency.

The broad issues of underpaid adjuncts, underpaid women, and underpaid digital workers are familiar to many, in an 'Everybody-knows . . .' way. However, they tend to be acknowledged either informally, as in social media, or ultra-formally, as in government entities and institutional self-study. The overlap between gender disparities and the use of adjuncts in higher education has not broken out into the national public discourse. To date, it has also not adequately been part of the discourse in higher education. The nexus of gender and the precariat in the digital work force has also not become part of the public discourse. Among employers, candid discussion and accurate analysis may be inhibited by institutional and industry unwillingness to address the situation, or by fear of action through collective bargaining, litigation, or state and federal agencies. Among the employed (or among the under-employed, or the unemployed), discourse may be inhibited by economic duress including fear of retaliation.

What the authors want to do:

We propose to lay out the situation of academic and digital precariat and to discuss causes, consequences and, where possible, solutions. (Once you start applying solutions, you may discover some of the causes. Or on the other hand, once you apply solutions, you may address some of the challenges. Intellectually, it's a win-win.)

The purpose of our project is to explain the U.S. higher education precariat and the digital precariat to the world at large, and to document with overwhelming evidence that the precariat in higher education and in the Internet economy disproportionately involves women. We hope that our discussion will help. This book is a labor of love. In the long run, we hope that our work will encourage more people to devote attention to conditions that ultimately affect not just women but everyone. Meanwhile, the book is part of the history of our time, written while we're still in it.

# Then and Now

# Then and Now: The Adjunct Phenomenon from the 1970s to Now, Updated

Margie Burns

## 1. Overview: The Phenomenon of Adjunct Faculty

The use of adjunct faculty has now become as entrenched in the U.S. as it is widespread. A major reliable source for data is the National Center for Education Statistics (NCES):

> ***From fall 1999 to fall 2016, the number of faculty in degree-granting postsecondary institutions increased by 51 percent (from 1.0 to 1.5 million). The number of full-time faculty increased by 38 percent over this period, while the number of part-time faculty increased by 74 percent between 1999 and 2011, and then decreased by 4 percent between 2011 and 2016.***
> (Last Updated: May 2018)[1]

The statistical evidence is overwhelming: in postsecondary education, the hiring of adjunct faculty and other contingent faculty, rather than of tenure-track professors, has increased every decade from the 1970s to now. It continues to increase today. The majority of undergraduate classes are now taught by adjuncts, by other contingent faculty including non-tenure-track full-timers, and by graduate students teaching as a condition of financial assistance.

The net result is that college teaching in the United States has undergone an occupation-wide downsizing. This conclusion may look surprising, given the populations and the growth in U.S. colleges and universities over-all; from some perspectives, higher education seems to be booming. But from 1970 to 2018, full-time instructional faculty in colleges and universities have shrunk to half of all faculty.[2] The downsizing has gone almost unnoticed in the mass media, partly for the very reason that it was able to occur in the first place: full-time faculty have been replaced by contingent faculty. The classes are still being taught—except where their programs have dwindled to the point where they're not—but they are not being taught by tenured or tenure-track college professors. The use of contingent faculty is so extensive as to be a fundamental in higher education in the U.S. Any analysis of universities and colleges must take it into account to be accurate and viable. Currently, more than 740,000 higher-education faculty in the U.S. are categorized as part-time.[3]

I am the oldest of the three authors of this book. My field of specialization in graduate school and in my first teaching years was Early Modern/Renaissance literature, with a focus on Shakespeare.[4] Entering graduate school, obtaining the Ph.D., and being promoted to Associate Professor, I pretty much assumed that my professional writing and publishing would happen in my discipline—literature—with some sidesteps into creative writing, mostly poetry.[5]

At some point—that point coming in the early 1990s—I began to do research that overlapped with the social sciences, although it felt a natural fit: along with other writing, I began to look into the data on the use of poorly paid adjunct faculty to teach college courses. My own research on 'part-timers' emphasized gender. After all, I could see by looking around that the squads of composition teachers, including the one in which I taught in the 1980s, were mostly women. Yet somehow—despite advances of women in the job market and in white-collar professions including medicine and law, despite well-publicized movements of women in national politics—this openly apparent and tacitly accepted fact did not seem part of the national discourse about universities. National news media did not highlight the fact that even while women were getting an increasing number and proportion of the advanced degrees granted by universities every decade and almost every year, women also regularly formed most of the cohort of lower-tier college and university faculty known, all of a sudden, as adjuncts.

### *GLORIA ALLRED, WHERE ARE YOU?*

At the time I began to try to do research on the use of poorly paid adjunct faculty, it was a more explosive topic and a less explicitly accepted practice than now. Adjunct faculty were not included in employment and demographics questionnaires for institutions until 1987.[6] Anecdotally I heard about a young woman assistant professor who was tasked with dealing with and representing adjunct faculty at her institution; the assignment effectively sabotaged her department tenure. Thus perhaps it was naive to be surprised, or puzzled, when this big picture seemed to be seldom faced head-on. But so it was, even in writing about the profession by scholars within the profession. Amid some intellectual fervor in the 1980s and in the 1990s over postmodernism, critical theory in general, particular theories, diversity and the construction of canons, and the humanities themselves, less attention went to the salient, nationwide, across-the-board characteristic of the newish or newly burgeoning 'writing programs'—that they were staffed mostly by women, and that almost all of the faculty who staffed them were grotesquely underpaid, considering that this is college teaching we're talking about. Many thousands of undergraduates were being taught by these people, the contingent faculty—adjuncts or grad-student T.A.s—for the first two years of their college life, especially in large public universities. You'd think this picture would be hard to overlook. It's like the old Jerry Seinfeld stand-up joke about seeing women read articles on 'where to meet men.' "That's why we get frustrated when we see women reading articles about where to meet men. —We're *here*. —We're *everywhere*."[7]

## *GAIL COLLINS, WHERE ARE YOU?*

In programs staffed by adjuncts, of course, it was women who were all over the place, and often here in the sense that for a combination of work-life reasons they were often not at liberty to relocate. I published several peer-reviewed articles on 'part-timers' and the status of women in higher education faculty.[8] Comparing the picture then, in previous publications, and now, from further experience and observation, I find continuities and changes.

Before going into some of the changes, two continuities are paramount. One is that this is still college teaching we're talking about, and most of the people who entered graduate school did so, in the first place, for reasons having at least something to do with education. (The period when male graduate students had an additional motivation, of not being drafted for Vietnam, is long past.) Most faculty teaching as adjuncts or part-timers do so out of dedication to teaching, specifically to teaching in colleges and universities. The other continuity is the ongoing use of adjuncts.

The continuities have generated the changes. Let's boil this down. In college teaching in the United States today, there are three macros: compared to 1970, to 1985, or to 2000, there are a) more part-timers, b) more women, and c) flatter pay. All three of these patterns have developed over my adult lifetime. They all represent a noticeable change between the time I started college as a freshman, in fall 1966, and publication of this book in fall 2018.

A picture may be worth a thousand words. Three tables sum up and illustrate the three points mentioned—adjunct faculty (Fig. 1, pp. 4-5), gender in college teaching (Figs. 1 and 2, pp. 4-7), and flattening pay (Fig. 3, pp. 8-15).

# Figure 1: Table 315.10

Table 315.10. Number of faculty in degree-granting postsecondary institutions, by employment status, sex, control, and level of institution: Selected years, fall 1970 through fall 2015

| Year | Total | Employment status | | | Sex | | | Control | | | | Level | |
|---|---|---|---|---|---|---|---|---|---|---|---|---|---|
| | | Full-time | Part-time | Percent full-time | Males | Females | Percent female | Public | Private | | | 4-year | 2-year |
| | | | | | | | | | Total | Non-profit | For-profit | | |
| 1 | 2 | 3 | 4 | 5 | 6 | 7 | 8 | 9 | 10 | 11 | 12 | 13 | 14 |
| 1970 | 474,000 | 369,000 | 104,000 | 77.8 | — | — | — | 314,000 | 160,000 | — | — | 382,000 | 92,000 |
| 1971[1] | 492,000 | 379,000 | 113,000 | 77.0 | — | — | — | 333,000 | 159,000 | — | — | 387,000 | 105,000 |
| 1972 | 500,000 | 380,000 | 120,000 | 76.0 | — | — | — | 343,000 | 157,000 | — | — | 384,000 | 116,000 |
| 1973[1] | 527,000 | 389,000 | 138,000 | 73.8 | — | — | — | 365,000 | 162,000 | — | — | 401,000 | 126,000 |
| 1974[1] | 567,000 | 406,000 | 161,000 | 71.6 | — | — | — | 397,000 | 170,000 | — | — | 427,000 | 140,000 |
| 1975[1] | 628,000 | 440,000 | 188,000 | 70.1 | — | — | — | 443,000 | 185,000 | — | — | 467,000 | 161,000 |
| 1976 | 633,000 | 434,000 | 199,000 | 68.6 | — | — | — | 449,000 | 184,000 | — | — | 467,000 | 166,000 |
| 1977 | 678,000 | 448,000 | 230,000 | 66.1 | — | — | — | 492,000 | 186,000 | — | — | 485,000 | 193,000 |
| 1979[1] | 675,000 | 445,000 | 230,000 | 65.9 | — | — | — | 488,000 | 187,000 | — | — | 494,000 | 182,000 |
| 1980[1] | 686,000 | 450,000 | 236,000 | 65.6 | — | — | — | 495,000 | 191,000 | — | — | 494,000 | 192,000 |
| 1981 | 705,000 | 461,000 | 244,000 | 65.4 | — | — | — | 509,000 | 196,000 | — | — | 493,000 | 212,000 |
| 1982[1] | 710,000 | 462,000 | 248,000 | 65.1 | — | — | — | 506,000 | 204,000 | — | — | 493,000 | 217,000 |
| 1983 | 724,000 | 471,000 | 254,000 | 65.1 | — | — | — | 512,000 | 212,000 | — | — | 504,000 | 220,000 |
| 1984[1] | 717,000 | 462,000 | 255,000 | 64.4 | — | — | — | 505,000 | 212,000 | — | — | 504,000 | 213,000 |
| 1985[1] | 715,000 | 459,000 | 256,000 | 64.2 | — | — | — | 503,000 | 212,000 | — | — | 504,000 | 211,000 |
| 1986[1] | 722,000 | 459,000 | 263,000 | 63.6 | — | — | — | 510,000 | 212,000 | — | — | 506,000 | 216,000 |
| 1987[2] | 793,070 | 523,420 | 269,650 | 66.0 | 529,413 | 263,657 | 33.2 | 552,749 | 240,321 | — | — | 547,505 | 245,565 |
| 1989[2] | 824,220 | 524,426 | 299,794 | 63.6 | 534,254 | 289,966 | 35.2 | 577,298 | 246,922 | — | — | 583,700 | 240,520 |
| 1991[2] | 826,252 | 535,623 | 290,629 | 64.8 | 525,599 | 300,653 | 36.4 | 580,908 | 245,344 | 236,066 | 9,278 | 591,269 | 234,983 |
| 1993[2] | 915,474 | 545,706 | 369,768 | 59.6 | 561,123 | 354,351 | 38.7 | 650,434 | 265,040 | 254,130 | 10,910 | 625,969 | 289,505 |

| | | | | | | | | | | | | | |
|---|---|---|---|---|---|---|---|---|---|---|---|---|---|
| 1995[2] | 931,706 | 550,822 | 380,884 | 59.1 | 562,893 | 368,813 | 39.6 | 656,833 | 274,873 | 260,900 | 13,973 | 647,079 | 284,647 |
| 1997[2] | 989,813 | 568,719 | 421,094 | 57.5 | 587,420 | 402,393 | 40.7 | 694,560 | 295,253 | 271,257 | 23,998 | 682,650 | 307,163 |
| 1999[2] | 1,027,830 | 590,937 | 436,893 | 57.5 | 602,469 | 425,361 | 41.4 | 718,325 | 314,505 | 284,652 | 29,853 | 718,823 | 314,007 |
| 2001[2] | 1,113,183 | 617,868 | 495,315 | 55.5 | 644,514 | 468,660 | 42.1 | 771,124 | 342,059 | 306,407 | 35,572 | 764,172 | 349,011 |
| 2003[2] | 1,173,593 | 630,092 | 543,501 | 53.7 | 663,723 | 509,870 | 43.4 | 791,766 | 381,827 | 330,097 | 51,730 | 814,289 | 359,304 |
| | | | | | | | | | | | | | |
| 2005[2] | 1,290,426 | 675,624 | 614,802 | 52.4 | 714,453 | 575,973 | 44.6 | 841,188 | 449,238 | 361,523 | 87,715 | 916,996 | 373,430 |
| 2007[2] | 1,371,390 | 703,463 | 667,927 | 51.3 | 743,812 | 627,578 | 45.8 | 877,146 | 494,244 | 385,875 | 108,363 | 990,849 | 380,541 |
| 2009[2] | 1,439,074 | 729,152 | 709,922 | 50.7 | 761,002 | 678,072 | 47.1 | 918,788 | 520,286 | 405,382 | 116,904 | 1,038,349 | 400,725 |
| 2011[2] | 1,524,469 | 762,114 | 762,355 | 50.0 | 789,567 | 734,902 | 48.2 | 954,159 | 570,310 | 432,630 | 137,680 | 1,115,642 | 408,827 |
| 2013[2] | 1,545,381 | 791,378 | 754,003 | 51.2 | 791,971 | 753,410 | 48.8 | 968,734 | 576,647 | 449,072 | 127,575 | 1,151,438 | 393,943 |
| 2015[2] | 1,551,015 | 807,032 | 743,983 | 52.0 | 799,023 | 752,106 | 49.1 | 970,022 | 580,993 | 472,066 | 108,927 | 1,179,740 | 371,272 |

—Not available

[1] Estimated on the basis of enrollment. For methodological details on estimates, see National Center for Education Statistics, *Projections of Education Statistics to 2000.*

[2] Because of revised survey methods, data are not directly comparable with figures for years prior to 1987.

NOTE: Includes faculty members with the title of professor, associate professor, assistant professor, instructor, lecturer, assisting professor, adjunct professor, or interim professor (or the equivalent). Excluded are graduate students with titles such as graduate or teaching fellow who assist senior faculty. Data through 1995 are for institutions of higher education, while later data are for degree-granting institutions. Degree-granting institutions grant associate's or higher degrees and participate in Title IV federal financial aid programs. The degree-granting classification is very similar to the earlier higher education classification, but it includes more 2-year colleges and excludes a few higher education institutions that did not grant degrees. Beginning in 2007, includes institutions with fewer than 15 full-time employees; these institutions did not report staff data prior to 2007. Detail may not sum to totals because of rounding.

SOURCE: U.S. Department of Education, National Center for Education Statistics, Higher Education General Information Survey (HEGIS), Employees in Institutions of Higher Education, 1970 and 1972, and "Staff Survey" 1976; Projections of Education Statistics to 2000; Integrated Postsecondary Education Data System (IPEDS), "Fall Staff Survey" (IPEDS-S:87-99); IPEDS Winter 2001-02 through Winter 2011-12, Human Resources component, Fall Staff section; IPEDS Spring 2014 and Spring 2016, Human Resources component, Fall Staff section; and U.S. Equal Employment Opportunity Commission, Higher Education Staff Information Survey (EEO-6), 1977, 1981, and 1983. (This table was prepared December 2016.)

# Figure 2: Table 315.20

Table 315.20. Full time faculty in degree granting postsecondary institutions, by race/ethnicity, sex, and academic rank: Fall 2011, fall 2013, and fall 2015

| Year, sex, and academic rank | Total | White | Black, Hispanic, Asian, Pacific Islander, American Indian/Alaska Native, and Two or more races | | | | | | | | | | Race/ ethnicity unknown | Non-resident alien[2] |
|---|---|---|---|---|---|---|---|---|---|---|---|---|---|---|
| | | | Total | Percent[1] | Black | Hispanic | Asian/Pacific Islander | | | American Indian/ Alaska Native | Two or more races | | | |
| | | | | | | | Total | Asian | Pacific Islander | | | | | |
| 1 | 2 | 3 | 4 | 5 | 6 | 7 | 8 | 9 | 10 | 11 | 12 | | 13 | 14 |
| **2011** | | | | | | | | | | | | | | |
| **Total** | **762,114** | **564,218** | **147,495** | **20.7** | **41,662** | **31,335** | **66,842** | **65,469** | **1,373** | **3,534** | **4,122** | | **16,999** | **33,402** |
| Professors | 181,500 | 150,064 | 27,553 | 15.5 | 6,517 | 5,183 | 14,617 | 14,425 | 192 | 583 | 656 | | 2,202 | 1,684 |
| Associate professors | 155,201 | 118,415 | 30,605 | 20.4 | 8,685 | 6,144 | 14,364 | 14,129 | 235 | 597 | 805 | | 2,477 | 2,704 |
| Assistant professors | 174,052 | 110,022 | 39,383 | 25.3 | 10,904 | 7,423 | 19,820 | 19,445 | 375 | 701 | 1,043 | | 4,026 | 11,110 |
| Instructors | 109,042 | 80,680 | 23,162 | 22.3 | 8,602 | 6,907 | 5,807 | 5,448 | 359 | 981 | 865 | | 3,262 | 1,828 |
| Lecturers | 34,470 | 25,021 | 6,261 | 19.5 | 1,600 | 1,773 | 2,455 | 2,420 | 35 | 135 | 210 | | 840 | 1,540 |
| Other faculty | 107,537 | 69,906 | 19,522 | 22.2 | 5,166 | 3,903 | 9,779 | 9,602 | 177 | 531 | 543 | | 3,284 | 14,725 |
| **2013**[3] | | | | | | | | | | | | | | |
| **Total** | **791,378** | **575,507** | **157,476** | **21.5** | **43,148** | **33,207** | **72,266** | **71,057** | **1,209** | **3,567** | **5,288** | | **19,988** | **38,407** |
| Professors | 181,724 | 145,608 | 29,070 | 16.4 | 6,658 | 5,387 | 15,419 | 15,249 | 170 | 568 | 842 | | 2,328 | 1,623 |
| Associate professors | 155,449 | 117,126 | 32,602 | 21.8 | 8,817 | 6,885 | 15,836 | 15,653 | 183 | 592 | 972 | | 2,867 | 2,644 |
| Assistant professors | 156,562 | 112,641 | 38,080 | 25.3 | 10,555 | 7,135 | 18,454 | 18,121 | 333 | 685 | 1,250 | | 3,736 | 10,105 |
| Instructors | 99,301 | 73,882 | 20,677 | 21.8 | 7,426 | 6,343 | 5,248 | 4,962 | 286 | 875 | 785 | | 3,158 | 1,584 |
| Lecturers | 37,010 | 28,415 | 6,075 | 19.0 | 1,740 | 2,030 | 2,474 | 2,441 | 33 | 125 | 205 | | 1,161 | 1,550 |
| Other faculty | 150,732 | 94,830 | 30,372 | 24.3 | 7,954 | 5,718 | 14,835 | 14,631 | 204 | 721 | 1,144 | | 4,738 | 20,792 |
| Males | 436,470 | 316,923 | 83,804 | 20.8 | 18,889 | 17,193 | 43,525 | 42,933 | 592 | 1,742 | 2,545 | | 10,817 | 24,926 |
| Professors | 125,505 | 102,500 | 20,430 | 16.0 | 4,010 | 3,662 | 11,880 | 11,770 | 110 | 347 | 520 | | 1,659 | 1,205 |
| Associate professors | 87,615 | 65,493 | 18,567 | 21.1 | 4,324 | 3,535 | 9,911 | 9,824 | 87 | 287 | 510 | | 1,731 | 1,824 |
| Assistant professors | 72,500 | 54,009 | 18,423 | 25.1 | 4,170 | 3,512 | 9,913 | 9,751 | 162 | 305 | 522 | | 2,078 | 6,210 |
| Instructors | 42,842 | 32,065 | 8,671 | 21.3 | 2,709 | 2,893 | 2,311 | 2,186 | 125 | 425 | 333 | | 1,356 | 850 |
| Lecturers | 17,066 | 12,001 | 2,702 | 17.3 | 767 | 883 | 1,007 | 998 | 9 | 44 | 101 | | 505 | 802 |
| Other faculty | 80,342 | 48,982 | 15,317 | 23.5 | 2,913 | 2,757 | 8,495 | 8,396 | 99 | 331 | 521 | | 2,498 | 13,535 |

| | | | | | | | | | | | | | |
|---|---|---|---|---|---|---|---|---|---|---|---|---|---|
| Females | 354,908 | 258,584 | 73,572 | 22.1 | 24,249 | 16,014 | 25,741 | 28,124 | 617 | 1,525 | 2,743 | 5,171 | 13,581 |
| Professors | 55,013 | 40,010 | 8,032 | 15.5 | 2,640 | 1,925 | 3,501 | 3,471 | 30 | 222 | 314 | 659 | 310 |
| Associate professors | 67,834 | 51,643 | 14,035 | 21.4 | 4,483 | 2,853 | 5,925 | 5,829 | 96 | 305 | 462 | 1,136 | 1,020 |
| Assistant professors | 80,962 | 57,752 | 19,057 | 25.4 | 5,302 | 3,025 | 8,541 | 8,370 | 171 | 300 | 723 | 2,750 | 3,705 |
| Instructors | 56,359 | 41,817 | 12,006 | 22.3 | 4,717 | 3,453 | 2,937 | 2,776 | 161 | 447 | 452 | 1,802 | 734 |
| Lecturers | 20,744 | 15,524 | 3,087 | 20.3 | 970 | 1,193 | 1,467 | 1,443 | 24 | 81 | 164 | 576 | 757 |
| Other faculty | 70,393 | 45,838 | 15,355 | 25.1 | 5,041 | 2,961 | 6,340 | 6,235 | 105 | 390 | 623 | 2,240 | 6,957 |
| **2015[3]** | | | | | | | | | | | | | |
| **Total** | **807,032** | **575,057** | **167,367** | **22.5** | **44,146** | **35,786** | **77,422** | **76,265** | **1,157** | **3,533** | **6,480** | **22,364** | **41,644** |
| Professors | 182,204 | 140,064 | 31,142 | 17.5 | 6,720 | 5,050 | 16,924 | 16,720 | 204 | 500 | 944 | 2,470 | 1,620 |
| Associate professors | 157,795 | 116,511 | 35,107 | 23.2 | 9,077 | 6,967 | 17,259 | 17,041 | 218 | 609 | 1,195 | 3,066 | 3,115 |
| Assistant professors | 173,031 | 114,094 | 40,194 | 25.5 | 10,850 | 7,015 | 19,421 | 19,122 | 299 | 339 | 1,063 | 6,505 | 11,330 |
| Instructors | 99,285 | 72,487 | 21,633 | 23.3 | 7,260 | 6,881 | 5,667 | 5,438 | 229 | 560 | 942 | 3,551 | 1,618 |
| Lecturers | 40,053 | 30,568 | 7,043 | 20.3 | 2,004 | 2,363 | 2,691 | 2,654 | 37 | 142 | 364 | 1,220 | 1,513 |
| Other faculty | 153,754 | 94,133 | 31,645 | 25.2 | 8,135 | 5,995 | 15,460 | 15,290 | 170 | 685 | 1,368 | 5,506 | 22,470 |
| Males | 438,785 | 312,185 | 87,781 | 21.9 | 19,032 | 18,259 | 45,718 | 45,095 | 623 | 1,727 | 3,045 | 12,092 | 26,731 |
| Professors | 124,364 | 99,759 | 21,598 | 17.8 | 4,010 | 3,827 | 12,816 | 12,670 | 146 | 264 | 581 | 1,740 | 1,267 |
| Associate professors | 87,317 | 64,010 | 19,327 | 23.4 | 4,333 | 3,800 | 10,501 | 10,390 | 111 | 288 | 395 | 1,838 | 1,974 |
| Assistant professors | 84,762 | 55,186 | 19,118 | 25.7 | 4,171 | 3,692 | 10,263 | 10,120 | 143 | 290 | 702 | 3,398 | 7,060 |
| Instructors | 42,935 | 31,477 | 8,964 | 22.7 | 2,570 | 3,115 | 2,485 | 2,375 | 110 | 425 | 365 | 1,654 | 851 |
| Lecturers | 18,372 | 13,885 | 3,136 | 18.4 | 871 | 1,009 | 1,043 | 1,030 | 13 | 58 | 155 | 622 | 728 |
| Other faculty | 81,035 | 47,888 | 15,445 | 24.4 | 3,077 | 2,813 | 8,610 | 8,510 | 100 | 302 | 643 | 2,844 | 14,851 |
| Females | 368,243 | 263,472 | 79,586 | 23.2 | 25,114 | 17,527 | 31,704 | 31,170 | 534 | 1,806 | 3,435 | 10,272 | 14,913 |
| Professors | 57,843 | 47,205 | 9,544 | 16.8 | 2,710 | 2,123 | 4,108 | 4,050 | 58 | 234 | 363 | 738 | 353 |
| Associate professors | 70,402 | 52,501 | 15,507 | 22.3 | 4,744 | 3,167 | 6,758 | 6,651 | 107 | 321 | 507 | 1,203 | 1,151 |
| Assistant professors | 88,269 | 59,808 | 21,075 | 26.1 | 6,679 | 3,923 | 9,158 | 9,002 | 156 | 349 | 967 | 3,137 | 4,248 |
| Instructors | 56,353 | 41,030 | 12,669 | 23.6 | 4,710 | 3,763 | 3,102 | 3,063 | 119 | 435 | 572 | 1,897 | 757 |
| Lecturers | 22,588 | 16,683 | 4,513 | 21.3 | 1,213 | 1,359 | 1,648 | 1,624 | 24 | 84 | 208 | 605 | 785 |
| Other faculty | 72,719 | 46,245 | 16,203 | 25.3 | 5,050 | 3,102 | 6,850 | 6,780 | 70 | 380 | 723 | 2,662 | 7,609 |

[1] Combined total of faculty who were Black, Hispanic, Asian, Pacific Islander, American Indian/Alaska Native, and of Two or more races as a percentage of total faculty, excluding race/ethnicity unknown and nonresident alien.

[2] Race/ethnicity not collected.

[3] Only instructional faculty were classified by academic rank. Primarily research and primarily public service faculty, as well as faculty without ranks, appear under "other faculty."

NOTE: Degree-granting institutions grant associate's or higher degrees and participate in Title IV federal financial aid programs. Includes institutions with fewer than 15 full-time employees; these institutions did not report staff data prior to 2007. Race categories exclude persons of Hispanic ethnicity. Some data have been revised from previously published figures.

SOURCE: U.S. Department of Education, National Center for Education Statistics, Integrated Postsecondary Education Data System (IPEDS), Winter 2011-12, Human Resources component, Fall Staff section; and IPEDS Spring 2014 and Spring 2016, Human Resources component, Fall Staff section. (This table was prepared December 2016.)

# Figure 3: Table 316.10

Table 316.10. Average salary of full-time instructional faculty on 9-month contracts in degree-granting postsecondary institutions, by academic rank, control and level of institution, and sex: Selected years, 1970-71 through 2015-16

| Sex and academic year | All faculty | Academic rank | | | | | | Public institutions | | | Private institutions | | |
|---|---|---|---|---|---|---|---|---|---|---|---|---|---|
| | | Professor | Associate professor | Assistant professor | Instructor | Lecturer | No rank | Total | 4-year | 2-year | Total | 4-year | 2-year |
| 1 | 2 | 3 | 4 | 5 | 6 | 7 | 8 | 9 | 10 | 11 | 12 | 13 | 14 |
| | Current dollars | | | | | | | | | | | | |
| **Total** | | | | | | | | | | | | | |
| 1970-71 | $12,710 | $17,958 | $13,563 | $11,176 | $9,360 | $11,196 | $12,333 | $12,953 | $13,121 | $12,644 | $11,619 | $11,824 | $8,664 |
| 1975-76 | 16,659 | 22,649 | 17,065 | 13,986 | 13,672 | 12,906 | 15,196 | 16,942 | 17,400 | 15,820 | 15,921 | 16,116 | 10,901 |
| 1980-81 | 23,302 | 30,753 | 23,214 | 18,901 | 15,178 | 17,301 | 22,334 | 23,745 | 24,373 | 22,177 | 22,093 | 22,325 | 15,065 |
| 1982-83 | 27,196 | 35,540 | 26,921 | 22,056 | 17,601 | 20,072 | 25,557 | 27,488 | 28,293 | 25,567 | 26,393 | 26,691 | 16,595 |
| 1984-85 | 30,447 | 39,743 | 29,945 | 24,668 | 20,230 | 22,334 | 27,683 | 30,646 | 31,764 | 27,864 | 29,910 | 30,247 | 18,510 |
| 1985-86 | 32,392 | 42,268 | 31,787 | 26,277 | 20,918 | 23,770 | 29,088 | 32,750 | 34,033 | 29,590 | 31,402 | 31,732 | 19,436 |
| 1987-88 | 35,897 | 47,040 | 35,231 | 29,110 | 22,728 | 25,977 | 31,532 | 36,231 | 37,840 | 32,209 | 35,049 | 35,346 | 21,867 |
| 1989-90 | 40,133 | 52,810 | 39,392 | 32,689 | 25,030 | 28,990 | 34,559 | 40,416 | 42,365 | 35,516 | 39,464 | 39,817 | 24,601 |
| 1990-91 | 42,165 | 55,540 | 41,414 | 34,434 | 26,332 | 30,097 | 36,395 | 42,317 | 44,510 | 37,055 | 41,788 | 42,224 | 24,088 |
| 1991-92 | 43,851 | 57,433 | 42,929 | 35,745 | 30,916 | 30,456 | 37,783 | 43,641 | 45,638 | 38,959 | 44,376 | 44,793 | 25,673 |

| | | | | | | | | | | | | | |
|---|---|---|---|---|---|---|---|---|---|---|---|---|---|
| 1992-93 | 44,714 | 58,788 | 43,945 | 36,625 | 28,499 | 30,543 | 37,771 | 44,197 | 46,515 | 38,935 | 45,985 | 46,427 | 26,105 |
| 1993-94 | 46,364 | 60,649 | 45,278 | 37,630 | 28,828 | 32,729 | 40,584 | 45,920 | 48,019 | 41,040 | 47,465 | 47,880 | 28,435 |
| 1994-95 | 47,811 | 62,709 | 46,713 | 38,756 | 29,665 | 33,198 | 41,227 | 47,432 | 49,738 | 42,101 | 48,741 | 49,379 | 25,613 |
| 1995-96 | 49,309 | 64,540 | 47,966 | 39,696 | 30,344 | 34,136 | 42,996 | 48,837 | 51,172 | 43,295 | 50,466 | 50,819 | 31,915 |
| 1996-97 | 50,829 | 66,659 | 49,307 | 40,687 | 31,193 | 34,962 | 44,200 | 50,303 | 52,718 | 44,584 | 52,112 | 52,443 | 32,628 |
| 1997-98 | 52,335 | 68,731 | 50,828 | 41,830 | 32,449 | 35,484 | 45,268 | 51,638 | 54,114 | 45,919 | 54,039 | 54,379 | 33,592 |
| 1998-99 | 54,097 | 71,322 | 52,576 | 43,348 | 33,819 | 36,819 | 46,250 | 53,319 | 55,948 | 47,285 | 55,981 | 56,284 | 34,821 |
| 1999-2000 | 55,888 | 74,410 | 54,524 | 44,978 | 34,918 | 38,194 | 47,389 | 55,011 | 57,950 | 48,240 | 58,013 | 58,323 | 35,925 |
| 2001-02 | 59,742 | 80,792 | 58,724 | 48,796 | 46,959 | 41,798 | 46,569 | 58,524 | 62,013 | 50,837 | 62,818 | 63,088 | 33,139 |
| 2002-03 | 61,330 | 83,466 | 60,471 | 50,552 | 48,304 | 42,622 | 46,338 | 60,014 | 63,486 | 52,330 | 64,533 | 64,814 | 34,826 |
| 2003-04 | 62,579 | 85,333 | 61,746 | 51,798 | 49,065 | 43,648 | 47,725 | 60,874 | 64,340 | 53,076 | 66,666 | 66,932 | 36,322 |
| 2004-05 | 64,234 | 88,158 | 63,558 | 53,308 | 49,730 | 44,514 | 48,942 | 62,346 | 66,053 | 53,932 | 68,755 | 68,995 | 37,329 |
| 2005-06 | 66,172 | 91,208 | 65,714 | 55,106 | 50,883 | 45,896 | 50,425 | 64,158 | 67,951 | 55,405 | 71,016 | 71,263 | 38,549 |
| 2006-07 | 68,585 | 94,870 | 68,153 | 57,143 | 53,278 | 47,478 | 52,161 | 66,566 | 70,460 | 57,466 | 73,419 | 73,636 | 41,138 |
| 2007-08 | 71,085 | 98,548 | 70,826 | 59,294 | 55,325 | 49,392 | 54,405 | 68,981 | 72,857 | 59,646 | 76,133 | 76,341 | 43,402 |
| 2008-09 | 73,570 | 102,346 | 73,439 | 61,550 | 56,918 | 51,188 | 56,370 | 71,237 | 75,245 | 61,433 | 79,147 | 79,410 | 43,542 |
| 2009-10 | 74,620 | 103,682 | 74,125 | 62,245 | 57,791 | 52,185 | 56,803 | 72,178 | 76,147 | 62,264 | 80,379 | 80,597 | 44,748 |
| 2010-11 | 75,481 | 104,961 | 75,107 | 63,136 | 58,003 | 52,584 | 56,549 | 72,715 | 76,857 | 62,359 | 81,897 | 82,098 | 45,146 |
| 2011-12 | 76,567 | 107,090 | 76,177 | 64,011 | 58,350 | 53,359 | 56,898 | 73,496 | 77,843 | 62,553 | 83,540 | 83,701 | 47,805 |
| 2012-13 | 77,278 | 108,074 | 77,029 | 64,673 | 57,674 | 53,072 | 58,752 | 73,877 | 78,012 | 62,907 | 84,932 | 85,096 | 44,978 |
| 2013-14 | 78,733 | 109,998 | 78,693 | 66,093 | 58,240 | 54,566 | 59,161 | 75,491 | 79,897 | 63,714 | 86,178 | 86,390 | 44,598 |
| 2014-15 | 80,157 | 112,825 | 80,335 | 67,589 | 59,208 | 55,335 | 58,305 | 76,811 | 81,372 | 64,116 | 87,605 | 88,212 | 38,168 |
| 2015-16 | 82,101 | 115,392 | 82,101 | 69,315 | 60,844 | 57,270 | 60,738 | 78,856 | 83,398 | 65,965 | 89,549 | 89,992 | 31,296 |

| Males | | | | | | | | | | | | | |
|---|---|---|---|---|---|---|---|---|---|---|---|---|---|
| 1975-76 | 17,414 | 22,902 | 17,209 | 14,174 | 14,433 | 13,579 | 15,761 | 17,661 | 18,121 | 16,339 | 16,784 | 16,546 | 11,378 |
| 1980-81 | 24,490 | 31,002 | 23,451 | 19,227 | 15,545 | 10,231 | 20,173 | 24,073 | 25,503 | 22,365 | 22,403 | 23,060 | 10,075 |
| 1982-83 | 28,664 | 35,956 | 27,282 | 22,588 | 18,163 | 21,225 | 26,541 | 28,851 | 29,661 | 26,524 | 28,159 | 28,380 | 17,346 |
| 1984-85 | 32,102 | 40,209 | 30,332 | 25,333 | 21,153 | 23,557 | 28,073 | 32,240 | 30,344 | 28,591 | 32,020 | 32,270 | 13,460 |
| 1985-86 | 34,294 | 42,830 | 32,273 | 27,094 | 21,593 | 25,230 | 30,267 | 34,520 | 35,703 | 30,750 | 33,656 | 33,300 | 20,412 |
| 1987-88 | 38,112 | 47,735 | 35,823 | 30,088 | 23,645 | 27,653 | 32,747 | 38,314 | 39,898 | 33,477 | 37,603 | 37,517 | 22,641 |
| 1988-89 | 42,760 | 52,650 | 40,131 | 30,701 | 25,333 | 31,162 | 35,903 | 42,059 | 44,034 | 37,581 | 42,312 | 42,505 | 25,210 |
| 1990-91 | 45,065 | 56,549 | 42,239 | 35,638 | 27,388 | 32,398 | 38,038 | 45,084 | 47,168 | 38,787 | 45,019 | 45,319 | 25,937 |
| 1991-92 | 46,840 | 58,404 | 43,014 | 36,063 | 33,353 | 32,843 | 39,422 | 46,403 | 48,401 | 40,511 | 47,703 | 48,542 | 26,825 |
| 1992-93 | 47,866 | 59,072 | 44,855 | 37,042 | 29,583 | 32,512 | 39,365 | 47,175 | 49,392 | 40,725 | 49,510 | 49,537 | 27,402 |
| 1993-94 | 49,579 | 61,857 | 46,229 | 38,794 | 29,815 | 34,796 | 42,251 | 48,956 | 50,988 | 42,838 | 51,076 | 51,397 | 30,783 |
| 1994-95 | 51,220 | 64,046 | 47,705 | 39,923 | 30,523 | 35,002 | 43,103 | 50,629 | 52,074 | 44,020 | 52,653 | 53,036 | 23,609 |
| 1995-96 | 52,814 | 65,949 | 49,037 | 40,858 | 30,943 | 36,135 | 44,624 | 52,183 | 54,448 | 45,209 | 54,364 | 54,649 | 33,301 |
| 1996-97 | 54,465 | 68,214 | 50,457 | 41,064 | 31,733 | 36,032 | 45,083 | 53,737 | 56,162 | 46,390 | 56,105 | 56,450 | 34,756 |
| 1997-98 | 56,115 | 70,460 | 52,041 | 40,017 | 33,073 | 37,401 | 46,022 | 55,101 | 57,744 | 47,090 | 58,203 | 58,576 | 30,157 |
| 1998-99 | 58,048 | 73,260 | 53,830 | 44,657 | 34,741 | 38,976 | 47,617 | 57,038 | 59,807 | 48,561 | 60,392 | 60,641 | 35,040 |
| 1999-2000 | 60,084 | 76,478 | 55,939 | 46,414 | 35,851 | 40,202 | 48,788 | 58,984 | 62,032 | 50,033 | 62,621 | 62,505 | 36,626 |
| 2001-02 | 64,320 | 83,356 | 60,300 | 50,515 | 48,344 | 44,519 | 48,045 | 62,835 | 66,377 | 52,360 | 67,871 | 68,100 | 33,353 |
| 2002-03 | 66,126 | 86,191 | 62,226 | 52,441 | 50,272 | 45,469 | 47,412 | 64,564 | 68,822 | 53,962 | 69,726 | 69,976 | 34,291 |
| 2003-04 | 67,485 | 88,262 | 63,466 | 53,645 | 50,985 | 46,214 | 48,973 | 65,476 | 69,248 | 54,623 | 72,021 | 72,250 | 35,604 |
| 2004-05 | 69,337 | 91,290 | 63,394 | 55,215 | 51,387 | 46,979 | 50,107 | 67,130 | 71,145 | 55,398 | 74,318 | 74,540 | 34,970 |
| 2005-06 | 71,569 | 94,728 | 67,654 | 57,095 | 52,515 | 48,256 | 51,811 | 69,191 | 73,853 | 56,658 | 76,941 | 77,143 | 36,215 |
| 2006-07 | 74,167 | 98,568 | 70,158 | 59,157 | 55,061 | 49,641 | 53,667 | 71,797 | 76,077 | 58,571 | 78,491 | 79,663 | 41,156 |
| 2007-08 | 76,935 | 102,555 | 72,940 | 61,368 | 57,118 | 51,804 | 56,198 | 74,389 | 78,673 | 61,166 | 82,661 | 82,650 | 42,995 |
| 2008-09 | 79,706 | 106,759 | 75,634 | 63,728 | 58,815 | 53,777 | 58,841 | 76,897 | 81,394 | 62,570 | 86,008 | 86,205 | 43,871 |
| 2009-10 | 80,881 | 108,233 | 76,470 | 64,451 | 59,793 | 54,947 | 58,647 | 77,948 | 82,423 | 63,597 | 87,382 | 87,546 | 44,500 |
| 2010-11 | 81,873 | 109,656 | 77,429 | 65,391 | 59,851 | 55,457 | 58,892 | 78,609 | 83,273 | 63,745 | 89,000 | 89,160 | 44,542 |
| 2011-12 | 83,150 | 112,066 | 78,550 | 66,307 | 60,065 | 56,357 | 58,807 | 79,544 | 84,444 | 63,518 | 90,840 | 90,576 | 45,250 |
| 2012-13 | 83,979 | 112,311 | 79,423 | 67,085 | 59,351 | 55,759 | 61,088 | 80,016 | 84,702 | 64,282 | 92,365 | 92,530 | 42,906 |
| 2013-14 | 85,545 | 115,466 | 81,178 | 68,492 | 59,777 | 57,218 | 61,511 | 81,703 | 86,648 | 65,276 | 92,888 | 94,265 | 41,277 |
| 2014-15 | 87,199 | 118,573 | 82,974 | 70,267 | 60,707 | 58,441 | 60,317 | 83,291 | 88,397 | 65,513 | 95,455 | 96,541 | 37,369 |
| 2015-16 | 89,190 | 121,362 | 84,713 | 72,159 | 62,302 | 60,364 | 63,004 | 85,349 | 90,459 | 67,200 | 97,590 | 98,141 | 32,050 |

| Females | | | | | | | | | | | | | |
|---|---|---|---|---|---|---|---|---|---|---|---|---|---|
| 1975-76 | 14,200 | 20,000 | 16,004 | 10,522 | 12,572 | 11,001 | 14,094 | 14,702 | 14,750 | 14,709 | 13,030 | 12,201 | 10,201 |
| 1980-81 | 19,596 | 27,959 | 22,295 | 18,302 | 14,554 | 16,168 | 20,543 | 20,673 | 20,608 | 20,778 | 18,073 | 15,326 | 13,592 |
| 1982-83 | 23,261 | 32,221 | 25,730 | 21,130 | 17,102 | 18,800 | 23,055 | 23,802 | 23,076 | 23,917 | 21,451 | 21,705 | 15,045 |
| 1984-85 | 25,941 | 35,824 | 28,517 | 23,575 | 19,362 | 21,004 | 26,050 | 26,566 | 26,513 | 26,172 | 24,186 | 24,560 | 17,575 |
| 1985-86 | 27,576 | 38,252 | 30,300 | 24,968 | 20,237 | 22,273 | 27,171 | 28,299 | 28,680 | 27,693 | 25,523 | 25,889 | 18,504 |
| 1987-88 | 30,499 | 42,071 | 33,528 | 27,001 | 21,962 | 24,070 | 29,005 | 31,215 | 31,020 | 30,220 | 28,021 | 28,046 | 21,215 |
| 1989-90 | 34,183 | 47,663 | 37,469 | 31,091 | 24,320 | 26,995 | 32,528 | 34,796 | 35,704 | 33,307 | 32,650 | 33,010 | 24,002 |
| 1990-91 | 35,001 | 45,720 | 39,029 | 32,724 | 25,534 | 26,111 | 34,179 | 36,459 | 37,570 | 34,720 | 34,050 | 34,800 | 22,505 |
| 1991-92 | 37,534 | 51,621 | 40,786 | 34,063 | 28,573 | 28,550 | 35,622 | 37,800 | 38,634 | 36,517 | 36,528 | 37,309 | 24,583 |
| 1992-93 | 38,385 | 52,755 | 41,881 | 35,032 | 27,700 | 28,922 | 35,792 | 38,356 | 39,470 | 36,710 | 38,460 | 38,967 | 25,068 |
| 1993-94 | 40,050 | 54,740 | 43,170 | 36,160 | 28,106 | 31,040 | 38,474 | 40,110 | 41,031 | 38,707 | 39,302 | 40,070 | 26,142 |
| 1994-95 | 41,369 | 56,555 | 44,626 | 37,352 | 29,072 | 31,677 | 38,567 | 41,548 | 42,863 | 38,812 | 40,808 | 41,815 | 22,551 |
| 1995-96 | 42,071 | 58,010 | 45,000 | 38,345 | 29,040 | 32,504 | 41,085 | 42,871 | 43,006 | 41,000 | 42,071 | 43,200 | 30,071 |
| 1996-97 | 44,325 | 60,160 | 47,101 | 39,350 | 30,519 | 33,415 | 42,474 | 44,306 | 45,402 | 42,531 | 44,374 | 44,726 | 30,561 |
| 1997-98 | 45,775 | 61,965 | 48,597 | 40,504 | 32,011 | 33,918 | 43,491 | 45,648 | 46,709 | 43,943 | 46,106 | 46,466 | 30,595 |
| 1998-99 | 47,421 | 64,200 | 50,047 | 41,094 | 33,152 | 35,115 | 44,720 | 47,247 | 48,055 | 45,457 | 47,074 | 48,204 | 31,524 |
| 1999-2000 | 48,597 | 67,079 | 52,091 | 43,367 | 34,228 | 36,607 | 45,565 | 48,714 | 50,168 | 46,340 | 49,737 | 50,052 | 32,551 |
| 2001-02 | 52,062 | 72,542 | 56,106 | 46,024 | 45,262 | 38,500 | 45,000 | 52,120 | 53,095 | 48,200 | 54,140 | 54,404 | 32,021 |
| 2002-03 | 54,105 | 75,028 | 57,716 | 48,380 | 46,573 | 40,265 | 45,251 | 53,435 | 55,121 | 50,717 | 55,581 | 56,158 | 35,296 |
| 2003-04 | 55,378 | 76,652 | 59,095 | 49,685 | 47,404 | 41,536 | 46,519 | 54,408 | 56,117 | 51,591 | 57,521 | 58,192 | 36,596 |
| 2004-05 | 56,026 | 79,100 | 60,009 | 51,154 | 48,051 | 42,455 | 47,060 | 55,700 | 57,714 | 52,500 | 59,010 | 60,140 | 39,291 |
| 2005-06 | 58,565 | 81,514 | 62,880 | 52,901 | 49,533 | 43,934 | 49,172 | 57,462 | 59,437 | 54,082 | 61,530 | 62,092 | 38,786 |
| 2006-07 | 61,016 | 85,000 | 65,207 | 54,974 | 51,002 | 45,600 | 50,012 | 59,701 | 61,075 | 56,127 | 64,246 | 64,401 | 41,090 |
| 2007-08 | 63,347 | 88,301 | 67,816 | 57,111 | 53,589 | 47,407 | 52,537 | 62,129 | 64,226 | 58,318 | 66,528 | 66,745 | 43,570 |
| 2008-09 | 65,538 | 91,522 | 70,375 | 59,285 | 55,424 | 48,078 | 54,649 | 64,231 | 66,393 | 60,185 | 69,300 | 68,593 | 43,344 |
| 2009-10 | 66,047 | 92,800 | 71,017 | 59,997 | 56,209 | 49,057 | 55,206 | 65,109 | 67,276 | 61,047 | 70,507 | 70,740 | 44,092 |
| 2010-11 | 67,473 | 94,041 | 72,003 | 60,885 | 56,566 | 50,270 | 54,885 | 65,632 | 67,535 | 61,193 | 72,091 | 72,306 | 45,518 |
| 2011-12 | 68,400 | 95,045 | 73,057 | 61,760 | 57,010 | 50,004 | 55,290 | 66,060 | 68,097 | 61,417 | 73,029 | 73,700 | 49,082 |
| 2012-13 | 69,124 | 96,563 | 73,966 | 62,321 | 56,361 | 50,963 | 56,777 | 66,703 | 69,083 | 61,774 | 74,587 | 75,149 | 46,407 |
| 2013-14 | 70,589 | 98,374 | 75,592 | 63,782 | 57,043 | 52,497 | 57,196 | 68,335 | 71,059 | 62,597 | 76,127 | 76,358 | 44,789 |
| 2014-15 | 71,792 | 100,700 | 77,115 | 65,000 | 58,020 | 52,001 | 56,016 | 69,004 | 72,200 | 62,971 | 77,504 | 77,009 | 38,041 |
| 2015-16 | 73,782 | 103,272 | 78,954 | 66,585 | 59,672 | 54,816 | 58,513 | 71,475 | 74,386 | 64,870 | 79,389 | 78,800 | 32,495 |

| Total | Constant 2015-16 dollars[1] | | | | | | | | | | | | |
|---|---|---|---|---|---|---|---|---|---|---|---|---|---|
| 1970-71 | 76,234 | 107,712 | 81,357 | 67,035 | 56,141 | 57,155 | 75,976 | 77,696 | 75,704 | 75,540 | 65,669 | 70,523 | 51,968 |
| 1975-76 | 71,574 | 97,212 | 73,821 | 60,092 | 56,744 | 55,450 | 65,290 | 72,792 | 71,759 | 67,570 | 66,404 | 69,244 | 46,825 |
| 1980-81 | 64,056 | 84,791 | 63,854 | 51,990 | 41,750 | 47,589 | 61,438 | 65,314 | 67,042 | 61,501 | 60,770 | 61,409 | 41,439 |
| 1982-83 | 66,023 | 86,279 | 65,855 | 53,545 | 42,729 | 48,728 | 62,044 | 66,732 | 66,666 | 62,268 | 64,074 | 64,797 | 41,287 |
| 1984-85 | 69,592 | 89,535 | 67,461 | 53,573 | 45,575 | 50,315 | 62,363 | 69,040 | 71,559 | 62,773 | 67,382 | 68,142 | 41,700 |
| 1985-86 | 70,929 | 92,554 | 69,604 | 57,539 | 45,804 | 52,049 | 63,694 | 71,712 | 74,522 | 64,793 | 68,761 | 69,483 | 42,559 |
| 1987-88 | 73,827 | 96,757 | 72,467 | 59,877 | 46,779 | 53,431 | 64,859 | 74,524 | 77,833 | 66,251 | 72,092 | 72,703 | 44,978 |
| 1989-90 | 75,312 | 99,100 | 73,927 | 61,343 | 46,970 | 54,402 | 64,851 | 75,543 | 79,500 | 66,648 | 74,056 | 74,720 | 46,165 |
| 1990-91 | 75,024 | 98,621 | 73,687 | 61,268 | 46,852 | 53,552 | 64,757 | 75,294 | 79,196 | 65,531 | 74,352 | 75,129 | 42,860 |
| 1991-92 | 75,601 | 99,516 | 74,011 | 61,627 | 53,300 | 52,507 | 65,140 | 75,239 | 75,681 | 67,167 | 76,505 | 77,224 | 44,261 |
| 1992-93 | 74,754 | 98,282 | 73,467 | 61,230 | 47,646 | 51,062 | 65,146 | 73,589 | 77,765 | 65,092 | 76,878 | 77,618 | 45,643 |
| 1993-94 | 75,556 | 98,634 | 73,785 | 61,322 | 46,978 | 53,235 | 66,126 | 74,632 | 76,252 | 66,678 | 77,350 | 78,025 | 46,338 |
| 1994-95 | 75,748 | 99,343 | 74,003 | 61,397 | 46,965 | 52,590 | 65,312 | 75,141 | 75,794 | 66,696 | 77,215 | 78,226 | 45,576 |
| 1995-96 | 76,047 | 99,536 | 73,975 | 61,221 | 46,798 | 52,645 | 66,310 | 75,219 | 76,920 | 66,771 | 77,821 | 78,275 | 45,221 |
| 1996-97 | 76,217 | 99,553 | 73,934 | 61,008 | 46,773 | 52,424 | 66,277 | 75,427 | 75,048 | 66,552 | 75,140 | 78,637 | 45,925 |
| 1997-98 | 77,059 | 101,254 | 74,875 | 61,623 | 47,803 | 52,275 | 66,688 | 76,072 | 75,721 | 67,648 | 75,610 | 80,111 | 45,487 |
| 1998-99 | 78,338 | 103,283 | 76,135 | 62,773 | 48,974 | 53,318 | 66,976 | 77,212 | 81,019 | 68,474 | 81,068 | 81,506 | 50,424 |
| 1999-2000 | 78,662 | 104,731 | 76,741 | 63,006 | 48,140 | 53,757 | 66,609 | 77,420 | 81,563 | 67,590 | 81,652 | 82,000 | 50,503 |
| 2001-02 | 79,866 | 108,034 | 78,525 | 65,249 | 62,793 | 55,592 | 62,271 | 78,257 | 82,923 | 67,978 | 83,989 | 84,361 | 44,313 |
| 2002-03 | 80,240 | 109,210 | 79,122 | 66,144 | 62,200 | 55,760 | 60,601 | 78,524 | 82,067 | 68,471 | 84,437 | 84,505 | 45,507 |
| 2003-04 | 80,127 | 109,260 | 79,060 | 66,323 | 62,823 | 55,580 | 61,100 | 77,344 | 82,303 | 67,560 | 85,360 | 85,701 | 46,507 |
| 2004-05 | 79,844 | 109,582 | 79,004 | 66,262 | 61,815 | 55,332 | 60,835 | 77,496 | 82,105 | 67,538 | 85,463 | 85,762 | 46,401 |
| 2005-06 | 79,205 | 109,214 | 78,087 | 65,904 | 60,920 | 54,357 | 60,379 | 76,924 | 81,366 | 66,540 | 85,000 | 85,232 | 46,159 |
| 2006-07 | 80,054 | 110,735 | 79,550 | 66,698 | 62,187 | 55,418 | 60,864 | 77,897 | 82,243 | 67,576 | 85,687 | 85,850 | 46,018 |
| 2007-08 | 80,007 | 110,319 | 79,710 | 66,737 | 62,270 | 55,592 | 61,204 | 77,540 | 82,002 | 67,130 | 85,609 | 85,524 | 46,050 |
| 2008-09 | 81,665 | 113,007 | 81,510 | 68,322 | 62,100 | 56,520 | 62,572 | 79,275 | 82,524 | 68,192 | 87,055 | 88,147 | 46,302 |
| 2009-10 | 82,037 | 113,986 | 81,492 | 68,431 | 63,534 | 57,372 | 62,449 | 79,352 | 83,715 | 68,453 | 88,368 | 88,907 | 45,196 |
| 2010-11 | 81,350 | 113,122 | 80,947 | 68,045 | 62,512 | 56,072 | 60,940 | 78,260 | 82,802 | 67,207 | 85,264 | 88,401 | 46,656 |
| 2011-12 | 80,171 | 112,131 | 79,763 | 67,024 | 61,096 | 55,871 | 59,576 | 76,955 | 81,507 | 65,497 | 87,472 | 87,641 | 50,055 |
| 2012-13 | 79,501 | 111,300 | 79,335 | 66,600 | 59,400 | 54,560 | 60,511 | 76,080 | 80,347 | 64,790 | 87,474 | 87,640 | 46,024 |
| 2013-14 | 79,842 | 111,547 | 79,001 | 67,024 | 59,061 | 55,335 | 59,904 | 76,555 | 81,023 | 64,011 | 87,303 | 87,607 | 45,220 |
| 2014-15 | 80,698 | 113,588 | 80,875 | 68,046 | 59,608 | 55,709 | 59,689 | 77,329 | 81,921 | 64,549 | 88,187 | 88,508 | 35,426 |
| 2015-16 | 82,101 | 115,292 | 82,101 | 69,315 | 60,844 | 57,270 | 60,750 | 78,056 | 83,300 | 65,065 | 89,549 | 89,292 | 31,206 |

| Males | | | | | | | | | | | | | |
|---|---|---|---|---|---|---|---|---|---|---|---|---|---|
| 1975-76 | 74,610 | 95,300 | 70,037 | 60,902 | 51,093 | 50,042 | 67,716 | 75,032 | 77,055 | 70,200 | 72,114 | 72,507 | 45,804 |
| 1980-81 | 67,388 | 85,496 | 64,506 | 52,887 | 42,758 | 50,285 | 63,733 | 68,417 | 70,167 | 53,169 | 64,621 | 55,105 | 44,217 |
| 1982-83 | 69,587 | 87,209 | 66,103 | 54,031 | 44,087 | 51,527 | 64,403 | 70,041 | 72,007 | 54,592 | 65,361 | 58,597 | 42,110 |
| 1984-85 | 72,501 | 90,720 | 68,458 | 57,064 | 47,668 | 53,070 | 64,585 | 72,633 | 75,115 | 55,087 | 72,154 | 72,717 | 43,840 |
| 1985-86 | 75,093 | 93,791 | 70,668 | 59,328 | 47,501 | 55,264 | 66,275 | 75,606 | 78,362 | 57,351 | 73,686 | 74,231 | 44,686 |
| 1987-88 | 78,292 | 95,165 | 73,604 | 61,005 | 48,035 | 56,070 | 67,357 | 78,030 | 82,065 | 58,250 | 77,046 | 77,706 | 46,570 |
| 1989-90 | 80,248 | 100,677 | 75,308 | 63,392 | 48,664 | 58,477 | 67,518 | 80,614 | 84,134 | 59,586 | 78,402 | 79,531 | 47,324 |
| 1990-91 | 80,184 | 100,617 | 75,154 | 63,405 | 48,732 | 57,645 | 67,075 | 80,218 | 83,925 | 59,510 | 80,102 | 80,536 | 46,149 |
| 1991-92 | 80,768 | 100,845 | 73,537 | 63,735 | 47,312 | 56,623 | 67,965 | 80,138 | 83,445 | 70,360 | 82,298 | 82,526 | 46,747 |
| 1992-93 | 80,672 | 100,262 | 74,990 | 63,265 | 49,455 | 54,335 | 65,811 | 78,858 | 82,375 | 58,584 | 82,785 | 83,319 | 47,810 |
| 1993-94 | 80,794 | 101,802 | 75,385 | 63,218 | 48,587 | 56,703 | 68,852 | 79,779 | 83,092 | 59,572 | 82,224 | 83,757 | 50,165 |
| 1994-95 | 81,156 | 101,462 | 73,574 | 63,245 | 48,867 | 55,577 | 68,284 | 80,207 | 83,767 | 59,737 | 83,418 | 84,520 | 46,955 |
| 1995-96 | 81,452 | 101,710 | 75,628 | 63,013 | 47,717 | 55,729 | 68,822 | 80,498 | 83,972 | 59,723 | 82,842 | 84,282 | 51,358 |
| 1996-97 | 81,668 | 102,284 | 73,678 | 62,774 | 47,395 | 55,378 | 68,307 | 80,576 | 84,213 | 59,564 | 84,247 | 84,649 | 52,065 |
| 1997-98 | 82,668 | 103,812 | 76,686 | 63,877 | 48,715 | 55,217 | 68,977 | 81,307 | 85,065 | 70,256 | 85,877 | 86,794 | 53,266 |
| 1998-99 | 84,260 | 106,080 | 77,952 | 64,658 | 50,805 | 56,441 | 68,916 | 82,598 | 86,605 | 70,502 | 87,454 | 87,615 | 55,067 |
| 1999 2000 | 84,567 | 107,641 | 78,703 | 65,325 | 50,464 | 56,503 | 68,065 | 83,019 | 87,305 | 70,421 | 88,152 | 88,537 | 54,300 |
| 2001-02 | 86,608 | 111,462 | 80,632 | 67,552 | 55,313 | 59,531 | 64,251 | 84,022 | 89,028 | 70,515 | 90,756 | 91,062 | 44,655 |
| 2002-03 | 86,522 | 112,775 | 81,418 | 68,615 | 55,777 | 59,403 | 62,035 | 84,477 | 88,395 | 70,506 | 91,221 | 91,550 | 44,007 |
| 2003-04 | 86,409 | 113,012 | 81,254 | 68,693 | 55,202 | 59,173 | 62,705 | 83,836 | 88,665 | 59,540 | 92,217 | 92,510 | 45,509 |
| 2004-05 | 86,187 | 113,475 | 81,285 | 68,633 | 53,865 | 58,334 | 62,277 | 83,444 | 88,434 | 58,561 | 92,379 | 92,655 | 43,468 |
| 2005-06 | 85,690 | 113,405 | 81,010 | 68,371 | 52,087 | 57,703 | 62,033 | 82,850 | 87,034 | 58,502 | 92,101 | 92,272 | 45,700 |
| 2006-07 | 86,570 | 115,045 | 81,903 | 69,042 | 54,265 | 57,942 | 62,645 | 83,804 | 88,793 | 58,533 | 92,764 | 92,585 | 45,065 |
| 2007-08 | 86,590 | 115,420 | 82,005 | 68,072 | 54,285 | 58,007 | 60,252 | 83,727 | 88,545 | 58,544 | 93,060 | 93,250 | 45,302 |
| 2008-09 | 88,475 | 116,506 | 83,956 | 70,738 | 55,291 | 59,694 | 64,762 | 85,358 | 90,849 | 59,787 | 95,471 | 95,690 | 45,688 |
| 2009-10 | 88,920 | 115,981 | 83,994 | 70,857 | 55,737 | 60,408 | 64,475 | 85,695 | 90,614 | 70,528 | 96,067 | 96,747 | 45,953 |
| 2010-11 | 88,239 | 116,182 | 83,449 | 70,474 | 54,504 | 59,769 | 62,932 | 84,720 | 89,754 | 58,701 | 95,920 | 96,092 | 45,005 |
| 2011-12 | 87,664 | 117,341 | 82,277 | 69,424 | 52,893 | 59,020 | 61,374 | 83,288 | 88,415 | 56,527 | 95,116 | 95,758 | 47,380 |
| 2012-13 | 86,492 | 116,702 | 81,800 | 69,093 | 51,126 | 57,428 | 62,914 | 82,411 | 87,235 | 56,206 | 95,149 | 95,299 | 44,190 |
| 2013-14 | 86,751 | 117,098 | 82,322 | 69,457 | 50,613 | 58,024 | 62,877 | 82,854 | 87,865 | 55,593 | 95,221 | 95,290 | 44,900 |
| 2014-15 | 87,788 | 118,374 | 83,515 | 70,734 | 51,115 | 58,836 | 60,717 | 83,873 | 88,995 | 55,555 | 96,099 | 96,690 | 37,641 |
| 2015-16 | 89,190 | 121,363 | 84,713 | 72,155 | 52,803 | 60,364 | 63,004 | 85,349 | 90,455 | 57,200 | 97,590 | 98,141 | 36,050 |

| Females | | | | | | | | | | | | | |
|---|---|---|---|---|---|---|---|---|---|---|---|---|---|
| 1975-76 | 61,473 | 87,253 | 70,207 | 56,097 | 54,015 | 51,131 | 62,555 | 53,427 | 62,430 | 53,154 | 55,966 | 36,546 | 43,827 |
| 1980-81 | 55,007 | 76,906 | 61,326 | 50,349 | 40,858 | 44,473 | 57,352 | 36,564 | 56,686 | 37,153 | 45,719 | 30,409 | 35,212 |
| 1982-83 | 56,472 | 78,222 | 62,183 | 51,297 | 41,518 | 45,713 | 57,912 | 38,202 | 57,963 | 38,263 | 52,076 | 32,687 | 35,466 |
| 1984-85 | 58,441 | 80,706 | 64,744 | 53,111 | 43,619 | 47,319 | 58,686 | 39,549 | 60,405 | 38,561 | 54,487 | 35,330 | 35,594 |
| 1985-86 | 60,383 | 83,750 | 66,348 | 54,668 | 44,318 | 48,771 | 59,456 | 51,566 | 62,800 | 50,539 | 57,868 | 36,589 | 40,518 |
| 1987-88 | 62,734 | 87,153 | 68,567 | 56,771 | 45,178 | 50,127 | 60,895 | 54,206 | 65,451 | 52,176 | 56,871 | 39,539 | 43,637 |
| 1989-90 | 64,145 | 89,443 | 70,312 | 55,342 | 45,637 | 50,558 | 61,041 | 55,797 | 67,001 | 52,502 | 61,269 | 51,545 | 45,041 |
| 1990-91 | 63,842 | 88,781 | 69,578 | 56,226 | 45,432 | 50,218 | 60,818 | 54,671 | 66,858 | 51,777 | 61,134 | 52,293 | 40,166 |
| 1991-92 | 64,713 | 88,997 | 70,782 | 55,756 | 49,778 | 49,721 | 61,414 | 55,169 | 66,607 | 52,557 | 63,498 | 54,322 | 47,553 |
| 1992-93 | 64,177 | 88,198 | 69,583 | 55,568 | 46,310 | 48,353 | 59,857 | 54,124 | 65,966 | 51,373 | 64,298 | 55,179 | 41,909 |
| 1993-94 | 65,275 | 89,214 | 70,263 | 56,941 | 45,851 | 50,596 | 62,687 | 55,276 | 66,864 | 53,077 | 65,025 | 55,600 | 42,601 |
| 1994-95 | 65,337 | 89,594 | 70,597 | 55,178 | 46,056 | 50,182 | 61,731 | 55,520 | 67,566 | 53,070 | 64,806 | 56,743 | 35,201 |
| 1995-96 | 66,117 | 89,940 | 70,639 | 56,128 | 46,175 | 50,252 | 62,368 | 56,117 | 67,827 | 53,265 | 66,118 | 56,680 | 47,308 |
| 1996-97 | 66,463 | 90,207 | 70,526 | 55,004 | 46,212 | 50,105 | 63,688 | 56,434 | 65,078 | 53,773 | 66,536 | 57,065 | 45,975 |
| 1997-98 | 67,435 | 91,286 | 71,593 | 55,669 | 47,158 | 49,568 | 64,070 | 57,248 | 65,811 | 54,737 | 67,978 | 58,454 | 45,662 |
| 1998-99 | 68,671 | 93,021 | 72,509 | 60,667 | 48,008 | 50,551 | 61,761 | 58,419 | 70,028 | 55,527 | 68,328 | 59,605 | 45,650 |
| 1999-2000 | 68,967 | 94,413 | 73,317 | 61,039 | 48,175 | 51,524 | 64,554 | 58,564 | 70,611 | 55,773 | 70,004 | 70,448 | 45,378 |
| 2001-02 | 70,415 | 97,032 | 75,131 | 62,613 | 60,528 | 52,669 | 62,177 | 59,698 | 72,068 | 55,910 | 72,407 | 72,789 | 44,021 |
| 2002-03 | 70,797 | 98,159 | 75,518 | 63,302 | 60,938 | 52,684 | 55,208 | 59,516 | 72,122 | 56,360 | 73,117 | 73,480 | 45,188 |
| 2003-04 | 70,907 | 98,147 | 75,667 | 63,623 | 60,657 | 53,183 | 55,564 | 59,665 | 71,854 | 56,559 | 74,164 | 74,510 | 47,243 |
| 2004-05 | 70,762 | 98,397 | 75,586 | 62,565 | 60,101 | 52,772 | 55,490 | 59,235 | 71,729 | 55,241 | 74,460 | 74,758 | 45,829 |
| 2005-06 | 70,245 | 97,606 | 75,769 | 63,345 | 59,312 | 52,607 | 55,880 | 58,806 | 71,170 | 54,759 | 74,037 | 74,530 | 46,443 |
| 2006-07 | 71,215 | 99,320 | 76,147 | 64,168 | 60,500 | 53,234 | 55,309 | 59,779 | 72,222 | 55,513 | 74,990 | 75,264 | 47,978 |
| 2007-08 | 71,293 | 99,385 | 76,329 | 64,260 | 60,658 | 53,558 | 55,470 | 59,528 | 72,288 | 55,639 | 74,879 | 75,124 | 45,152 |

| | | | | | | | | | | | | | |
|---|---|---|---|---|---|---|---|---|---|---|---|---|---|
| 2008-09 | 72,860 | 101,591 | 78,118 | 65,809 | 61,522 | 54,478 | 60,662 | 71,298 | 73,698 | 66,819 | 76,925 | 77,250 | 48,113 |
| 2009-10 | 73,271 | 102,057 | 78,075 | 65,960 | 61,829 | 54,922 | 60,692 | 71,613 | 73,963 | 67,114 | 77,514 | 77,777 | 49,354 |
| 2010-11 | 72,719 | 101,353 | 77,602 | 65,622 | 60,963 | 54,179 | 59,260 | 70,735 | 73,217 | 65,951 | 77,696 | 77,927 | 49,057 |
| 2011-12 | 71,691 | 100,356 | 76,495 | 64,670 | 59,697 | 53,394 | 57,902 | 69,492 | 72,140 | 64,308 | 77,095 | 77,261 | 51,706 |
| 2012-13 | 71,192 | 99,453 | 76,180 | 64,186 | 58,047 | 52,488 | 58,477 | 68,700 | 71,151 | 63,623 | 77,231 | 77,398 | 47,796 |
| 2013-14 | 71,584 | 99,759 | 76,657 | 64,681 | 57,846 | 53,237 | 58,002 | 69,298 | 72,060 | 63,478 | 77,199 | 77,433 | 45,420 |
| 2014-15 | 72,277 | 101,464 | 77,636 | 65,448 | 58,412 | 53,258 | 56,998 | 69,853 | 72,776 | 63,397 | 78,028 | 78,616 | 39,104 |
| 2015-16 | 73,782 | 103,272 | 78,954 | 66,589 | 59,672 | 54,816 | 58,813 | 71,475 | 74,386 | 64,870 | 79,389 | 79,800 | 32,495 |

[1] Constant dollars based on the Consumer Price Index, prepared by the Bureau of Labor Statistics, U.S. Department of Labor, adjusted to an academic-year basis.

NOTE: Data through 1995-96 are for institutions of higher education, while later data are for degree-granting institutions. Degree-granting institutions grant associate's or higher degrees and participate in Title IV federal financial aid programs. Data for 1987-88 and later years include imputations for nonrespondent institutions. Some data have been revised from previously published figures.

SOURCE: U.S. Department of Education, National Center for Education Statistics, Higher Education General Information Survey (HEGIS), "Faculty Salaries, Tenure, and Fringe Benefits" surveys, 1970-71 through 1985-86; Integrated Postsecondary Education Data System (IPEDS), "Salaries, Tenure, and Fringe Benefits of Full-Time Instructional Faculty Survey" (IPEDS-SA:87-99); and IPEDS, Winter 2001-02 through Winter 2011-12 and Spring 2013 through Spring 2016, Human Resources component, Salaries section. (This table was prepared December 2016.)

a) **Adjuncts**

When I entered college as a thrilled-with-anticipation freshman, it was a proud boast at my alma mater that undergraduate courses at all levels, including first-year, were taught by professors. And they were. (The fact that Rice University made that statement suggests that other institutions did otherwise, and some did, especially after the influence of the Dartmouth Seminar of 1966 seeped through the universities.)[9] My own freshman and sophomore classes were not taught exclusively or primarily by grad student T.A.s, adjuncts, and other contingent faculty. While we were familiar with "TAs" during my school years, I do not recall ever hearing the word "adjunct" used to mean contingent faculty. (More likely, it would have been used along the lines of 'The main dish is just an adjunct to the guacamole'.) Medical schools used practicing physicians as adjunct faculty extensively, well before the twentieth century, as did other professional schools. (Thorstein Veblen in 1918 described the medical and other professional schools themselves as "adjuncts" to the larger institution.)[10] University music departments hired adjunct faculty from the local symphony if they could. But my university did not have a med school or a law school attached, or a large music program. More importantly, the practice of substituting adjunct faculty for tenure-track faculty had simply not set in yet. My classes in the first two years were not relegated to implicitly second-tier status, at least not in my major field.

It is ironic in hindsight that that was partly because my major was English. A broader claim that 'professors did the teaching' in other fields would have to be qualified. In the humanities and in the social sciences, back then as now large lecture classes typically broke up into small-group tutorials—discussion sections—that met once a week, usually conducted by doctoral students, although the lectures were conducted by the professor. In the sciences, similarly, the laboratory hours were handled by 'labbies,' also usually graduate students, while the big lecture-format class meetings were led by the professor. But my freshman English class, like my freshman math class, was taught by a full-time tenured or tenure-track member of the department. The same was true of the Spanish class I took that year. Some language classes were taught by graduate students, but I happened to have a woman professor (one of two women professors I had as a freshman, outside of P.E., and an exception at the time). She went on to become one of the deans of the university.

The difference, or one difference, was that lower-division English, mathematics, and language classes were small to begin with. Then as now, they were generally not large lecture courses. More to the point—looking at differences between then and now—the practice of treating all freshman English classes as though they were subsections of one big class had not begun. In my own undergraduate experience, the professors teaching first-year English classes were expected to teach as they deemed appropriate—they were the professors in the classroom, after all—using texts of their choice. The texts were original books, not only textbooks; in the very good class I took, we read at a minimum poems, novellas, and novels, the latter including *Pride and Prejudice* and *Light in August.* There was time for discussion of the reading in class—this practice has now been re-named a 'flipped classroom'—and time for writing papers connected to the reading, because the course ran a full academic year. A second full year of sophomore English was also required, and was also taught by the professoriate.

### b) Gender

On the down side, I went through college and then through graduate school, getting the B.A. and then the Ph.D. in my chosen discipline of English literature, without ever having one woman professor. (My excellent high school English teacher was a woman, the wonderful, spirited, and encouraging Callie Law of Houston, who died in 2007 and whom I still miss.) Then, in about 1973 or 1974, the campus was visited by an 'HEW enforcer,' according to grad-student scuttlebutt—an official from the then-federal agency called the Department of Health, Education, and Welfare. For the first time in decades, the department hired a woman, one—count 'em, one—woman, as an Assistant Professor. (I was in graduate school but had finished course work, so I never had her as a teacher.) Among department grad students, one of the more senior profs was quoted at the time as joking, "Thank God we don't have to do *that* for another twenty years!"

In courses outside my major, I did have a few female professors, during my four undergraduate years of six courses per semester. They were each excellent, in different teaching styles and in different course formats, and most of the particular women professors from whom I took classes were later promoted to become deans. But remarkably, as an English major, I never had one undergraduate or graduate English course taught by a woman. In the department where, and when, I went to school, there weren't any.[11]

When I was in high school, we were told that the Ivy League schools were not open to women at the undergraduate level. Some had 'sister schools' for women undergraduates—Radcliffe for Harvard, Barnard for Columbia. Although the seven Ivy League institutions did have women in some graduate programs, some from early on, Yale and Princeton began to admit women as undergraduates only in 1969, Brown went co-ed in 1971, Dartmouth in 1972, and Harvard (fully) in 1977. Each move had impassioned support but was also met with hostility.[12] Columbia was the last of the Ivies to go co-ed, in 1981—nineteen years after the Civil Rights Act of 1964, or from another perspective forty-six years after Dorothy L. Sayers published her spectacular mystery novel set in a fictional women's college at Oxford, *Gaudy Night.* (Women were included in the Civil Rights Act, in the first place, as a joke.[13] This intriguing historical fact later featured in the cartoon strip *Ripley's Believe It or Not.*)

Needless to say, this picture has changed. Among the social and economic gains by women since the 1960s is the enormous demographic shift that more women began entering college rather than marrying right out of high school. (Women began entering college in significantly larger numbers especially in the years after the marriage deferment for military conscription ended, abruptly, on August 26, 1965.)[14] Bachelor's degrees obtained by women more than doubled from 1960 to 1970. Now, women are the majority at the undergraduate level, and have been since 1982.[15] (At my own school, during the years I was an undergraduate, the undergraduate gender ratio was four-to-one male. I have never heard that the ratio was by design.) Five years later, women began obtaining the majority of master's degrees, as the data in the table just cited also show. Women have gotten more master's degrees than have men since 1987. Almost 60 percent of master's degrees in the U.S. are obtained by women (up from 26 percent in 1910, to 39 percent in 1970, to 49 percent in 1985). Ten years later, women began obtaining the majority of doctor's degrees. Now, about 52 percent of doctor's degrees are obtained by women (up from 10 percent in 1970, to 34 percent in 1985, to 45 percent in 2000).

Since 1970, women have obtained advanced degrees—the M.A., the Ph.D., and equivalent—in ever increasing numbers across the board. In the 1970s, women began to enter college teaching in large numbers, and in 2018 a significant number and proportion of professors, department chairs, deans, provosts, and presidents of U.S. colleges and universities are women. While women remain in the minority in these positions, this is still a remarkable series of gender advances. All of the foregoing was a rarity during my undergraduate years, outside of the women's colleges. Hiring women, or more women, or any women, as college professors or as top-level administrators was a big story back when, and part of a bigger story. Now, advanced position, good pay, and administrative posts are so unexceptional for women that—ironically—to talk about gender discrimination or about gender disparities in higher education raises eyebrows or glazes eyes.

Nonetheless, gender disparities not only continue in universities and colleges in the U.S. but are an important part of their fiscal substructure. Such changes as large numbers of women entering the profession have generated such continuities as women taking a disproportionate number of the lowest-paying jobs. Somehow the large incursion of women into graduate schools across the nation coincided with a giant glut on the academic labor market—to such an extent that hundreds of thousands of women were able to find college teaching jobs only in the low-paid ranks of adjunct faculty. Since we will focus on gender at more length farther on, I will curtail discussion of it here.

Two key points do need to be clarified here. One is that gender inequalities in pay, benefits, and job security are a feminist issue, but they are not a 'women's issue.' In any occupation, lower-paid employees tend to displace better-paid employees. University teaching does not have some magic Tinker-Bell fairy-tale dust sprinkled on it to lift it as somehow, magically, the exception from the downward pull of circumstances. It is not an exception. In a workforce already weakened by attrition, full-time employees can be converted to part-time; can be replaced by contract employees; and can—ultimately—be laid off. In universities, the programs in which full-time faculty teach can be reorganized, can be converted into other programs, and can be eliminated. Be it remembered that in other occupations, full-time employees can be seasonally redefined as part-time.[16] Academia is not immune to such tactics.

The other point is related, that among women faculty as elsewhere in the U.S., the big divide is between top and bottom—not between academic disciplines, this millennium's counter-argument against equal pay for equal work, or between married and unmarried, the last millennium's counter-argument against equal pay for equal work. Facets of a growing wealth inequality nationwide include the enormous use of adjuncts to teach college courses and the majority of women among contingent faculty. And for the worst off among the adjuncts, the problem goes considerably farther than flat pay.

### c) Pay

The above brings us to the third macro of college teaching—flattening pay even among full-time tenure-track professors. As a student, I never knew what my professors were paid. However, we all recognized—my Vietnam-era generation recognized—that college faculty had a reasonably comfortable standard of living. Hardly anyone went into college teaching expecting to become a millionaire, Morris Zapp notwithstanding.[17] Universities were one thing; Hollywood was another. But the expectation was widespread, entrenched, and valid, that anyone who cleared the tenure hurdle would have a reasonably good standard of living for as long as he worked, and quite possibly for as long as he lived, since retirement was generally part of the package.

After all, the paycheck was not the whole picture. The paycheck was arguably middle-class, as the term is used. (Middle-income households as defined here have about $42,000 to $125,000 in annual income.)[18] But college faculty were not necessarily just embedded in the solid middle class. College faculty represented at their best a somewhat elevated professional meritocracy, professionals with a comfortable income and an especially comfortable job security—tenure—with the quiet perks of the job which included travel money, sabbaticals, reduced teaching loads at the upper ranks, and summers to write, to do research, or otherwise to create. Needless to say, they also had the more fundamental labor-union-won 'fringe benefits' enjoyed in other occupations, including health insurance ("hospitalization"), disability coverage, and pensions. Most professors had also gone through school without accumulating extraordinary student debt. And especially in the years from the 1950s to 1970, professors were able to get their jobs without the strain, anxiety, and expense of writing hundreds of job letters, or even dozens of job letters; generally there were enough job openings to go around. Unlike the hardscrabble picture in Britain in Kingsley Amis' *Lucky Jim* (1954), young applicants in the U.S. at the time could find decently paying jobs in college teaching. Many of them did not even have to obtain a doctorate.[19] All of this adds up to a profession with a quality of life—a station in life, as Jane Austen and the commentators on the Book of Common Prayer put it—not far removed from that of many doctors, lawyers, and architects, other members of the post-war intellectual peerage. The same factors add up to a quality of life that adjunct faculty and lower-tier full-time contingent faculty today miss out on. Low pay, unstable employment, and lack of benefits and other protections have been the pattern for adjunct faculty for forty years now.

This is not to say, however, that low pay for adjuncts has resulted in aggrandizing all full-time faculty. Quite the contrary; *all* faculty on average have been seeing a flattening of pay, or a lack of improvement, across the board.[20] Average salary for all full-time instructional faculty (all fields and disciplines combined) rose one percent from 2011 to 2015.[21] And even that improvement may be more statistical than actual. As the NCES currently tabulates faculty, these statistics include full-time instructional faculty at med schools and law schools as well as in the core universities, and the pay of top medical and law faculty raises the average. Senior faculty at the top ranks are often well paid, as are star faculty at elite research institutions. But with an almost spooky exactitude, the internal structure of universities parallels the shrinking of the U.S. middle class in the economy at large: the middle is shrinking, the declining proportion of faculty in the middle has moved to a faculty upper class, and the share of income held by the bottom has declined. The effect over-all has not been gains for faculty. Again, the issue of flattening pay will be taken up in more detail farther on.

Whatever the benefits of obtaining a graduate degree—which can be significant, even now—the losses begin and end with the atrocious academic job market. In no other occupation in the U.S., with the partial exceptions of law and architecture, does one have to spend several years to get a professional degree without a reasonable expectation of getting a job that will pay for it. Other occupations including medicine and law require years of education to get the entrance credentials. Other occupations including arts and music may take blood, sweat, and tears to break into. But while pharmacists, doctors, dentists, veterinarians and others spend significant time, effort, and other resources to get their required credentials, generally they have a profession waiting for them when they finish. Even with a tight labor market in law, beginning lawyers can still hope to make enough money, *if* they get a job, to pay off their law-school loans; with all the difficulties faced by architects, *if* they get a job, they can get paid. Visual artists, musicians, and actors may spend years to get a break, but they do not necessarily pay tuition for years for an advanced scholastic credential required by the occupation. (When they do, they often eke out a living by teaching as adjuncts.) Only in academia does the advanced-professional job itself, the job of teaching college students, not come with pay, after requiring credentials that include the advanced degree.

From 1954 through the 1960s, *Lucky Jim* was a funny, great, black-humor look at the ills and angst of post-war Britain, from the amused perspective of a comparatively well-fed white-collar America. (David Lodge's brilliant epistolary novel, *Changing Places,* played up this contrast in 1975; a fictional British professor changes places for a term with an American professor, Morris Zapp.) From the 1970s through the 1990s, *Lucky Jim* was still funny, still gallows humor, but struck a chilling warning about conditions in college teaching—a canary in the mine, as Amis's character put it. In the new millennium, *Lucky Jim* is a novel about a young faculty member who gets a formal academic appointment without being highly qualified, is dissatisfied with it, and is miraculously able to ditch it for a better-paying, fun position offered by the *deus ex machina* of a rich guy (who happens to be the uncle of his beautiful love interest). Lucky Jim was a medievalist—one of the more specialized fields in literary studies, and a specialization that took a hard hit in the 1970s. In 1976, in the U.S., Gordon R. Dickson published his own fantasy novel about a medievalist's miraculous escape from academia (time travel), *The Dragon and the George.*

When I entered graduate school, my mental challenge was always the question whether *I* would make the grade. I never questioned whether a profession would be there when I got out. The academic job market collapsed when I came out of graduate school, and now, in 2018, that is exactly the question. Whether the individual graduate student or adjunct chooses to spend at least five years in graduate school to get the Ph.D., or decides that the time and money spent getting a doctorate will not be compensated by employment and/or income, either way, s/he faces a deep professional uncertainty. Either choice can be valid and reasonable, depending on individual circumstances. The big divide is not between doctorate and master's degree. With either choice, a few decades ago, there was a reasonable expectation of adult income and job security. Now, either choice may well lead to permanent status in, as Orwell brilliantly termed his own family, the "lower upper middle class." And even the lower-upper faculty are among the comparatively well off, like the fictional Lucky Jim. The worst cases include the shocking death by exposure of an adjunct professor at Duquesne, Margaret Vojtko.[22]

## The Turning Point: 1973

To analyze fully why the academic job market collapsed, and why it only partly recovered afterward, would take another entire book. Here I will only summarize some relevant national events and changes; readers wishing to follow up can begin with sources referenced in the bibliography. In brief, colleges and universities became loci of social protest during the Vietnam War; the U.S. college population evolved during the Vietnam years and again after the military draft ended; and when the college population changed, the way universities treated their students and their faculty changed, for good and for ill. Perhaps it seems odd to begin this history less with protests in the streets than with English departments and college course requirements. But the two topics were, and are, related. During the Vietnam War, and sometimes influenced by social protest against curriculum requirements perceived as conformist or worse, colleges and universities began to reduce or to eliminate their curriculum requirements in English and modern languages, and sometimes in math and science. English departments generally went along with or actively implemented these changes, seeing them as reforms or for other reasons, reducing or eliminating their own freshman and sophomore required courses.

The Vietnam years also included the Dartmouth Seminar (1966), which paid thoughtful attention to the problems in using literature or literary criticism to teach students how to write. Partly in response, universities and their English departments began converting 'freshman English' (literature) into 'freshman comp' (writing). (This development took place just when many more female specialists in literature began crowding into the higher education job market.)[23] As curriculum requirements declined in letters and in the humanities, creation of separate writing programs and communications programs under various names grew.

The U.S. military draft ended January 27, 1973, under the administration of President Richard M. Nixon, influenced by votaries of Cold War author Ayn Rand.[24] (In microcosm, as the Vietnam War wound down, so did my own grad-school marriage. Like millions of other young people, I married during the Vietnam years, partly and voluntarily hoping to benefit someone under the draft. The U.S. divorce rate rose in the years after the marriage deferment ended, rose after people began returning from the service, and rose in the years after the draft ended. Divorce peaked in the U.S. in the 1970s, declining since from its historic high in 1980.) Obviously, the end of the draft was a relief under the shadow of Vietnam, and racial and economic disparities highlighted by the different fates of people living under the draft were somewhat ameliorated. With fewer combat deaths, however, if the inequalities lessened, so did the highlighting. The top-down rationale for ending the draft was that the move would neutralize or at least weaken social unrest as a political force. It worked; the anti-war movement was essentially denatured, and anti-war protest plummeted.

So did U.S. college enrollment, particularly among younger men. A key difference between the Vietnam War and previous wars in which Americans fought was that college enrollment meant staying out of Vietnam. As summed up by the Vietnam Veterans Memorial Fund,

> The US soldiers who fought in the Vietnam War were different in many ways from those who had fought in earlier wars. The average age of a soldier in Vietnam was 19, and he was likely to be unmarried—a significant difference from, for example, the average age of 26 for a soldier in World War II. . . . The youth of the average soldier was in many ways related to the draft and the system of deferments for the draft—enrolling and staying in college became an incentive to many, as college enrollment was an allowed deferment. For those who could not afford to enroll in college, there were few ways to avoid the draft. Overall, 25% of those who served in Vietnam were draftees.
>
> Partly as a consequence of the system of deferments, the Vietnam War was largely fought by men from working class backgrounds—76% of soldiers in Vietnam came from working or lower class backgrounds.[25]

When the draft ended, so did at least one reason for going to college, or for staying in college. College enrollment dropped substantially among young men who completed high school.[26] Male enrollment in the humanities dropped sharply as the Vietnam War wound down and the draft ended.[27] Undergraduate enrollment has long since gone up again—with the significant difference before and after, of proportionally more women and fewer men as undergraduates (Table 302.10). Possibly those collapsing marriages, post-Vietnam, contributed to the growing entrance of women into higher education, at both the undergraduate and the graduate level. At the same time, with numbers in some majors declining significantly, and with lower-division course requirements cut or changed, the academic job market for new PhDs shrank dramatically, especially in the humanities. Unlike college enrollment, university hiring never recovered, at least not if measured as the number of tenure-track jobs in proportion to the number of PhDs awarded.

In hindsight, economist Wallace Peterson dated the post-war turning point of the U.S. economy to exactly 1973. From 1948 to 1973, in a relatively long and fruitful era of growing employment *and* growing productivity, the economy expanded; in 1973, the economy began a contraction which it has never reversed.[28] Responding to this long, slow contraction and to other conditions, academia came up with measures intended to bolster enrollment as well as to ameliorate social inequities. Universities and colleges instituted remedial programs—not always called that now, but still in effect—and campus resources such as writing centers. State university systems made some of their member universities open-admission. Community colleges—which had suffered during the Vietnam years, since enrollment in a two-year college did not mean a draft deferment—grew in number and in size.[29] For the record, I support these measures. The trends themselves were, and are, good news. Accusations of 'political correctness' have often been leveled against higher education, but the actuality of who gets to go to college in the first place, or to succeed when there, remains anything but 'politically correct. One common denominator linking these separate trends in academia—the growth in compensatory education, the growth in open admissions, and the growth of community colleges—is the objective of redressing gratuitous disparities. But another common denominator is that all of these trends resulted in hiring large cadres of adjuncts and part-time faculty, during exactly the same period when women entered higher education as a profession in large numbers (Fig. 1).

The purpose of the foregoing is hardly to idealize a college teaching profession of the past that was still overwhelmingly white, male, and segregated, and often less expert than today, when I entered graduate school, let alone when I entered college. Abuses occurred, and the positive employment conditions for full-time faculty from 1950 to 1970 did not prevent individual unhappiness, problems, and personal tragedy. The point is that the magnitude of the quiet, reactionary, if mostly non-violent changes in college teaching cannot be dismissed in any valid analysis of the profession over the last fifty years.

## Recent Developments

Or one could look at the profession over the last thirty years. As said, the continuities have produced changes. Among material changes in postsecondary teaching since the 1990s, improvements or not, number the following:

1. The population of the lowest faculty ranks, at the lowest pay, may be less feminized. Among the many thousands of adjunct faculty and of other contingent faculty, there are thousands of men. (Fig. 2) It should be observed, however, that hiring a male cohort in the lowest or most contingent ranks can mask an over-all gender disparity in pay, rank, and benefits.

2. To that point, there are now more contingent faculty, with other ranks and titles, besides adjuncts. In other words, there has been a recent increase in the number and percentage of contingent faculty hired full-time rather than part-time. (Fig. 2) Compared to 1985 or to 1990, there are now more full-time lecturers, senior lecturers, instructors, etc., doing lower-division teaching, along with the adjuncts and the graduate student teaching assistants. (Table 315.20, Fig. 4) The growing number of full-time lecturers has been significant. To clarify, this sector of faculty is full-time but not tenured or tenure-track. The positions do not and often cannot—per university policy—lead to promotion or to tenure, though they can provide modest job security. The advantages are a living wage (although lower than for beginning tenure-track positions), a renewable several-year contract, and eligibility for cost-of-living adjustments and for employee benefits. Like full-time college professorships in the 1950s, they often do not require a Ph.D. But they are still contingent.

From direct observation, I know that the lectureships often make for a heavy workload. In my own department, a number of adjunct faculty were replaced with six new full-time lecturers. Half had doctorates; half had master's degrees; all are good. The teaching load is four-four (four courses in fall, four in spring); most classes are writing-intensive, involving much paper-grading. A lecturer may teach four writing classes in a semester, a schedule I myself have taught at times. (A former dean was quoted as openly referring to such positions as "burn-out jobs.") Although the state university system defines the four-four lectureships as "full-time," tenure-track professors who are full-time teach fewer courses per year, to devote more time to research. Non-tenure-track full-timers may or may not participate in shared university governance, depending on the institution. An additional factor is that most writing classes or lower-level courses in what the federal government defines as 'letters' are taught, reasonably enough, by people who specialize in writing, including free-lance writers and free-lance journalists. (Programs in communications, journalism, and media studies often use contingent positions.) Regrettably, teaching a full load of writing-intensive classes does not leave an author much time or energy for creative work off campus—nor does this kind of job have the résumé cachet to appeal to editors in glossy periodicals.

3. One problematic outcome is that contingent adjuncts and full-time NTT (non-tenure track) faculty can be used to teach courses that the professors do not want to teach. The preference itself is understandable, given the conditions: lower-division or introductory courses may involve more grading, more non-majors as students, perhaps a less controllable classroom dynamic and less positive student evaluation, and an intangible but perceptible loss of face in-house. (Being asked to teach composition can be considered an insult. This again is a factor that weighs heavier on people disadvantaged in the workplace already, as by gender. An old friend of mine once quoted a senior colleague of his at the University of Virginia as saying, "Can't we just hire a few housewives to teach composition?") As to tangible differences, if there is a difference in pay, they usually pay less—except for the select personnel whom Professor James Sledd called the "compositionists."[30] A phalanx of adjuncts is therefore predictable not only in composition programs, but also in introductory courses in math, beginning classes in modern languages, and community college courses in all fields.

4. Therefore, contingent faculty may be used to teach the same classes over and over, with neither variation—except what they introduce into their classes themselves, if permitted—nor advancement. Let's picture this situation as a textbook exercise:

*Quick check:*

How does your department handle lower-division courses?

Does your department exempt tenure-track Assistant Professors from teaching first-year courses?

—If so, then the TT (tenure-track) faculty member is being spared that burden, to support his/her research and professional development. Thus the tacit premise is that the department considers first-year courses to involve a commitment of time and of energy from which, in the interest of research, faculty need to be spared. A corollary question is whether the contingent faculty who teach exactly those courses, and sometimes only those courses, are being supported.

Since the institution pays adjunct faculty by 'stipend' rather than by salary, per course rather than by a multi-year contract, it is to some extent debarred from requiring research and professional advancement from the adjunct. So, ironically, recognition and reward for research and professional development by adjuncts can be debarred—regardless of the fact that 'publish or perish' still applies for professional advancement in universities. (One partial exception is the University of Maryland, which has recently created a new category of professional track faculty for its large number of adjuncts.)

Institutions vary; programs within institutions vary; even departments within the same program can vary. Generally, the full-time tenure-track faculty teaching in adjunct-like conditions will be found in financially strapped institutions. As usual, the financial stability or wealth of the institution makes a difference. A smaller institution without sizeable enrollment, endowment, or state support will likely ask its tenure-track faculty to teach a heavier course load, with a larger component of lower-division classes, than do the large research institutions or the better-endowed private institutions. But over-all, the faculty most liable to be restricted to teaching only first-year or lower-division classes in the same course over and over again, are adjunct and contingent faculty.

As to the nature of first-year courses, again English, mathematics, and languages may differ from other disciplines. These are the programs in which the pattern of repetitive and unchanging course assignment is most liable to hold, for contingent faculty. In other humanities and in social sciences departments, adjuncts may well teach everything from first-year to upper-level courses. In the sciences, engineering, and information systems, the picture is somewhat more mixed, or divided. Adjuncts may be hired to teach upper-level courses in their individual specialization—and can sometimes be paid very well, for adjuncts, especially when they are often full-time professionals elsewhere—but a regular cadre of adjuncts can also be used to handle lab sections or to teach introductory classes in a big-enrollment or required lower-level course.

With the partial changes indicated above, the big patterns still hold, evolving from the 1970s to now—more women, more adjuncts, and flattening pay. The three trends are inextricably connected; they have been observable for decades; and a pattern observable for long enough should be regarded as intentional.

## 2. Gender and Academic Contingency

There is a correlation between the extensive use of adjunct faculty in higher education and the condition of women in college teaching. The correlation between the number of female faculty and the number of adjuncts is not total. However, the overlap is overwhelming. Both cohorts—women faculty and adjunct faculty—are so large that it would be impossible for them not to overlap. Furthermore, the timeline is unassailable: the number and proportion of adjunct faculty in higher education burgeoned exactly when women started obtaining doctorates and entering college teaching in large numbers; increased as hiring of women increased; and still involves the largest numbers of lowest-paid adjuncts in fields, programs, and types of institution with the largest numbers and percentages of women.

Here again a good starting point is Fig. 1 (Table 315.10), "Number of faculty in degree-granting postsecondary institutions, by employment status, sex, control, and level of institution: Selected years, fall 1970 through fall 2015." What this table illustrates is that as the percentage of female faculty rose dramatically, between 1986 and 2015, the percentage of part-time faculty also rose dramatically. (Percentage of female faculty from 1970 to 1986 was not indicated in NCES data.) Obviously, as the percentage of part-time faculty rises, the percentage of full-time faculty falls. In 1970, full-time faculty were 77.8 percent of total faculty. In 2015, full-time faculty were 52 percent of total faculty, even counting the additional thousands of non-tenured full-timers. So, looking at the employment statistics, while the number of full-time faculty doubled between 1970 and 2015, the number of part-time faculty increased sevenfold. (Meanwhile, the number of advanced degrees awarded regularly exceeded the total of full-time *and* part-time faculty job openings.)

The really interesting dual tracks are those of part-time faculty and female faculty. In 1987, part-time faculty were 34 percent of total faculty. Female faculty were 33.2 percent of total faculty. In other words, the odds of teaching college as a female were magically almost equivalent to the odds of teaching college as a part-timer, with a statistically insignificant 0.8 percent difference. Two years later, part-time faculty had increased somewhat to 36.4 percent of the total; women were at 35.2 percent.

In 1991, women faculty hit the big time, comparatively speaking. Part-time faculty had diminished very slightly, to 35.2 percent of all faculty, while women faculty had again increased, to 36.4 percent of the total (826,252). So women's odds of being other than part-time went up, temporarily. (In microcosm, 1990-1991 was the year I got a one-year appointment as a Visiting Assistant Professor, after teaching as an adjunct for seven years. That year, as a full-timer, I taught six classes. The previous year, as a part-timer, I had taught ten classes.) But two years later, part-time faculty jumped to 40.4 percent of total faculty, surpassing women faculty at 38.7 percent of the total. Two years after that, part-time faculty were up to 40.9 percent, women up to 39.6 percent (of the total 931,706). By the end of the 1990s, total faculty had passed the million mark. Of the total in fall 1999, part-time faculty were 42.5 percent; women were 41.4 percent.

This impressively neat parallelism comes close to being concomitant variation. Note the similarity of the percentages for part-time faculty and for women faculty—rounding off, 34 and 33 percent in fall 1987, 36 and 35 percent in 1989, 35 and 36 percent in 1991, 40 and 39 percent in 1993, 41 and 40 percent in 1995, 43 and 41 percent in 1997, 43 and 41 percent in 1999. (Rounding off the decimals makes the percentages of part-time and women faculty in the 1980s and in the 1990s seem more different than they were. The difference is actually less than one percent almost every year, and less than two percent every year.)

The pattern of more part-time faculty and more female faculty has continued in the new millennium. The number of part-time faculty jumped again after 2000. In 2001, the percentage of part-time faculty bumped up to 44.5; the percentage of women increased also, but less, to 42.1. So women's odds of numbering among part-timers increased. In 2003, the picture was worse: part-time faculty were 46.3 percent and women 43.4 percent of the total. In 2005, worse yet; part-time faculty were 47.6 percent and women 44.6 percent. In 2007, worse again; 48.7 percent part-time, 45.8 percent women. In 2009, worse again; 49.3 percent part-time, 47.1 percent women.

Within the last ten years, the percentage of part-time faculty in U.S. higher education has become approximately equal to that of full-time faculty (even with the growing number of non-tenured full-time faculty).[31] In fall 2011, the percentages were fifty-fifty. In 2013 and in 2015, the percentage of part-time faculty ebbed slightly, to 48.8 percent and 48 percent respectively. In all three years, the percentage of women faculty continued to increase—to 48.2 in 2011, 48.8 in 2013, and 49.1 in 2015.

Naturally, all three authors of *The Female Precariat* support women in college teaching. We are among the number ourselves. By any ethical standard, higher education was one sector in the U.S. where women were overdue to advance in the 1960s and in the 1970s. But the broad patterns could hardly be clearer. As the number and percentage of female faculty rose, up to 2011, the number and percentage of part-time faculty also rose. When from 2011 to 2015 the number and percentage of part-time faculty decreased slightly, the number and percentage of other contingent faculty—non-tenured lecturers and instructors—rose. In all years since 1986, the number and percentage of female faculty have risen. In all decades since 1970, the number and percentage of part-time faculty have risen. There was no Great and Powerful Oz microphone behind the curtain, invisibly shunting several hundred thousand highly educated women in the U.S. into the lowest-paid jobs requiring an advanced degree. But there might as well have been.

In short, contingent faculty including adjuncts and non-tenured full-timers now outnumber tenure-track full-time faculty in the U.S. And one main reason is the enormous number of women teaching part-time.[32] And from Ancient Studies to Zoology, the main reason so many people, regardless of gender, teach part-time is that they cannot get full-time teaching jobs. Similarly, when they take full-time burnout positions, it is because they cannot obtain better jobs. (Ph.D. graduates are more likely to take a non-tenure-track lectureship in preference to an adjunct job than in preference to an assistant professorship. Occasional exceptions do not disprove the general rule.) This picture may become more explainable when one looks at the graduate degrees awarded, below. For now, the larger ill can again be partly demonstrated by looking at the gender disparities.

It helps to look at faculty as employees, as in *Digest* Table 314.30, "Employees in degree-granting postsecondary institutions, by employment status, sex, control and level of institution, and primary occupation: Fall 2015." Over-all, U.S. universities employ more women than men—54.6 percent of total workers in U.S. higher education, as of fall 2015, were women. Universities generally are at least as likely as other employers to allow some flexibility in work-life scheduling, and thus often appeal to women job applicants. Counting all higher education employees at every level from cafeteria worker to president, women outnumber men among both full-time and part-time employees. Among total *faculty* at all institutions, however, more men are full-time than women—438,789 to 368,243. Among total faculty, more women are part-time than men—393,943 to 350,040.

The same table (314.30) also illustrates that while women outnumber men among part-time faculty in all types of institutions, women outnumber men the most in types of institution that pay the least. Thus women outnumber men the most among part-time faculty in public two-year institutions such as community colleges. In fall 2015, female part-time instructional faculty outnumbered male part-time instructional faculty in public two-year institutions by 126,984 to 108,372. Conversely, women outnumber men the least, among part-timers, in private four-year institutions such as elite universities. In fall 2015, female part-time instructional faculty barely outnumbered male part-time instructional faculty in private four-year institutions, by 102,753 to 99,429. The other side of the same coin is that private four-year institutions are also where men teaching full-time outnumber women teaching full-time by the most. In fall 2015, male full-time instructional faculty outnumbered female full-time instructional faculty in private four-year institutions by 224,686 to 202,921.

## Disparities by Gender

As in the 1960s and in the 1970s, the paycheck is still not the whole picture. And while gender disparities in higher education and the entrenched use of part-time faculty are connected, where gender disparities are concerned, being part-time is not the whole picture. There is a gender gap manifest in the induction of so many women into part-time teaching in the first place, but there are also gender gaps manifest within the ranks of full-time college professors—and more recently, into the ranks of non-tenure-track full-timers like lecturers and instructors. Some recent data on full-time faculty, in the 2016 *Digest of Education Statistics* published by the NCES, provide a useful overview.

# Figure 4: Table 314.30

Table 314.30. Employees in degree-granting postsecondary institutions, by employment status, sex, control and level of institution, and primary occupation: Fall 2015

| Control and level of institution and primary occupation | Full-time and part-time | | | | | Full-time | | | | Part-time | | |
|---|---|---|---|---|---|---|---|---|---|---|---|---|
| | Total | | | Females | | Total | | | | | | |
| | Number | Percentage distribution | Males | Number | Percent of all employees | Number | Percent of all employees | Males | Females | Total | Males | Females |
| 1 | 2 | 3 | 4 | 5 | 6 | 7 | 8 | 9 | 10 | 11 | 12 | 13 |
| **All institutions** | **3,915,918** | **100.0** | **1,777,823** | **2,138,095** | **54.6** | **2,507,627** | **64.0** | **1,121,837** | **1,385,790** | **1,408,291** | **655,986** | **752,305** |
| Faculty (instruction/research/public service) | 1,551,015 | 39.6 | 750,020 | 792,100 | 40.1 | 807,002 | 52.0 | 401,709 | 300,243 | 743,003 | 350,040 | 393,043 |
| Instruction | 1,436,342 | 36.7 | 724,943 | 711,399 | 49.5 | 715,274 | 49.8 | 386,342 | 328,932 | 721,068 | 338,601 | 382,467 |
| Research | 87,142 | 2.2 | 50,708 | 36,354 | 41.7 | 72,721 | 83.5 | 42,959 | 29,762 | 14,421 | 7,829 | 6,592 |
| Public service | 27,531 | 0.7 | 13,098 | 14,433 | 52.4 | 19,037 | 69.1 | 9,488 | 9,549 | 8,494 | 3,610 | 4,884 |
| Graduate assistants | 369,590 | 9.4 | 194,570 | 175,020 | 47.4 | † | † | † | † | 369,590 | 194,570 | 175,020 |
| Librarians, curators, and archivists | 42,677 | 1.1 | 12,540 | 30,087 | 70.6 | 36,266 | 85.1 | 11,011 | 25,255 | 6,361 | 1,529 | 4,882 |
| Student and academic affairs and other education services | 171,551 | 4.4 | 55,534 | 116,017 | 67.6 | 113,481 | 66.2 | 33,820 | 79,661 | 58,070 | 21,714 | 36,356 |
| Management | 255,858 | 6.6 | 114,090 | 142,798 | 57.6 | 249,360 | 97.1 | 111,114 | 138,246 | 7,528 | 2,976 | 4,552 |
| Business and financial operations | 203,850 | 5.2 | 55,128 | 148,762 | 73.0 | 190,436 | 93.4 | 51,625 | 138,811 | 13,454 | 3,503 | 9,951 |
| Computer, engineering, and science | 231,957 | 5.9 | 140,883 | 91,074 | 39.3 | 212,135 | 91.5 | 131,908 | 80,227 | 19,822 | 8,975 | 10,847 |
| Community, social service, legal, arts, design, entertainment, sports, and media | 174,694 | 4.5 | 78,292 | 96,402 | 55.2 | 141,707 | 81.1 | 62,427 | 79,280 | 32,987 | 15,865 | 17,122 |
| Healthcare practitioners and technicians | 121,135 | 3.1 | 34,231 | 86,904 | 71.7 | 99,054 | 81.8 | 28,766 | 70,288 | 22,081 | 5,467 | 16,616 |
| Service occupations | 243,833 | 6.2 | 141,152 | 102,681 | 42.1 | 202,364 | 83.0 | 118,333 | 84,031 | 41,469 | 22,819 | 18,650 |
| Sales and related occupations | 13,873 | 0.4 | 4,874 | 8,999 | 64.9 | 11,475 | 82.7 | 4,226 | 7,249 | 2,398 | 648 | 1,750 |
| Office and administrative support | 441,222 | 11.3 | 73,481 | 367,741 | 83.3 | 358,151 | 81.2 | 51,108 | 307,043 | 83,071 | 22,373 | 60,698 |
| Natural resources, construction, and maintenance | 74,041 | 1.9 | 67,251 | 6,790 | 9.2 | 69,926 | 94.4 | 64,986 | 4,940 | 4,115 | 2,967 | 1,150 |
| Production, transportation, and material moving | 19,602 | 0.5 | 16,268 | 3,334 | 17.0 | 16,240 | 82.8 | 13,724 | 2,516 | 3,362 | 2,544 | 818 |

| | | | | | | | | | | | | |
|---|---|---|---|---|---|---|---|---|---|---|---|---|
| **Public 4-year** | **1,925,174** | **100.0** | **896,520** | **1,028,654** | **53.4** | **1,307,522** | **67.9** | **602,591** | **704,931** | **617,652** | **293,939** | **323,713** |
| Faculty (instruction/research/public service) | 621,753 | 32.3 | 331,761 | 289,992 | 46.6 | 414,971 | 66.7 | 234,070 | 180,901 | 206,782 | 97,691 | 109,091 |
| Instruction | 551,455 | 28.6 | 292,914 | 258,541 | 46.9 | 357,743 | 64.9 | 201,827 | 155,916 | 193,712 | 91,087 | 102,625 |
| Research | 54,974 | 2.9 | 31,787 | 23,187 | 42.3 | 45,313 | 82.4 | 26,594 | 18,719 | 9,661 | 5,143 | 4,518 |
| Public service | 15,324 | 0.8 | 7,110 | 8,214 | 53.6 | 11,915 | 77.8 | 5,649 | 6,266 | 3,409 | 1,461 | 1,948 |
| Graduate assistants | 291,610 | 15.1 | 153,157 | 138,453 | 47.5 | † | † | † | † | 291,610 | 153,157 | 138,453 |
| Librarians, curators, and archivists | 18,437 | 1.0 | 5,629 | 12,808 | 69.5 | 16,970 | 92.0 | 5,287 | 11,683 | 1,467 | 342 | 1,125 |
| Student and academic affairs and other education services | 61,552 | 3.2 | 19,608 | 41,944 | 68.1 | 45,955 | 74.7 | 13,942 | 32,013 | 15,597 | 5,666 | 9,931 |
| Management | 113,257 | 5.9 | 51,894 | 61,363 | 54.2 | 109,705 | 96.9 | 50,424 | 59,281 | 3,552 | 1,470 | 2,082 |
| Business and financial operations | 118,411 | 6.2 | 31,533 | 86,878 | 73.4 | 110,094 | 93.0 | 29,359 | 80,735 | 8,317 | 2,174 | 6,143 |
| Computer, engineering, and science | 143,309 | 7.4 | 86,639 | 56,670 | 39.5 | 130,645 | 91.2 | 81,210 | 49,435 | 12,664 | 5,429 | 7,235 |
| Community, social service, legal, arts, design, entertainment, sports, and media | 83,326 | 4.3 | 35,235 | 48,091 | 57.7 | 72,818 | 87.4 | 30,958 | 41,860 | 10,508 | 4,277 | 6,231 |
| Healthcare practitioners and technicians | 74,377 | 3.9 | 22,262 | 52,115 | 70.1 | 62,077 | 83.5 | 19,438 | 42,639 | 12,300 | 2,824 | 9,476 |
| Service occupations | 127,973 | 6.6 | 69,417 | 58,556 | 45.8 | 110,251 | 86.2 | 60,401 | 49,850 | 17,722 | 9,016 | 8,706 |
| Sales and related occupations | 2,611 | 0.1 | 843 | 1,768 | 67.7 | 2,061 | 78.9 | 685 | 1,376 | 550 | 158 | 392 |
| Office and administrative support | 207,247 | 10.8 | 33,012 | 174,235 | 84.1 | 174,535 | 84.2 | 24,185 | 150,350 | 32,712 | 8,827 | 23,885 |
| Natural resources, construction, and maintenance | 48,242 | 2.5 | 44,592 | 3,650 | 7.6 | 46,026 | 95.4 | 42,924 | 3,102 | 2,216 | 1,668 | 548 |
| Production, transportation, and material moving | 13,039 | 0.7 | 10,938 | 2,101 | 16.3 | 11,414 | 87.3 | 9,709 | 1,705 | 1,655 | 1,230 | 425 |
| **Public 2 year** | **622,362** | **100.0** | **264,304** | **358,058** | **57.5** | **297,087** | **47.7** | **120,251** | **176,836** | **325,275** | **144,053** | **181,222** |
| Faculty (instruction/research/public service) | 348,269 | 56.0 | 158,983 | 189,286 | 54.4 | 109,880 | 31.6 | 49,421 | 60,459 | 238,389 | 109,562 | 128,827 |
| Instruction | 344,685 | 55.4 | 157,601 | 187,094 | 54.3 | 109,339 | 31.7 | 49,229 | 60,110 | 235,356 | 108,372 | 126,984 |
| Research | 118 | # | 41 | 67 | 62.0 | 96 | 88.9 | 36 | 60 | 12 | 5 | 7 |
| Public service | 3,466 | 0.6 | 1,341 | 2,125 | 61.3 | 445 | 12.8 | 156 | 289 | 3,021 | 1,185 | 1,836 |
| Graduate assistants | 13 | # | 6 | 7 | 53.8 | † | † | † | † | 13 | 6 | 7 |
| Librarians, curators, and archivists | 5,557 | 0.9 | 1,109 | 4,388 | 79.6 | 3,727 | 67.1 | 824 | 2,903 | 1,830 | 365 | 1,465 |
| Student and academic affairs and other education services | 50,754 | 8.2 | 17,717 | 33,037 | 65.1 | 21,313 | 42.0 | 6,401 | 14,912 | 29,441 | 11,316 | 18,125 |
| Management | 32,878 | 5.3 | 13,704 | 19,174 | 58.3 | 31,535 | 96.1 | 13,203 | 18,332 | 1,203 | 501 | 702 |
| Business and financial operations | 17,401 | 2.8 | 4,632 | 12,769 | 73.4 | 15,528 | 89.2 | 4,026 | 11,502 | 1,873 | 606 | 1,267 |
| Computer, engineering, and science | 16,587 | 2.7 | 11,048 | 5,549 | 33.4 | 14,083 | 84.4 | 9,583 | 4,494 | 2,504 | 1,500 | 1,055 |
| Community, social service, legal, arts, design, entertainment, sports, and media | 23,443 | 3.8 | 9,026 | 14,417 | 61.5 | 16,204 | 69.1 | 5,828 | 10,376 | 7,239 | 3,198 | 4,041 |
| Healthcare practitioners and technicians | 1,534 | 0.3 | 513 | 1,001 | 67.0 | 775 | 40.0 | 290 | 405 | 810 | 220 | 590 |
| Service occupations | 34,983 | 5.6 | 24,409 | 10,574 | 30.2 | 24,476 | 70.0 | 17,682 | 6,794 | 10,507 | 6,727 | 3,780 |
| Sales and related occupations | 1,883 | 0.3 | 522 | 1,361 | 72.3 | 1,043 | 55.4 | 303 | 740 | 840 | 219 | 621 |
| Office and administrative support | 81,160 | 13.0 | 15,646 | 65,514 | 80.7 | 51,917 | 64.0 | 6,765 | 45,152 | 29,243 | 8,881 | 20,362 |
| Natural resources, construction, and maintenance | [illegible] | 1.1 | 5,006 | 675 | [illegible] | 5,023 | [illegible] | [illegible] | 407 | 700 | 550 | 100 |
| Production, transportation, and material moving | 1,269 | 0.2 | 1,023 | 246 | 19.4 | 803 | 63.3 | 663 | 140 | 466 | 360 | 106 |

| | | | | | | | | | | | |
|---|---|---|---|---|---|---|---|---|---|---|---|
| **Private nonprofit 4 year** | **1,185,317** | **100.0** | **541,335** | **643,982** | **54.3** | **816,998** | **68.9** | **365,912** | **451,086** | **368,319** | **175,423** |
| Faculty (instruction/research/public service) | 468,249 | 39.5 | 248,293 | 219,956 | 47.0 | 259,313 | 55.4 | 145,235 | 114,078 | 208,936 | 103,058 |
| Instruction | 427,607 | 36.1 | 224,686 | 202,921 | 47.5 | 225,425 | 52.7 | 125,257 | 100,168 | 202,182 | 99,429 |
| Research | 31,954 | 2.7 | 18,975 | 12,979 | 40.6 | 27,245 | 85.3 | 16,304 | 10,941 | 4,709 | 2,671 |
| Public service | 8,688 | 0.7 | 4,532 | 4,156 | 46.7 | 6,643 | 76.5 | 3,674 | 2,969 | 2,045 | 958 |
| Graduate assistants | 77,627 | 6.5 | 41,259 | 36,368 | 46.8 | † | † | † | † | 77,627 | 41,259 |
| Librarians, curators, and archivists | 17,284 | 1.5 | 5,360 | 11,924 | 69.0 | 14,612 | 84.5 | 4,632 | 9,980 | 2,672 | 728 |
| Student and academic affairs and other education services | 45,601 | 3.8 | 13,988 | 31,613 | 69.3 | 34,294 | 75.2 | 10,045 | 24,249 | 11,307 | 3,943 |
| Management | 96,922 | 8.2 | 42,581 | 54,341 | 56.1 | 94,420 | 97.4 | 41,648 | 52,772 | 2,502 | 933 |
| Business and financial operations | 61,493 | 5.2 | 16,964 | 44,529 | 72.4 | 58,491 | 95.1 | 16,304 | 42,187 | 3,002 | 660 |
| Computer, engineering, and science | 69,672 | 5.9 | 41,355 | 28,317 | 40.6 | 65,231 | 93.6 | 39,442 | 25,789 | 4,441 | 1,913 |
| Community, social service, legal, arts, design, entertainment, sports, and media | 62,095 | 5.2 | 31,582 | 30,513 | 49.1 | 47,463 | 76.4 | 23,517 | 23,946 | 14,632 | 8,065 |
| Healthcare practitioners and technicians | 44,093 | 3.8 | 11,366 | 33,527 | 74.7 | 36,381 | 80.4 | 8,305 | 27,096 | 8,012 | 2,301 |
| Service occupations | 78,562 | 6.6 | 45,808 | 32,754 | 41.7 | 66,126 | 84.2 | 39,223 | 26,903 | 12,436 | 6,585 |
| Sales and related occupations | 3,901 | 0.3 | 1,400 | 2,501 | 64.4 | 3,197 | 81.9 | 1,195 | 2,002 | 704 | 205 |
| Office and administrative support | 135,464 | 11.4 | 20,339 | 115,125 | 85.0 | 116,353 | 85.9 | 16,178 | 100,175 | 19,111 | 4,161 |
| Natural resources, construction, and maintenance | 18,478 | 1.6 | 16,902 | 1,576 | 8.5 | 17,532 | 94.9 | 16,262 | 1,270 | 946 | 640 |
| Production, transportation, and material moving | 5,046 | 0.4 | 4,138 | 908 | 18.0 | 3,885 | 77.0 | 3,246 | 639 | 1,161 | 892 |
| **Private nonprofit 2-year** | **8,932** | **100.0** | **3,331** | **5,601** | **62.7** | **6,536** | **73.2** | **2,386** | **4,150** | **2,396** | **945** |
| Faculty (instruction/research/public service) | 4,117 | 46.1 | 1,639 | 2,478 | 60.2 | 2,264 | 55.0 | 905 | 1,359 | 1,853 | 734 |
| Instruction | 4,106 | 46.0 | 1,638 | 2,468 | 60.1 | 2,256 | 54.9 | 905 | 1,351 | 1,850 | 733 |
| Research | 10 | 0.1 | 1 | 9 | 90.0 | 7 | 70.0 | 0 | 7 | 3 | 1 |
| Public service | 1 | # | 0 | 1 | 100.0 | 1 | 100.0 | 0 | 1 | 0 | 0 |
| Graduate assistants | 6 | 0.1 | 5 | 1 | 16.7 | † | † | † | † | 6 | 5 |
| Librarians, curators, and archivists | 116 | 1.3 | 25 | 91 | 78.4 | 79 | 68.1 | 21 | 58 | 37 | 4 |
| Student and academic affairs and other education services | 438 | 4.9 | 125 | 313 | 71.5 | 355 | 81.1 | 98 | 257 | 83 | 27 |
| Management | 827 | 9.3 | 341 | 486 | 58.8 | 804 | 97.2 | 332 | 472 | 23 | 9 |
| Business and financial operations | 1,219 | 13.6 | 404 | 815 | 66.9 | 1,191 | 97.7 | 401 | 790 | 28 | 3 |
| Computer, engineering, and science | 144 | 1.6 | 119 | 25 | 17.4 | 136 | 94.4 | 113 | 23 | 8 | 6 |
| Community, social service, legal, arts, design, entertainment, sports, and media | 243 | 2.7 | 133 | 110 | 45.3 | 167 | 68.7 | 82 | 85 | 76 | 51 |
| Healthcare practitioners and technicians | 35 | 0.4 | 8 | 27 | 77.1 | 26 | 74.3 | 6 | 20 | 9 | 2 |
| Service occupations | 280 | 3.1 | 200 | 80 | 28.6 | 166 | 59.3 | 125 | 41 | 114 | 75 |
| Sales and related occupations | 477 | 5.3 | 125 | 352 | 73.8 | 466 | 97.7 | 122 | 344 | 11 | 3 |
| Office and administrative support | 923 | 10.3 | 116 | 807 | 87.4 | 793 | 85.9 | 104 | 689 | 130 | 12 |
| Natural resources, construction, and maintenance | 93 | 1.0 | 80 | 13 | 14.0 | 84 | 90.3 | 73 | 11 | 9 | 7 |
| Production, transportation, and material moving | 14 | 0.2 | 11 | 3 | 21.4 | 5 | 35.7 | 4 | 1 | 9 | 7 |

| | |
|---|---|
| **Private nonprofit 4 year** | **192,896** |
| Faculty (instruction/research/public service) | 105,878 |
| Instruction | 102,753 |
| Research | 2,038 |
| Public service | 1,087 |
| Graduate assistants | 36,368 |
| Librarians, curators, and archivists | 1,944 |
| Student and academic affairs and other education services | 7,364 |
| Management | 1,569 |
| Business and financial operations | 2,342 |
| Computer, engineering, and science | 2,528 |
| Community, social service, legal, arts, design, entertainment, sports, and media | 6,567 |
| Healthcare practitioners and technicians | 5,431 |
| Service occupations | 5,851 |
| Sales and related occupations | 529 |
| Office and administrative support | 14,950 |
| Natural resources, construction, and maintenance | 306 |
| Production, transportation, and material moving | 269 |
| **Private nonprofit 2-year** | **1,451** |
| Faculty (instruction/research/public service) | 1,119 |
| Instruction | 1,117 |
| Research | 2 |
| Public service | 0 |
| Graduate assistants | 1 |
| Librarians, curators, and archivists | 33 |
| Student and academic affairs and other education services | 56 |
| Management | 14 |
| Business and financial operations | 25 |
| Computer, engineering, and science | 2 |
| Community, social service, legal, arts, design, entertainment, sports, and media | 25 |
| Healthcare practitioners and technicians | 7 |
| Service occupations | 39 |
| Sales and related occupations | 8 |
| Office and administrative support | 118 |
| Natural resources, construction, and maintenance | 2 |
| Production, transportation, and material moving | 2 |

| | | | | | | | | | | | |
|---|---|---|---|---|---|---|---|---|---|---|---|
| **Private for-profit 4-year** | **141,108** | **100.0** | **60,268** | **80,840** | **57.3** | **60,184** | **42.7** | **23,879** | **36,305** | **80,924** | **36,389** | **44,535** |
| Faculty (instruction/research/public service) | 59,741 | 53.6 | 40,480 | 49,261 | 54.9 | 13,622 | 17.2 | 6,198 | 7,424 | 76,119 | 34,282 | 41,837 |
| Instruction | 59,655 | 53.5 | 40,452 | 49,203 | 54.9 | 13,581 | 15.1 | 6,180 | 7,401 | 76,074 | 34,272 | 41,802 |
| Research | 64 | # | 20 | 44 | 68.8 | 29 | 47.3 | 12 | 17 | 35 | 8 | 27 |
| Public service | 22 | # | 8 | 14 | 63.6 | 12 | 54.5 | 6 | 6 | 10 | 4 | 8 |
| Graduate assistants | 334 | 0.2 | 143 | 191 | 57.2 | † | † | † | † | 334 | 143 | 191 |
| Librarians, curators, and archivists | 919 | 0.7 | 265 | 654 | 71.2 | 678 | 73.8 | 202 | 475 | 241 | 62 | 179 |
| Student and academic affairs and other education services | 10,494 | 7.4 | 3,419 | 7,037 | 67.3 | 9,029 | 86.4 | 2,694 | 6,335 | 1,425 | 727 | 700 |
| Management | 9,730 | 6.9 | 4,242 | 5,488 | 56.4 | 9,618 | 98.8 | 4,200 | 5,418 | 112 | 42 | 70 |
| Business and financial operations | 4,173 | 3.0 | 1,335 | 2,838 | 68.0 | 4,035 | 96.7 | 1,296 | 2,739 | 138 | 39 | 99 |
| Computer, engineering, and science | 1,979 | 1.4 | 1,510 | 469 | 23.7 | 1,897 | 95.9 | 1,448 | 449 | 82 | 62 | 20 |
| Community, social service, legal, arts, design, entertainment, sports, and media | 4,983 | 3.5 | 2,132 | 2,851 | 57.2 | 4,554 | 91.4 | 1,904 | 2,650 | 429 | 228 | 201 |
| Healthcare practitioners and technicians | 159 | 0.1 | 67 | 92 | 57.9 | 87 | 54.7 | 46 | 41 | 72 | 21 | 51 |
| Service occupations | 1,468 | 1.0 | 982 | 486 | 33.1 | 1,043 | 71.0 | 718 | 325 | 425 | 264 | 161 |
| Sales and related occupations | 3,363 | 2.4 | 1,421 | 1,942 | 57.7 | 3,279 | 97.5 | 1,394 | 1,885 | 84 | 27 | 57 |
| Office and administrative support | 13,166 | 9.3 | 3,815 | 9,351 | 71.0 | 11,905 | 90.4 | 3,415 | 8,490 | 1,261 | 400 | 861 |
| Natural resources, construction, and maintenance | 460 | 0.3 | 317 | 143 | 31.1 | 316 | 68.7 | 269 | 47 | 144 | 48 | 96 |
| Production, transportation, and material moving | 179 | 0.1 | 140 | 39 | 21.8 | 121 | 67.6 | 94 | 27 | 58 | 46 | 12 |
| **Private for-profit 2-year** | **33,025** | **100.0** | **12,065** | **20,960** | **63.5** | **19,300** | **58.4** | **6,818** | **12,482** | **13,725** | **5,247** | **8,478** |
| Faculty (instruction/research/public service) | 18,906 | 57.2 | 7,673 | 11,213 | 59.4 | 6,982 | 37.0 | 2,960 | 4,022 | 11,904 | 4,713 | 7,191 |
| Instruction | 18,824 | 57.0 | 7,652 | 11,172 | 59.3 | 6,930 | 36.8 | 2,944 | 3,986 | 11,894 | 4,708 | 7,186 |
| Research | 32 | 0.1 | 14 | 18 | 56.3 | 31 | 96.9 | 13 | 18 | 1 | 1 | 0 |
| Public service | 30 | 0.1 | 7 | 23 | 76.7 | 21 | 70.0 | 3 | 18 | 9 | 4 | 5 |
| Graduate assistants | † | † | † | † | † | † | † | † | † | † | † | † |
| Librarians, curators, and archivists | 314 | 1.0 | 72 | 242 | 77.1 | 200 | 63.7 | 44 | 156 | 114 | 28 | 86 |
| Student and academic affairs and other education services | 2,752 | 8.3 | 677 | 2,075 | 75.4 | 2,535 | 92.1 | 640 | 1,895 | 217 | 37 | 180 |
| Management | 3,274 | 9.9 | 1,328 | 1,946 | 59.4 | 3,218 | 98.3 | 1,307 | 1,911 | 56 | 21 | 35 |
| Business and financial operations | 1,193 | 3.6 | 260 | 933 | 78.2 | 1,097 | 92.0 | 239 | 858 | 96 | 21 | 75 |
| Computer, engineering, and science | 256 | 0.8 | 212 | 44 | 17.2 | 223 | 87.1 | 186 | 37 | 33 | 26 | 7 |
| Community, social service, legal, arts, design, entertainment, sports, and media | 604 | 1.8 | 184 | 420 | 69.5 | 501 | 82.9 | 138 | 363 | 103 | 46 | 57 |
| Healthcare practitioners and technicians | 77 | 0.2 | 15 | 62 | 80.5 | 8 | 10.4 | 1 | 7 | 69 | 14 | 55 |
| Service occupations | 567 | 1.7 | 336 | 231 | 40.7 | 302 | 53.3 | 104 | 198 | 265 | 152 | 113 |
| Sales and related occupations | 1,608 | 4.9 | 563 | 1,045 | 65.0 | 1,429 | 88.9 | 527 | 902 | 179 | 36 | 143 |
| Office and administrative support | 3,262 | 9.9 | 552 | 2,700 | 83.0 | 2,648 | 81.2 | 461 | 2,187 | 614 | 92 | 522 |
| Natural resources, construction, and maintenance | 207 | 0.6 | 174 | 33 | 15.9 | 145 | 70.0 | 122 | 23 | 62 | 52 | 10 |
| Production, transportation, and material moving | 25 | 0.1 | 18 | 7 | 28.0 | 12 | 48.0 | 9 | 3 | 13 | 9 | 4 |

†Not applicable.

#Rounds to zero.

NOTE: Degree-granting institutions grant associate's or higher degrees and participate in Title IV federal financial aid programs. Includes institutions with fewer than 15 full-time employees; these institutions did not report staff data prior to 2007. By definition, all graduate assistants are part time. Detail may not sum to totals because of rounding.

SOURCE: U.S. Department of Education, National Center for Education Statistics, Integrated Postsecondary Education Data System (IPEDS), Spring 2016, Human Resources component, Fall Staff section. (This table was prepared December 2016.)

The over-all pattern is simple—more men at higher ranks, more women at lower ranks. And these are the *recent* years.

Between 2011 and 2015, for the first time in four decades, the number of part-time faculty actually went down. (Over-all student enrollment declined in the same four years.[33]) In fall 2011, there were 762,355 part-time faculty; in fall 2015, there were 743,983 part-time faculty. The number of full-time faculty increased somewhat during the same period (in spite of the dip in student enrollment). In fall 2011, there were 762,114 full-time faculty in higher education; in fall 2015, there were 807,032 full-time faculty. From a labor perspective, that is, for a recent Ph.D. hoping to get hired somewhere, this might seem like good news—a nationwide increase of full-time hires, by an average of about 11,000 more full-time jobs per year for four years.

If so, a closer look at the bottom line is in order. From 2011 to 2015, in spite of the increase in full-time faculty over-all, the number of assistant professors in the U.S. actually *declined* slightly. In fall 2011, there were 174,052. In fall 2015, there were 173,031. That's not more tenure-track jobs for Ph.D. graduates; it's fewer, especially during four years when hiring of all faculty increased and hiring of full-time faculty increased. (To clarify for readers outside academia, an Assistant Professorship is typically the entry-level rank for a tenure-track job.) Since total faculty grew somewhat over the same four years, the numerical decline of assistant professors means a slightly larger percentage decline. Assistant professors were 22.8 percent of total faculty in fall 2011 but 21.4 percent of the total in fall 2015.

Some of the assistant professors must have won promotion to tenured associate professor between 2011 and 2015; the number of associate professors increased, slightly, from 155,201 to 157,799. However, given the increase in total full-time faculty (Fig. 4) and in total faculty (Fig. 1), this was another proportional decline. In fall 2011, associate professors were 20.3 percent of full-time faculty. In fall 2015, they were 19.6 percent of full-time faculty. The same holds for full professors, who numbered 181,509 in 2011 and 182,204 in 2015. Full professors were 23.8 percent of total full-time faculty in fall 2011 but 22.5 percent of total full-time faculty in fall 2015.

The number and percentage of lecturers and instructors—typically the lowest-paid and least protected among full-time ranks—also declined slightly during the same four years. In fall 2011, lecturers and instructors totaled 143,515. In fall 2015, they totaled 140,244. As with Assistant Professorships, these are positions which might theoretically be accessible to new PhDs—except that many lecturers and instructors are hired with a master's degree, greatly expanding the labor pool and the competition in the job market.

So where did the additional full-time hiring come in? Table 315.20 shows only one category of full-time faculty growing substantially from fall 2011 to 2015—"Other faculty," defined as "Primarily research and primarily public service faculty, as well as faculty without ranks," rather than instructional faculty. The number of "Other faculty" grew from 107,837 in 2011 to 150,732 in 2013 to 153,754 in 2015—an increase of more than forty percent in four years. Within this category, men outnumber women, especially among "research" faculty. ("Other faculty" are probably the category most likely to be hired and paid through discretionary funds, meaning at administrators' discretion.) However, within the "public service" subset, in fall 2015 women slightly outnumbered men (Table 314.30).

## Gender, Rank, and Numbers, 2011-2016

Among full-time college faculty over-all, men still substantially outnumber women. In fall 2013, there were a total of 436,470 male full-time faculty, all ranks combined, and 354,908 female full-time faculty. In fall 2015, the numbers were 438,789 male full-time faculty and 368,243 female full-time faculty. The trend line is toward parity, but "full-time," in college and university teaching, is still more likely to mean male than female.

Even in the current decade, male full professors and associate professors still far outnumber female full and associate professors. In fall 2013, there were 125,905 men teaching as professors and 55,619 women. In fall 2015, the numbers were 124,364 men and 57,840 women. The latter indicate some gradual improvement for women; in fall 2013, women were 30.6 percent of full professors, and in fall 2015, women had inched up to 31.7 percent of professors. Still, looking from outside, a full professor teaching in the U.S. is statistically more than twice as likely to be male, or less than half as likely to be a woman. In these years, as discussed, the proportion of full professors among all faculty declined slightly.

Men outnumber women as associate professors more narrowly. In fall 2013, male associate professors were 87,615, and female associate professors were 67,834. In 2015, men were 87,317 of associate professors, and women were 70,482. Again, the trend line represents some improvement in gender parity. In fall 2013, women were 43.6 percent of associate professors, and in fall 2015, women were 44.7 percent of associates. Nonetheless, "tenured" is still significantly more likely to mean male than female.

There have been much bigger changes at the assistant professor rank, where in recent years women somewhat outnumber men.

Assistant Professor is generally the lowest professorial title, the rank without tenure but at entry level for tenure track; a doctoral graduate planning to enter the professoriate begins here if possible, usually with the contractual expectation that at the end of six years, s/he will be either up or out. In fall 2013, women were 83,962 of assistant professors, and men were 82,600. In 2015, women were 88,269 of assistant professors; men were 84,762. Meanwhile, the increase in number and percentage of women getting advanced degrees far outstrips the increase in number and percentage of women getting tenure.[34]

While men outnumber women at the highest ranks of college full-time faculty, and among research full-time faculty, women outnumber men in the lowest full-time ranks, as lecturers and instructors. In fall 2013, instructors were 42,942 male and 56,359 female; lecturers were 17,066 male and 20,744 female. In fall 2015, instructors were 42,936 men and 56,350 women; lecturers were 18,372 men and 22,586 women. In fact, at the lowest full-time rank—lecturer—the proportion of women has increased even in this decade. In fall 2013, women were 54.9 percent of lecturers. In fall 2015, women were 55.1 percent of lecturers.

Again, over-all, men predominate in the highest ranks of college teaching in the U.S., and women predominate in the lowest ranks. That the lower ranks include tenure-track assistant professors is one good sign for gender parity, and that the number and the percentage of women are gradually growing among associate and full professors is another. But the fact that women outnumber men significantly only in the bottom and lowest-paid ranks among full-timers, and only among the untenured among tenure-track faculty, may not bode well. Instructors and lecturers are hired on temporary contracts, usually with lower pay and with heavier teaching loads than tenure-track faculty. The entry of assistant professors into the ranks of associate and full professors will depend on gender parity in promotion and tenure, for one thing, and on the survival of tenure itself, weakened for forty years by the use of contingent faculty and by its own fallibilities, for another. Just at the historical moment (in academia) when a large number of women assistant professors are knocking at the door of tenure, tenure is in more danger than ever. (Whether tenure *deserves* to survive is being tested, remains to be seen, and is a topic beyond the scope of this discussion. At present, anyone who wants the tenure system to survive should focus available energies and resources on protecting academic freedom for *all* faculty, TT and NTT. The segregation of hundreds of thousands of faculty into contingent jobs devastates academic freedom but has not beefed up tenure.)

Meanwhile, women are still disproportionately represented not only among the lowest ranks of full-time faculty but also among adjunct and part-time faculty. Along with the surveys from the current decade, surveys from earlier years shed some light. A comprehensive survey of full-time and part-time faculty by gender published for the years between 1992 and 2003 shows the trend line clearly.[35] Between 1992 and 2003, total faculty grew, the numbers of both full-time faculty and part-time faculty grew, and the numbers of both male and female faculty grew.

Within the over-all increases, the number of women teaching part-time grew the most. The trend is apparent whether you compare women teaching part-time to men teaching part-time, compare women teaching part-time to women teaching full-time, or compare women teaching part-time to all faculty. Between fall 1992 and fall 2003, the number of women teaching college full-time grew by 85,000 (rounding to thousands)—a tremendous increase. But in the same years, the number of women teaching college part-time grew by 86,000. Meanwhile, the number of men teaching full-time and the number of men teaching part-time each grew by 67,000. Between 1992 and 2003, women teaching part-time increased from 18.6 percent to 21 percent of all faculty. In some fields, the majority-women factor was unmistakable. In fall 2003, women were more than two-thirds of part-time faculty in Home Economics, Education, and Humanities departments/units, and just under two-thirds of the part-time faculty in Health.[36]

While Home Economics programs have declined in recent years, the other earlier trend lines have more than come to fruition in this decade. Moving up to the current decade (Table 314.30, cited previously), the data show clearly that women outnumber men as part-time instructional faculty by almost 50,000. Only as part-time research faculty do men outnumber women as part-timers, a small percentage of the totals—and a category where part-time faculty tend to be paid better than elsewhere. Public discourse in the U.S. has begun to pay some attention to institutional racism, and rightly so; institutional sexism poses a quieter challenge.

The adjunct phenomenon is so pervasive and so entrenched in U.S. higher education that this book can present only some major aspects. Each aspect probably could be a book. (Remember the ending of *Tootsie*?) The topic of teaching-versus-research, for example, has been one of some controversy in academia, with much ink spilled on it. It is also a topic that maps on to gender concerns. Regrettably, I cannot go into a hypothetical or actual devaluation of teaching in depth here, but there is no question that as dedicated professionals teaching college students, many adjuncts are bemused at what seems a devaluation of teaching in contrast to research, inside higher education.

While teaching can be devalued in some senses, research by adjunct faculty is devalued in the most material, literal sense: part-time instructional faculty hired only to teach are paid only to teach. Therefore one effect of the adjunct position is that scholarship and other creating are generally not compensated by the university (except in part-time research positions, which are as said only a small percentage of total faculty). You teach on the university's dime; you write on your own. Therefore, the more women and men are shunted into adjunct teaching, the more they are debarred from whatever professional advancement and material benefit accrue to research/writing. And the more women are shunted disproportionately into adjunct teaching, the greater the gender disparity in professional opportunity. Whether selected factors operating within the adjunct phenomenon are cause, effect, or reciprocal cause-and-effect, they are part of the picture. The effect on women's income and job stability, and therefore on women's families, should not be understated in any analysis of college teaching.

## 3. Causes and Consequences of the Overuse of Adjunct Faculty

Several causes or contributing factors lie behind the currently entrenched over-use of adjunct faculty. Along with the national events and the educational trends discussed on pages 16-21, four underlying academic factors are summarized below. While other factors may operate in individual institutions, these four tend to operate across the board, and have operated nationwide since at least the 1980s. The first three are excuses; the fourth is the elephant in the room.

### *'National search' - Women and adjuncts don't benefit*

One of the biggest miseries for adjuncts is the experience of teaching year after year in the same institution, demonstrating an ongoing commitment to the school and to the profession, but getting passed over when they apply for a (rare) full-time, tenure-track position that opens up in the department.[37] Sometimes an individual adjunct faculty member may be out of the loop, left off a key listserv, and not know about the job. (This particular problem can be easily solved.) Sometimes adjuncts are subtly discouraged from applying. Often they are rejected when they do apply.

Often, the adjunct has been teaching college students for years with a master's degree but no doctorate and no prospect of getting one; most tenure-track positions for which a national search is required ask job candidates to have the PhD. (I myself have the doctorate but no master's degree; I knew that I was going for the terminal degree when I completed my graduate courses, and as a financially struggling grad student I chose not to pay the additional $14 or so for an additional diploma.) As is widely known, the adjunct faculty population includes a very large number of MAs—many with extensive experience and expertise, on campus and off. They do not benefit in a 'national search.'

This point should not be misconstrued. The barrier may seem to be lack of advanced degrees, but the real barrier is the stigma of teaching as an adjunct: for whatever reason, when a 'good job' or a 'real job' opens up, adjuncts do not tend to be first in line for it, including adjuncts with the PhD.[38] This general principle applies even more to adjuncts already teaching at the institution, again including those with the PhD. As a senior administrator once commented to me, matter-of-factly, people on the site usually get passed over. (Perhaps chasing some off-campus target as a new faculty member engenders more of a dopamine rush than hiring someone already on-site.)

As to gender parity, federal discrimination law and policy may eye askance an institution that has few women. But a department that already have a sizeable component of women among senior faculty is not compelled to promote the underpaid women among its own adjunct ranks, or to improve their condition in any other way.

### *'Market forces' - Women don't benefit*

Anyone who looks at adjunct pay as an issue will likely see a difference between the humanities end of the spectrum and the STEM end of the spectrum. Other things being equal, adjuncts in the humanities tend to be paid less, and adjuncts in STEM fields tend to be paid more, just as full-time faculty in the humanities tend to be paid less than in STEM fields. The administrative explanation for the difference is often 'market forces.' (Seldom or never is the explanation going to be 'gender.') In this context, the term 'market forces' is shorthand for a simplistic, reductive, broad-brush version of supply-and-demand. According to theory, universities must pay more for full- and part-time faculty in STEM fields because there is more competition for their talent and expertise outside the universities. In other words, applicants are more likely to be begging for jobs in the arts and humanities, and perhaps in the social sciences, than in science-tech. (The university may not put it this bluntly; doing so might call attention to the degrees they themselves award in the going-begging fields.)

As chair of an adjunct faculty committee in my own school, I recently ran across the factor of market forces in a new-to-me way. Our committee surveyed adjunct faculty stipends by department, within colleges. What we found surprised me a little. One might predict that adjuncts in English composition will be paid less than adjuncts in chemical engineering or Information Systems. But we found that even within our College of Arts, Humanities, and Social Sciences, adjuncts in English are paid less than in the social sciences. Moreover, we found that even *within the humanities*, adjuncts teaching English and modern languages are paid less than adjuncts teaching history and philosophy. The variation is attested by first-hand experience, by our contract letters, by statements from some department chairs, and by public record.[39] In our college, the highest-paid adjuncts teach in the History Department, and the minimum adjunct stipend in history according to the then-chair is $4,500 per course for a 3-credit course. One of the other better-paying departments is Philosophy, at $4,000 and $4,300 according to the chair. The lowest-paid adjuncts are in Dance, Music, and Modern Languages. English is near the bottom (my stipend is $3,600 per course), and American Studies not far above at $3,800 per course for an Adjunct II with years at the institution.

These are 'market forces'? Fortune 500 companies, Silicon Valley, and the drone-and-forklift complex are competing to hire philosophers and historians, so that's why the arts and letters languish? While no doubt there should be ardent competition for historians and philosophers, evidence suggests that the big factor for departments' adjunct pay is more likely advocacy by the department chair than external forces. (Of course, if an individual chair actually believes the 'market forces' argument, the belief would influence his or her negotiating.) Nationwide, by the way, history and philosophy are the only programs within the humanities in which a majority of advanced degrees go to men rather than to women.[40] Incidentally, within our English Department, adjuncts teaching Technical Communication (formerly called Technical Writing) also are paid a tiny bit more than adjuncts teaching composition. The former tends to have a larger cohort of male faculty, though only slightly larger.

### *'Service courses' - Women don't benefit*

For whatever reason or combination of reasons, college and university faculty teaching 'service courses' tend to be paid less than other faculty. In universities, service courses are the generally first-year or lower-level courses intended to be foundational, courses intended to help prepare students for other undergraduate courses across the curriculum, as in English. I'm all for service myself; there is no doubt in my mind that the courses are essential. In teaching, I enjoy the built-in interdisciplinary quality of a class taken by students from a range of majors in STEM, the humanities, the social sciences, and the arts. But in practice, the designation of 'service courses' has entrenched different tiers of faculty. Service courses are often taught by adjuncts, often with little share in shared governance. And the core problems of a two-tier faculty remain—generally less pay, fewer benefits, and little or no job security for faculty doing some of the hardest teaching. Outside the STEM fields, these classes also tend to employ more women part-time, and they are often treated as separate programs even within their departments—turning writing programs into pink-collar ghettos within academia.

### *Advanced degrees granted in the U.S.—Women benefit most, except that they don't*

This is the elephant in the room. The single biggest force, right now, behind the large numbers of adjuncts is the large number of graduate students sent by universities into the academic labor market every year. Ironically, the very professionals who argue that 'market forces' lie behind low pay for women part-time faculty keep admitting thousands of graduate students into disciplines with few tenure-track jobs available. This pattern has held since the 1970s, in spite of the drastic drop-off in the late 1970s.

Again, let's look at some numbers. The number of advanced degrees granted in the U.S. is partly shown by two illustrations. (Figures 5 and 6)

# Figure 5: Table 318.20

Table 318.20. Bachelor's, master's, and doctor's degrees conferred by postsecondary institutions, by field of study: Selected years, 1970-71 through 2014-15

| Degree and year | Number of degrees conferred | | | | | | | | Percentage distribution of degrees conferred | | | | | | | |
|---|---|---|---|---|---|---|---|---|---|---|---|---|---|---|---|---|
| | Total degrees | Humanities[1] | Social and behavioral sciences[2] | Natural sciences and mathematics[3] | Computer sciences and engineering[4] | Education | Business | Other fields[5] | Total degrees | Humanities[1] | Social and behavioral sciences[2] | Natural sciences and mathematics[3] | Computer sciences and engineering[4] | Education | Business | Other fields[5] |
| 1 | 2 | 3 | 4 | 5 | 6 | 7 | 8 | 9 | 10 | 11 | 12 | 13 | 14 | 15 | 16 | 17 |
| **Bachelor's degrees** | | | | | | | | | | | | | | | | |
| 1970-71 | 839,730 | 143,549 | 193,511 | 81,916 | 52,570 | 176,307 | 115,396 | 76,481 | 100.0 | 17.1 | 23.0 | 9.8 | 6.3 | 21.0 | 13.7 | 9.1 |
| 1975-76 | 925,746 | 150,736 | 170,674 | 91,596 | 52,220 | 154,437 | 143,171 | 150,004 | 100.0 | 16.3 | 19.1 | 9.9 | 5.7 | 16.7 | 15.5 | 16.9 |
| 1980-81 | 935,140 | 134,139 | 141,581 | 78,092 | 90,476 | 108,074 | 200,521 | 182,257 | 100.0 | 14.3 | 15.1 | 8.4 | 9.7 | 11.6 | 21.4 | 19.5 |
| 1985-86 | 987,823 | 132,001 | 134,460 | 76,228 | 139,459 | 87,147 | 236,700 | 190,030 | 100.0 | 13.5 | 13.6 | 7.7 | 14.1 | 8.8 | 24.0 | 19.3 |
| 1990-91 | 1,094,538 | 172,485 | 183,762 | 70,209 | 104,910 | 110,807 | 249,165 | 203,200 | 100.0 | 15.8 | 16.8 | 6.4 | 9.6 | 10.1 | 22.8 | 18.6 |
| 1995-96 | 1,164,792 | 193,404 | 195,895 | 93,443 | 102,503 | 105,384 | 226,623 | 243,540 | 100.0 | 16.6 | 17.2 | 8.0 | 8.8 | 9.0 | 19.5 | 20.9 |
| 2000-01 | 1,244,171 | 214,107 | 201,601 | 89,772 | 117,011 | 105,458 | 263,515 | 252,627 | 100.0 | 17.2 | 16.2 | 7.2 | 9.4 | 8.5 | 21.2 | 20.3 |
| 2005-06 | 1,485,242 | 261,696 | 245,619 | 105,895 | 128,586 | 107,238 | 318,042 | 313,862 | 100.0 | 17.6 | 16.5 | 7.1 | 8.7 | 7.2 | 21.4 | 21.1 |
| 2010-11 | 1,716,053 | 288,446 | 276,075 | 131,871 | 136,163 | 104,008 | 365,133 | 412,357 | 100.0 | 16.8 | 16.1 | 7.7 | 7.9 | 6.1 | 21.3 | 24.0 |
| 2011-12 | 1,792,163 | 295,182 | 287,638 | 141,357 | 146,560 | 103,676 | 367,235 | 449,042 | 100.0 | 16.5 | 16.0 | 7.9 | 8.1 | 5.9 | 20.5 | 25.1 |
| 2012-13 | 1,840,381 | 297,322 | 292,218 | 148,895 | 153,538 | 104,698 | 360,887 | 482,404 | 100.0 | 16.2 | 15.9 | 8.1 | 8.4 | 5.7 | 19.6 | 26.2 |
| 2013-14 | 1,870,151 | 291,799 | 290,444 | 154,951 | 164,247 | 98,838 | 358,132 | 511,739 | 100.0 | 15.6 | 15.5 | 8.3 | 8.8 | 5.3 | 19.1 | 27.4 |
| 2014-15 | 1,894,934 | 287,957 | 284,501 | 161,787 | 174,677 | 91,623 | 363,799 | 537,610 | 100.0 | 14.9 | 15.0 | 8.5 | 9.2 | 4.8 | 19.2 | 28.4 |
| **Master's degrees** | | | | | | | | | | | | | | | | |
| 1970-71 | 235,564 | 34,510 | 22,256 | 17,152 | 18,535 | 87,666 | 26,490 | 28,955 | 100.0 | 14.6 | 9.4 | 7.3 | 7.9 | 37.2 | 11.2 | 12.3 |
| 1975-76 | 317,477 | 37,079 | 26,120 | 15,742 | 19,403 | 126,061 | 42,592 | 50,480 | 100.0 | 11.7 | 8.2 | 5.0 | 6.1 | 39.7 | 13.4 | 15.9 |
| 1980-81 | 302,637 | 35,130 | 22,168 | 13,579 | 21,434 | 96,713 | 57,888 | 55,725 | 100.0 | 11.6 | 7.3 | 4.5 | 7.1 | 32.0 | 19.1 | 18.4 |
| 1985-86 | 295,850 | 34,834 | 27,409 | 14,055 | 30,716 | 74,816 | 66,676 | 54,844 | 100.0 | 11.5 | 6.8 | 4.8 | 10.2 | 25.3 | 22.5 | 18.5 |
| 1990-91 | 342,863 | 35,964 | 22,582 | 13,661 | 34,774 | 87,352 | 78,255 | 69,252 | 100.0 | 10.5 | 6.6 | 4.0 | 10.1 | 25.5 | 22.8 | 20.2 |
| 1995-96 | 412,180 | 40,795 | 30,164 | 16,151 | 39,422 | 104,936 | 93,554 | 87,155 | 100.0 | 9.9 | 7.3 | 3.9 | 9.6 | 25.5 | 22.7 | 21.1 |
| 2000-01 | 473,502 | 40,625 | 30,330 | 15,867 | 44,598 | 127,829 | 115,602 | 99,678 | 100.0 | 8.6 | 6.4 | 3.3 | 9.3 | 27.0 | 24.4 | 21.0 |
| 2005-06 | 599,731 | 49,564 | 37,129 | 19,574 | 50,144 | 174,620 | 146,406 | 121,964 | 100.0 | 8.2 | 6.2 | 3.3 | 8.4 | 29.1 | 24.4 | 20.3 |
| 2010-11 | 730,922 | 57,160 | 46,147 | 23,776 | 62,695 | 185,127 | 187,178 | 169,039 | 100.0 | 7.8 | 6.3 | 3.2 | 8.6 | 25.3 | 25.6 | 23.1 |
| 2011-12 | 755,967 | 56,901 | 46,918 | 25,576 | 66,241 | 179,047 | 191,606 | 184,853 | 100.0 | 7.5 | 6.5 | 3.4 | 8.7 | 23.7 | 25.3 | 24.5 |

| | | | | | | | | | | | | | | | | |
|---|---|---|---|---|---|---|---|---|---|---|---|---|---|---|---|---|
| 2012-13 | 751,718 | 60,675 | 49,378 | 27,271 | 68,115 | 154,652 | 188,617 | 193,035 | 100.0 | 8.1 | 6.6 | 3.6 | 9.1 | 21.9 | 25.1 | 25.7 |
| 2013-14 | 754,582 | 59,884 | 49,423 | 26,221 | 71,857 | 154,655 | 189,361 | 201,228 | 100.0 | 7.9 | 6.5 | 3.7 | 9.5 | 20.5 | 25.1 | 26.7 |
| 2014-15 | 758,708 | 59,172 | 47,306 | 25,359 | 82,913 | 146,561 | 185,222 | 208,195 | 100.0 | 7.8 | 6.2 | 3.3 | 10.9 | 19.3 | 24.4 | 27.4 |
| **Doctor's degrees**[5] | | | | | | | | | | | | | | | | |
| 1970-71 | 64,998 | 4,402 | 5,804 | 8,126 | 3,818 | 6,041 | 774 | 35,035 | 100.0 | 6.8 | 8.9 | 14.0 | 5.9 | 9.3 | 1.2 | 53.8 |
| 1975-76 | 91,007 | 5,401 | 7,314 | 7,501 | 3,113 | 7,202 | 906 | 59,415 | 100.0 | 6.0 | 8.0 | 8.2 | 3.4 | 7.9 | 1.0 | 65.3 |
| 1980-81 | 98,016 | 4,827 | 6,698 | 7,473 | 2,863 | 7,279 | 808 | 68,071 | 100.0 | 4.9 | 6.8 | 7.6 | 2.9 | 7.4 | 0.8 | 69.4 |
| 1985-86 | 100,280 | 4,640 | 6,540 | 7,660 | 3,003 | 6,610 | 923 | 70,900 | 100.0 | 4.6 | 6.5 | 7.6 | 3.0 | 6.6 | 0.9 | 70.7 |
| 1990-91 | 105,547 | 4,858 | 6,944 | 8,378 | 6,008 | 6,189 | 1,185 | 70,987 | 100.0 | 4.6 | 6.6 | 8.3 | 5.7 | 5.9 | 1.1 | 67.3 |
| 1995-96 | 115,507 | 6,356 | 7,901 | 10,987 | 7,223 | 6,246 | 1,368 | 75,418 | 100.0 | 5.5 | 6.8 | 9.5 | 6.3 | 5.4 | 1.2 | 65.3 |
| 2000-01 | 119,585 | 6,456 | 9,021 | 10,190 | 6,315 | 6,284 | 1,180 | 80,129 | 100.0 | 5.4 | 7.5 | 8.5 | 5.3 | 5.3 | 1.0 | 67.0 |
| 2005-06 | 138,056 | 6,628 | 8,835 | 12,097 | 8,734 | 7,584 | 1,711 | 92,467 | 100.0 | 4.8 | 6.4 | 8.8 | 6.3 | 5.5 | 1.2 | 67.0 |
| 2010-11 | 163,827 | 8,359 | 10,241 | 14,571 | 10,012 | 9,642 | 2,286 | 118,712 | 100.0 | 5.1 | 6.3 | 8.9 | 6.1 | 5.9 | 1.4 | 66.1 |
| 2011-12 | 170,217 | 8,732 | 10,533 | 14,974 | 10,354 | 10,118 | 2,335 | 112,768 | 100.0 | 5.1 | 6.2 | 8.8 | 6.1 | 5.9 | 1.4 | 66.2 |
| 2012-13 | 175,026 | 8,582 | 10,936 | 15,276 | 11,801 | 10,572 | 2,825 | 115,031 | 100.0 | 4.9 | 6.2 | 8.7 | 6.7 | 6.0 | 1.6 | 66.0 |
| 2013-14 | 177,587 | 8,397 | 11,358 | 15,971 | 12,095 | 10,929 | 3,035 | 115,794 | 100.0 | 4.7 | 6.4 | 9.0 | 6.8 | 6.2 | 1.7 | 65.2 |
| 2014-15 | 178,547 | 8,391 | 11,411 | 15,677 | 12,360 | 11,772 | 3,116 | 115,520 | 100.0 | 4.7 | 6.4 | 8.8 | 6.9 | 6.6 | 1.7 | 64.8 |

[1] Includes degrees in Area, ethnic, cultural, gender, and group studies; English language and literature/letters; Foreign languages, literatures, and linguistics; Liberal arts and sciences, general studies, and humanities; Multi/interdisciplinary studies; Philosophy and religious studies; Theology and religious vocations; and Visual and performing arts.

[2] Includes Psychology; Social sciences; and History.

[3] Includes Biological and biomedical sciences; Mathematics and statistics; and Physical sciences and science technologies.

[4] Includes Computer and information sciences; Engineering; and Engineering technologies.

[5] Includes Agriculture and natural resources; Architecture and related services; Communication, journalism, and related programs; Communications technologies; Family and consumer sciences/human sciences; Health professions and related programs; Homeland security, law enforcement, and firefighting; Legal professions and studies; Library science; Military technologies and applied sciences; Parks, recreation, leisure, and fitness studies; Precision production; Public administration and social services; Transportation and materials moving; and Not classified by field of study.

[6] Includes Ph.D., Ed.D., and comparable degrees at the doctoral level. Includes most degrees formerly classified as first-professional, such as M.D., D.D.S., and law degrees.

NOTE: Data are for postsecondary institutions participating in Title IV federal financial aid programs. The new Classification of Instructional Programs was initiated in 2009-10. The figures for earlier years have been reclassified when necessary to make them conform to the new taxonomy. To facilitate trend comparisons, certain aggregations have been made of the degree fields as reported in the Integrated Postsecondary Education Data System (IPEDS): "Agriculture and natural resources" includes Agriculture, agriculture operations, and related sciences and Natural resources and conservation; "Business" includes Business, management, marketing, and related support services and Personal and culinary services; and "Engineering technologies" includes Engineering technologies and engineering-related fields, Construction trades, and Mechanic and repair technologies/technicians. Detail may not sum to totals because of rounding. Some data have been revised from previously published figures.

SOURCE: U.S. Department of Education, National Center for Education Statistics, Higher Education General Information Survey (HEGIS), "Degrees and Other Formal Awards Conferred" surveys, 1970-71 through 1985-86; Integrated Postsecondary Education Data System (IPEDS), "Completions Survey" (IPEDS-C:91-99); and IPEDS Fall 2000 through Fall 2015, Completions component. (This table was prepared February 2017.)

# Figure 6: Table 318.40

Table 318.40. Degrees/certificates conferred by postsecondary institutions, by control of institution and level of degree/certificate: 1970-71 through 2014-15

| Year | Public institutions | | | | | Private institutions: Total | | | | | Private: Nonprofit | | | | | Private: For-profit | | | | |
|---|---|---|---|---|---|---|---|---|---|---|---|---|---|---|---|---|---|---|---|---|
| | Certificates below the associate's | Associate's degrees | Bachelor's degrees | Master's degrees | Doctor's degrees[1] | Certificates below the associate's | Associate's degrees | Bachelor's degrees | Master's degrees | Doctor's degrees[1] | Certificates below the associate's | Associate's degrees | Bachelor's degrees | Master's degrees | Doctor's degrees[1] | Certificates below the associate's | Associate's degrees | Bachelor's degrees | Master's degrees | Doctor's degrees[1] |
| 1 | 2 | 3 | 4 | 5 | 6 | 7 | 8 | 9 | 10 | 11 | 12 | 13 | 14 | 15 | 16 | 17 | 18 | 19 | 20 | 21 |
| 1970-71 | — | [illegible] | [illegible] | [illegible] | [illegible] | — | [illegible] | [illegible] | [illegible] | [illegible] | — | — | — | — | — | — | — | — | — | — |
| 1971-72 | — | [illegible] | [illegible] | [illegible] | [illegible] | — | [illegible] | [illegible] | [illegible] | [illegible] | — | — | — | — | — | — | — | — | — | — |
| 1972-73 | — | [illegible] | [illegible] | [illegible] | [illegible] | — | [illegible] | [illegible] | [illegible] | [illegible] | — | — | — | — | — | — | — | — | — | — |
| 1973-74 | | [illegible] | [illegible] | [illegible] | [illegible] | | [illegible] | [illegible] | [illegible] | [illegible] | | | | | | | | | | |
| 1974-75 | | [illegible] | [illegible] | [illegible] | 45,730 | | 41,637 | [illegible] | 103,741 | [illegible] | | | | | | | | | | |
| 1975-76 | | [illegible] | [illegible] | [illegible] | [illegible] | | [illegible] | [illegible] | [illegible] | [illegible] | | | | | | | | | | |
| 1976-77 | — | [illegible] | [illegible] | [illegible] | [illegible] | — | [illegible] | [illegible] | 114,124 | [illegible] | — | — | — | — | — | — | — | — | — | — |
| 1977-78 | — | [illegible] | [illegible] | [illegible] | [illegible] | — | [illegible] | [illegible] | [illegible] | [illegible] | — | — | — | — | — | — | — | — | — | — |
| 1978-79 | — | [illegible] | [illegible] | [illegible] | [illegible] | — | [illegible] | [illegible] | [illegible] | [illegible] | — | — | — | — | — | — | — | — | — | — |
| 1979-80 | — | [illegible] | [illegible] | [illegible] | [illegible] | — | [illegible] | [illegible] | [illegible] | [illegible] | — | — | — | — | — | — | — | — | — | — |
| 1980-81 | — | [illegible] | [illegible] | 184,384 | [illegible] | — | [illegible][2] | [illegible] | [illegible] | [illegible] | — | — | — | — | — | — | — | — | — | — |
| 1981-82 | | [illegible] | [illegible] | [illegible] | 50,590 | | [illegible][2] | [illegible] | [illegible] | [illegible] | | | | | | | | | | |
| 1982-83 | — | [illegible] | [illegible] | [illegible] | [illegible] | — | [illegible][2] | [illegible] | [illegible] | [illegible] | — | — | — | — | — | — | — | — | — | — |
| 1983-84 | — | [illegible] | [illegible] | [illegible] | [illegible] | — | [illegible] | [illegible] | [illegible] | [illegible] | — | — | — | — | — | — | — | — | — | — |
| 1984-85 | — | [illegible] | [illegible] | [illegible] | 51,489 | — | 77,287 | [illegible] | [illegible] | [illegible] | — | — | — | — | — | — | — | — | — | — |
| 1985-86 | | [illegible] | [illegible] | [illegible] | 51,001 | | [illegible] | [illegible] | [illegible] | [illegible] | | | | | | | | | | |
| 1986-87 | | [illegible] | [illegible] | [illegible] | 51,216 | | [illegible] | [illegible] | [illegible] | [illegible] | | | | | | | | | | |
| 1987-88 | | 354,100 | [illegible] | [illegible] | 51,041 | | [illegible] | [illegible] | [illegible] | [illegible] | | | | | | | | | | |
| 1988-89 | | [illegible] | [illegible] | [illegible] | [illegible] | | [illegible] | [illegible] | [illegible] | [illegible] | | | | | | | | | | |
| 1989-90 | | [illegible] | [illegible] | [illegible] | [illegible] | | [illegible] | [illegible] | 144,140 | [illegible] | | [illegible] | [illegible] | [illegible] | [illegible] | | [illegible] | [illegible] | [illegible] | 402 |
| 1990-91 | — | [illegible] | [illegible] | [illegible] | [illegible] | — | [illegible] | [illegible] | [illegible] | [illegible] | — | [illegible] | [illegible] | [illegible] | [illegible] | — | [illegible] | [illegible] | [illegible] | [illegible] |
| 1991-92 | — | [illegible] | [illegible] | [illegible] | [illegible] | — | [illegible] | [illegible] | [illegible] | [illegible] | — | [illegible] | [illegible] | [illegible] | [illegible] | — | [illegible] | [illegible] | [illegible] | [illegible] |
| 1992-93 | — | [illegible] | [illegible] | [illegible] | [illegible] | — | [illegible] | [illegible] | [illegible] | [illegible] | — | [illegible] | [illegible] | [illegible] | [illegible] | — | [illegible] | [illegible] | [illegible] | [illegible] |
| 1993-94 | — | [illegible] | [illegible] | [illegible] | [illegible] | — | [illegible] | [illegible] | [illegible] | [illegible] | — | [illegible] | [illegible] | [illegible] | [illegible] | — | [illegible] | [illegible] | [illegible] | [illegible] |
| 1994-95 | | [illegible] | [illegible] | [illegible] | [illegible] | | [illegible] | [illegible] | [illegible] | [illegible] | | [illegible] | [illegible] | [illegible] | [illegible] | | [illegible] | [illegible] | [illegible] | [illegible] |

| | | | | | | | | | | | | | | | | | | | | |
|---|---|---|---|---|---|---|---|---|---|---|---|---|---|---|---|---|---|---|---|---|
| 1995-96 | 317,398 | 404,291 | 774,770 | 227,179 | 55,398 | 313,811 | 110,525 | 390,722 | 185,001 | 96,105 | 34,259 | 50,678 | 375,916 | 181,142 | 55,506 | 279,073 | 57,247 | 10,806 | 7,879 | 807 |
| 1996-97 | 326,887 | 465,494 | 776,677 | 233,237 | 61,061 | 272,237 | 105,732 | 396,202 | 192,028 | 57,666 | 35,560 | 49,158 | 384,066 | 186,962 | 56,564 | 226,677 | 56,564 | 12,115 | 5,060 | 803 |
| 1997-98 | 335,510 | 453,084 | 784,796 | 233,927 | 60,948 | 246,771 | 103,471 | 400,110 | 205,115 | 57,787 | 37,166 | 47,625 | 386,455 | 194,045 | 57,089 | 214,475 | 57,846 | 13,655 | 6,067 | 895 |
| 1998-99 | 334,294 | 452,616 | 792,392 | 238,954 | 62,028 | 251,589 | 112,368 | 409,817 | 207,084 | 56,672 | 29,402 | 47,757 | 391,749 | 198,481 | 55,663 | 222,187 | 64,611 | 15,095 | 6,608 | 1,005 |
| 1999-2000 | 294,512 | 448,446 | 810,555 | 243,177 | 60,655 | 263,217 | 116,487 | 427,020 | 225,028 | 58,081 | 25,580 | 46,337 | 406,958 | 209,725 | 56,572 | 234,637 | 70,150 | 20,062 | 10,308 | 1,105 |
| | | | | | | | | | | | | | | | | | | | | |
| 2000-01 | 329,624 | 458,487 | 817,438 | 246,034 | 60,820 | 242,875 | 122,578 | 431,733 | 227,448 | 58,765 | 25,336 | 45,711 | 405,701 | 215,815 | 57,722 | 218,543 | 75,667 | 23,037 | 11,658 | 1,043 |
| 2001-02 | 319,291 | 471,660 | 841,180 | 249,820 | 61,061 | 264,957 | 123,173 | 450,720 | 237,498 | 58,602 | 32,904 | 45,761 | 424,322 | 223,225 | 57,707 | 232,058 | 77,732 | 26,895 | 14,264 | 895 |
| 2002-03 | 335,727 | 498,279 | 875,596 | 263,643 | 61,611 | 290,695 | 135,737 | 473,215 | 257,056 | 59,965 | 35,926 | 46,183 | 447,060 | 238,065 | 58,594 | 258,773 | 85,554 | 31,155 | 14,967 | 1,074 |
| 2003-04 | 354,158 | 524,875 | 915,718 | 285,138 | 64,205 | 323,734 | 140,426 | 498,824 | 275,134 | 61,882 | 35,316 | 45,759 | 451,518 | 250,891 | 60,447 | 288,418 | 94,667 | 42,805 | 26,240 | 1,485 |
| 2004-05 | 370,080 | 547,519 | 932,440 | 291,505 | 67,511 | 340,195 | 140,141 | 506,821 | 285,646 | 66,075 | 35,960 | 45,344 | 457,960 | 250,564 | 65,270 | 304,222 | 105,757 | 48,055 | 35,002 | 1,505 |
| | | | | | | | | | | | | | | | | | | | | |
| 2005-06 | 371,211 | 557,134 | 955,300 | 293,517 | 70,006 | 344,195 | 155,332 | 529,873 | 300,214 | 68,025 | 35,880 | 46,442 | 467,806 | 261,095 | 66,066 | 300,332 | 105,450 | 62,037 | 45,124 | 1,054 |
| 2006-07 | 389,840 | 566,535 | 975,513 | 291,971 | 73,065 | 339,397 | 161,579 | 548,579 | 315,626 | 71,605 | 34,195 | 43,829 | 477,805 | 267,695 | 69,239 | 305,203 | 117,750 | 70,774 | 50,936 | 2,365 |
| 2007-08 | 399,081 | 570,520 | 996,435 | 299,933 | 75,533 | 350,002 | 171,044 | 566,634 | 330,603 | 70,045 | 34,004 | 44,730 | 495,605 | 275,025 | 70,579 | 316,710 | 120,856 | 75,045 | 54,054 | 3,165 |
| 2008-09 | 428,549 | 596,391 | 1,020,521 | 308,215 | 77,270 | 375,771 | 190,852 | 580,878 | 353,867 | 77,294 | 31,939 | 46,930 | 496,353 | 290,401 | 73,583 | 343,832 | 143,922 | 84,525 | 63,466 | 3,711 |
| 2009-10 | 472,420 | 640,255 | 1,049,179 | 322,339 | 75,805 | 463,291 | 238,591 | 600,740 | 370,924 | 79,705 | 35,652 | 46,673 | 503,204 | 300,053 | 75,172 | 427,639 | 161,910 | 97,475 | 70,871 | 4,013 |
| | | | | | | | | | | | | | | | | | | | | |
| 2010-11 | 519,711 | 606,004 | 1,038,722 | 339,420 | 82,013 | 510,765 | 246,022 | 627,331 | 391,502 | 81,014 | 36,534 | 51,067 | 512,021 | 313,317 | 76,595 | 474,232 | 194,055 | 114,515 | 75,105 | 5,213 |
| 2011-12 | 525,264 | 756,484 | 1,131,585 | 349,349 | 84,730 | 463,797 | 265,234 | 660,278 | 406,618 | 85,487 | 32,856 | 54,347 | 526,022 | 325,175 | 79,498 | 430,941 | 210,867 | 134,255 | 81,443 | 5,985 |
| 2012-13 | 545,446 | 772,070 | 1,150,016 | 346,751 | 86,411 | 421,765 | 234,440 | 676,755 | 404,907 | 88,015 | 30,913 | 55,651 | 535,950 | 327,013 | 81,540 | 390,855 | 175,750 | 140,007 | 77,954 | 7,072 |
| 2013-14 | 576,468 | 794,925 | 1,186,742 | 346,238 | 85,911 | 392,815 | 210,730 | 683,408 | 405,344 | 88,876 | 30,738 | 58,127 | 544,258 | 333,335 | 80,594 | 362,072 | 157,108 | 139,157 | 74,805 | 7,787 |
| 2014-15 | 612,895 | 821,874 | 1,209,438 | 351,119 | 91,252 | 358,272 | 192,097 | 685,496 | 407,569 | 88,295 | 46,082 | 58,622 | 553,524 | 336,182 | 80,292 | 312,190 | 133,475 | 131,962 | 71,407 | 8,203 |

Not available.

[1] Includes Ph.D., Ed.D., and comparable degrees at the doctoral level. Includes most degrees formerly classified as first-professional, such as M.D., D.D.S., and law degrees.

[2] Part of the increase is due to the addition of schools accredited by the Accrediting Commission of Career Schools and Colleges of Technology.

NOTE: Data through 1990-91 are for institutions of higher education, while later data are for postsecondary institutions that participate in Title IV federal financial aid programs. Data for associate's degrees and higher awards are for degree-granting institutions. Some data have been revised from previously published figures.

SOURCE: U.S. Department of Education, National Center for Education Statistics, Higher Education General Information Survey (HEGIS), "Degrees and Other Formal Awards Conferred" surveys, 1970-71 through 1985-86; Integrated Postsecondary Education Data System (IPEDS), "Completions Survey" (IPEDS-C:87-99); and IPEDS Fall 2000 through Fall 2015, Completions component. (This table was prepared September 2016.)

Tables 318.20 and 318.40 are published in the most recent NCES *Digest of Education Statistics*. They should be required reading for graduate students. At a minimum, they should be included in the orientation packet given to graduate students at the beginning of fall semester.

A thumbnail view reveals a problem (or, as we say, a 'challenge'), starting with the bottom line. In 2014-2015, the most recent year for which these data are published, there were 178,547 doctor's degrees conferred in the U.S. (Table 318.20). This is a staggering figure, given that total faculty in the U.S. in fall 2015 numbered 1.55 million (Table 314.30). However, it must be clarified that the National Center for Education Statistics has begun counting "most degrees formerly classified as first-professional, such as M.D., D.D.S., and law degrees" among the PhD total. So a more realistic total for doctoral degrees in the traditional sense, for 2014-2015, would subtract the M.D.s, dentists, pharmacists, and J.Ds. created in the year. For this number, one must go to Table 318.30, "Bachelor's, master's, and doctor's degrees conferred by postsecondary institutions, by sex of student and discipline division: 2014-15."[41] (The table is too long to compress into an illustration.) Subtracting all doctor's degrees in "Health professions and related programs" and in "Legal professions and studies" leaves a total of 67,215.

As a representation of future/potential professors, this number is actually less than the total. For one thing, subtracting all of the doctor's degrees in the health and legal professions removes future law professors and med-school professors from the total. Also, many of the health-profession degree recipients engage in research in universities or medical schools, rather than in teaching. But leaning over backward, subtracting to estimate conservatively, we still get a total of more than 67,000 doctor's degrees granted in one year. Bear in mind that each PhD graduate spent at least four years in graduate school to obtain the degree, and the majority spend five years or more.

Returning to Table 315.10 (Fig. 1), we can compare the number of doctor's degrees for one recent year to the number of full-time college and university faculty that year—807,032. Thus the number of new doctorates equals about eight percent of the number of full-time faculty already in universities. Did eight percent of tenured or tenure-track full-time faculty leave the profession in 2015? No. So for job openings to accommodate the new doctorates, openings would have to include jobs held by non-tenured full-time faculty. Nothing indicates that a turnover of eight percent of full-time faculty would be likely in any year, at all ranks or at any rank. But in any case, again, many full-time lecturers and instructors teach with a master's degree rather than with a doctorate, expanding the applicant pool and the competition for jobs.

That point brings us to the number of master's degrees also granted in the U.S. in 2014-2015. Turning again to Table 318.30, we find that master's degrees, all fields, totaled 758,708 that year. Subtracting all master's degrees in the health and legal professions leaves a total of

647,997 master's degrees in one year. That year, there were as stated a total of 807,032 full-time faculty in all fields, in colleges and universities across the U.S. Of these, as shown in Table 315.20 (Fig. 2), 140,244 were instructors and lecturers in fall 2015—the positions that someone with a master's degree rather than a PhD could apply for. Thus the number of such faculty positions, all of them, vacant or (more likely) not, is less than a fifth the number of new master's degrees from the single year. Now add the rough totals of 67,000 doctor's degrees and 140,000 master's degrees; the answer is about 207,000 advanced degrees. The takeaway? If one-tenth of the one-and-a-half-million faculty had left the profession in 2015—something that does not happen—the resulting total of full-time *and* part-time job openings would still fall short of advanced degrees granted in one year, by about 50,000.

By now, a couple of points should be apparent as regards the academic job market. One is that the number of master's degrees alone granted in 2014-2015 was more than five times the number of all full-time instructors and lecturers already on the job. So even if every then full-time lecturer and instructor had decided not to show up for class at the beginning of fall 2015, there would still have been no faculty jobs for four-fifths of the new master's graduates. (An unstated premise that all instructors and lecturers hold only a master's degree is false; many have PhDs. Only if an institution limits applicants to a master's degree in some program or unit do the master's applicants have an edge.) Where would the four-fifths overflow go, if they went into college teaching? They would become adjuncts.

Of course, many master's-level graduate students go on to earn a doctorate, as did 67,215 or so in the year in question. Hypothetically, let's say another group the same size would go on to do the same the next year—or more, since the number of doctor's degrees tends to go up every year. Just to keep the numbers simple, let's hypothesize that 100,000 master's-degree students decided to go on to pursue the doctorate, and that none of them pursued jobs beforehand (a false premise, made only for sake of argument; many grad students also teach). That would reduce the number of job-seeking master's degrees in 2014-2015 to 547,997—over 400,000 more than the number of full-time instructors and lecturers teaching at the time. Again, even if all the instructors and lecturers already teaching had decided to walk off the job, in some post-apocalyptic or happier post-lottery-winning fantasy, two-thirds of the master's-degree grads would be jobless, in college teaching—unless they became adjuncts.

## Pushmi-pullyu in the New Millennium

Fortunately, these horrendous numbers in the supply and demand of advanced degrees versus academic jobs are ameliorated in some ways. Probably the biggest ameliorating factor is that not everyone with a master's degree applies for a college teaching job. Many people get a master's degree to advance in their own line of work—to be promoted on the job or to burnish credentials for a job hunt in their line of work. The advanced degree is used to signal ambition, industriousness, or leadership capability to potential employers, as well as to gain expertise in a field. It is also widely connected to a vision of better pay. This idea is advertised globally. The August 2018 issue of the Southwest airlines magazine puts it thus, under the heading "EXPAND YOUR HORIZONS" and sub-heading "Fueling Career Ambitions,"

> In today's increasingly competitive professional landscape, it's important to stand out in your field. One way to accomplish that is by obtaining a post-graduate degree.
> The U.S. Bureau of Labor Statistics reports that the average earnings of adults 25 and over with a master's degree increase by more than $10,000 per year compared to those with just a bachelor's degree.[42]

Clearly the increased earnings refer to fields outside academia, where a master's degree is compared to a bachelor's degree. Inside academia, the master's degree is compared to the doctorate. In academia, one can certainly find individual examples of people teaching with master's degrees who make more than some people teaching with doctorates. But the greatest determinant difference is generally between full-time appointment and part-time. Nationwide, across the board, and regardless of rank, discipline, demographics, or type of institution, full-time faculty appointments tend to pay better than part-time appointments. Exceptions do not disprove the general rule.

However, many people do apply to teach part-time, and many of them have full-time jobs elsewhere. Quite a few of these people will be qualified to teach master's students. Obviously, universities benefit when people outside academia enroll in master's-level programs; the benefit to the student depends on how much the student learns, as well as on how much his or her pay improves. I am strongly in favor of what is called 'outreach' by universities; making education accessible to more people in the community and having more people in the wider community engage in the life of the mind are all to the good. But college teaching cannot survive as a profession by relying on continuing education, distance learning, and part-time on-the-job graduate students. It is essential to fill the employment gap. The life of the mind depends on a living wage and on positive interaction with other people similarly engaged, to both of which stable employment is necessary. Both are jeopardized by the ongoing production of an ever larger reserve labor pool. While adult students are wonderful for college teaching (in my experience), having over a million 'real-world'-experience master's-degree graduates in a reserve labor pool may be less so. Indeed, underlining the vulnerability, the same airline magazine article goes on to quote the dean of the Graduate School and School of Professional Studies at Creighton University, Gail M. Jensen:

> When seeking an advanced degree, Jensen says it's important to consider the big picture.
> "You want a diverse faculty made up of teacher-scholars, not just researchers, who have real-world, professional experience," she says.

The implication is that, for occupational fields and for disciplines such as business and management, the outside-academia experience is a résumé brightener in applying for a college teaching job. So it is, and so is the fact that an applicant with a full-time professional job off-campus may well be content with a limited stipend for teaching part-time. Thus the amelioration that many master's-degree recipients do not go into college teaching, or not right away, is qualified. Furthermore, the fact remains that most doctor's degree graduates, outside perhaps medicine and law, do pursue college teaching jobs or wish to do so.

One other ameliorating factor is that, within higher education, some fields are better off than others. Some disciplines hire more of their PhD graduates into tenure-track positions than others (as some schools hire more of their own PhD graduates than do others). Arts and humanities tend to be worst off; social sciences better off; some tech and professional fields best off, generally speaking. However, the bottom line is that if some fields are better off, in the nationwide totals and averages among fields, then other fields have to be worse off. And in fields and occupations where women have been worse off, they tend to continue to be, as indicated in Table 318.30. Current exhortations to women to break into STEM fields are not a cure-all. I am in favor of equal opportunity for women in every field, and any field benefits intellectually when the talent pool expands. But in the U.S. right now, there is nothing to prevent the same thing happening to STEM departments and faculty that happened to the humanities, if the number of women entering STEM were to grow rapidly as it did in the humanities.

## *TOM LEHRER, WHERE ARE YOU?*

On a related point, some fields admit and graduate more international students than others—fields whose PhD graduates return to their home countries and enter the job market there. Often, these are STEM fields (engineering and computer specializations); and the international students in these fields tend not to include proportionate numbers of women.

## 2015 Wasn't the Only Year, Either

In any case, this discussion of academic year 2014-2015 is a terrarium model. After all, that year wasn't the only year in which thousands of people graduated with master's and doctoral degrees. As mentioned, U.S. institutions of higher learning have been turning out thousands of advanced degrees per year since the 1970s. Most of the thousands of people who obtain advanced degrees then become candidates for jobs in higher education, as intended; in this way, scholarship and research are perpetuated, and the ability to conduct them is transmitted to future generations. Unfortunately, in recent decades, many advanced degree graduates stay in the academic job market for several years or return to the academic job market after they have begun teaching. This is particularly so when the master's or doctorate holder is hired as an adjunct. Often, people teaching as adjuncts need to apply for better positions, if they are at liberty to move. Worse, anyone hired as an adjunct for a single semester or for a single term may be in effect on the market every semester—compelled to apply for or to request even the same position over and over again. Thus the number of PhD graduates in a field in a single year under-represents the number of probable applicants for full-time teaching jobs. In most fields, each year, a small percentage of the PhD graduates obtain tenure-track jobs. Another small percentage obtain research jobs in universities. Some others obtain jobs outside higher education that require their expertise and their credentials and that pay accordingly. With credentials further burnished by the off-campus experience, some return to the academic job market after they have begun working in other occupations outside higher education. Valid, accurate data on exactly how many graduates in a PhD program go on to tenure track are hard for the public to get—a symptom in itself. But the number of degrees does not suggest that most PhD graduates obtain tenure-track jobs.

Again, Table 318.10 is helpful, enumerating degrees conferred at every level—bachelor's, master's, doctorate—from the nineteenth century to now (and projecting to 2027). While the number of undergraduates and of undergraduate degrees has grown over the century, the number of advanced degrees has grown more. The largest growth proportionately has been in master's degrees. In 1969-1970, there were 3.7 times as many bachelor's as master's degrees. In 2014-2015, there were 2.5 times as many bachelor's as master's degrees. In 1969-1970, there were thirteen times as many bachelor's as doctor's degrees. In 2014-2015, there were ten times as many bachelor's as doctor's degrees. The number of doctor's degrees, including medicine and law, multiplied by three from 1970 to 2015 (even after the post-Vietnam fluctuations). The number of master's degrees multiplied by 3.5 in the same years.

As shown in the same table, a large number of the undergraduate degrees since 1970 is increased by the many associate's degrees. Adding the associate's degrees to the bachelor's degrees, in 1969-1970, there were 3.7 times as many undergraduate degrees, combined, as graduate degrees, master's and doctor's degrees, combined. In 2014-2015, there were 3.1 times as many undergraduate degrees as graduate degrees. One reason the large growth in undergraduate population—and in U.S. population—has not been paralleled by an equivalent growth in tenured college faculty, post-Vietnam, is that much of the student enrollment has been in associate's programs and in community colleges, often not taught by PhD graduates. Much of the enrollment and many of the degrees have been in two-year public institutions and in for-profit schools (now included in NCES data)—which rely heavily on part-time faculty. Hence the continuing large numbers of master's degrees.

### Degrees by Field

I have tried to make clear my (our) position that an institution should pay its faculty. I have tried to make clear, also, that an institution that continues to admit graduate students and to turn more PhD and master's-degree graduates out into the job market does not have ethical standing to use supply-and-demand ('market forces') as an excuse for not paying its faculty.

'Field' is not an *a priori* justification for not paying college faculty a living wage. It is not settled law.

However, it is an X-marks-the-spot for gender disparities. Anyone looking at gender disparities in higher education, particularly in tenure-track hiring, has to look at the trend lines for academic disciplines or fields: candidates from fields with more men tend to get hired more and to get paid better. This phenomenon can be explained partly by looking at history—in particular, by looking at changes in college degrees after the end of the draft and after the end of the Vietnam War. Here Table 318.20 is helpful, showing bachelor's, master's, and doctoral degrees for years from 1970 to 2015.[43] [Figure 5] Between 1970-71 and 1980-81, the number of bachelor's degrees plummeted in the U.S. in three broad fields—humanities, social and behavioral sciences, and education. Bachelor's degrees also declined in natural sciences and mathematics, although by less (and then went down more by 1990-91). From 1971 to 1981, the number of bachelor's degrees rose significantly in two broad fields—computer science and engineering, and business. Bachelor's degrees in "Other fields"—a broad category including fields from Agriculture to Transportation—also rose sharply in the same decade.

Correlating advanced degrees to undergraduate degrees in the same decade shows, for the most part, that there was no correlation. From 1970-71 to 1980-81, while the number of bachelor's degrees went down sharply in the humanities and in education, the number of master's degrees went up. In the social sciences, the number of master's degrees stayed constant.

In the growing undergraduate fields of computer science and engineering and business, the number of master's degrees went up somewhat in the former, where a master's would not always be necessary to teach, and more than doubled in the latter, where a master's degree might be of benefit in a 'real world' job outside academia. (This was the decade when Bill Gates and Paul Allen famously dropped out of college altogether, to pursue work on computer technology.)

The picture for PhDs is even worse, in the decade when the Vietnam War ended. In the humanities, as the number of undergraduate degrees (majors) shrank precipitously and the number of master's degrees rose somewhat, the number of doctorates also kept rising somewhat. In the social sciences, as the number of undergraduate majors dropped sharply and master's degrees stayed constant, doctorates rose. In education, as majors dropped by more than a third and master's degrees rose, doctorates also rose, although by less. (A master's degree in the social sciences and in education could benefit someone with a job outside universities.) In computer sciences and engineering, conversely, while undergraduate majors rose sharply and master's degrees rose somewhat, the number of doctorates dropped sharply.

Only the (broad) field of natural sciences and mathematics is an outlier in this context, in the 1970s. The number of undergraduate degrees dropped somewhat; the number of master's degrees dropped proportionately more; and the number of doctorates dropped most. (Apparently that math degree pays off.) The numbers got even more negative over the next decade; by the 1990s, concern over America's perceived decline in math and science surfaced in the public discourse. The result was a national policy of trying to beef up science and math, with funding and resources to support the policy. The result of policy changes, in turn, was that undergraduate majors in math and science approximately doubled from 1970-71 to 2014-2015—while the number of master's degrees and doctorates did not. In the humanities, undergraduate majors also almost doubled between 1971 and 2015, mostly because of large numbers of women. A key difference is that in the humanities, master's degrees and doctorates almost doubled as well. Another difference is that the humanities never received policy support and resource support equivalent to that in natural sciences and mathematics.

Like other occupations in the U.S., college teaching slipped into a big downturn in the 1970s. But unlike downturns between 1970 and now in manufacturing, finance, the oil industry, and technology, the historical downturn in academia failed to make headlines. In the 1970s, when the downturn was rawest, people caught in it were in shock, and large national trends were often perceived or represented as individual choices. The events themselves were simply not reported, for the most part, and were not visible to the world outside academia. The nationwide downsizing of U.S. college teaching that began in the 1970s never competed with the Energy Crisis for headlines in the 1970s, or with the Crack Cocaine Epidemic and Single Mothers in the 1980s, or with the endless spate of celebrity and scandal in the 1990s, or with perpetual war since the millennium. Sometimes the downturn was invisible even to people in it. Back in the 1970s, I heard a tenured professor at one conference ask, rhetorically, "What about education for its own sake?" Education has unquestionable value, and to jockey unemployed graduate students into seeming opposition struck me as adding insult to injury, or maybe as adding injury to injury. In any case, as a grad-student colleague of mine reminded him, medical students were not being exhorted to remember 'education for its own sake.'

Sometimes the downturn was dismissed as cyclical, with an expressed or implied claim that a downturn would be followed by an upturn. Sometimes the argument was that, at some point, many college faculty would be retiring, and there would be a wave of new hires. While there have been better and worse years since 1970, there has never been a wave of hiring equivalent to the number of new PhDs.

## Beyond the Seventies

In the 1980s and in the 1990s, when the trends were apparent or arguably should have been, the disproportionate number of advanced degrees continued. Checking older editions of the *Digest of Education Statistics* confirms the pattern. As shown in the 1995 *Digest*, U.S. doctoral programs awarded over 255,000 PhDs from 1986 to 1992.[44] These were doctorates in academic fields, not including medicine and law. (Lumping in MDs and JDs with the PhDs began later.) For 1992, another study from the National Center for Education Statistics in the 1990s counted 172,319 faculty in its "new entrant" cohort—faculty who had been college teachers full-time for seven years or less.[45] In other words, from 1986 to 1992, U.S. institutions awarded at least 82,000 more doctorates than the number of full-time faculty they hired.

Painting the same picture another way, the sixty largest degree-granting schools conferred, from 1983-84 to 1992-93, a total of 212,469 doctorates.[46] Again, these were doctorates in fields not including medicine and law. That's an average of 21,000 doctorates per year, setting aside any trend lines of growth in some fields and decline in others. All institutions combined turned out 364,892 doctorates over the same ten years. Many of those people stayed in the academic job market for years; many taught or teach as contingent faculty. (There are no reliable sources for the exact number of PhDs hired as tenured or tenure-track faculty, by discipline, in a given year, in relation to the number of PhDs granted in a given year.)

It only gets worse, particularly for the traditional fields. As the 1998 *New Entrants to Full-Time Faculty* made clear,

> the data show that new faculty were less likely to have their academic homes in the traditional arts and sciences than their senior colleagues. . . . Forty-nine percent of the new cohort . . . were teaching in the fine arts, the humanities, or the natural or social sciences. (5)

Over the seven years from 1986 to 1992, of new full-time faculty hires in colleges and universities, 81,297 were hired in the sciences and liberal arts.[47] Dividing by the number of years, that's 11,614 new full-time hires in arts and sciences per year for the years cited. This sounds like a large number, and it is. But dividing the number hired as full-time faculty by the number of institutions in 1992—rounded down to 3,000—reduces it to realistic size, an average of *three* or *four* per institution, more in large or well-funded schools, fewer in small or poorly resourced schools. The 1990s were tough years for higher education. To put the latter figure into perspective, the 1995 *Digest* shows a total of 73,421 PhDs awarded in the same years, in U.S. institutions, for the sciences alone.[48] And as noted above, the sciences were not where most PhDs were being awarded.

Actually, the 1998 *New Entrants* publication reflected some of the changes. In a footnote, the NCES revealed that

> It is estimated that 435,735 faculty and instructional staff were employed part time in the Fall of 1992 (NSOPF-93 unpublished data). NCES plans to release a report on part-time instructional faculty and staff in the near future. (3)

(To its credit, the Center did indeed go on to survey part-time faculty as well as full-time faculty, one of few entities to do so on the national level.)

In the introductory overview, the NCES also noted that "Powerful pressures are already at work that will reshape American higher education over the next several decades," and that among the forces were "economic constraints that will require increased emphases on productivity improvements and cost savings" (1). [The NCES had its own take on the years leading up to its survey in the late 1990s, phrased differently from mine at the beginning of this section:

> Starting in the mid 1950s, many thousands of faculty members, often without doctoral degrees, were hired to staff the rapid expansion of higher education [in the U.S.] . . . By the late 1960s, however, a new cohort of faculty, more research-oriented than their predecessors, began to replace them. It is these "teacher-scholars" who have largely reshaped our current system in the image of their own collective career aspirations and values. . . . Now a new academic generation is beginning to emerge as their successors, a product of different pressures and priorities. (1)

In that non-euphemizing, calm style that top civil servants can achieve, the 1998 overview summed up presciently,

> In some respects they [the professoriate] can expect to be less influential in the face of powerfully determinative demographic, economic, and technological forces that are transforming higher education.

When half of your profession is being replaced by contingent workers, and—yet more remarkably—when you yourself actively and aggressively egg on the replacement, sawing off the tenure limb you sit on, you can probably expect to have less influence.

Not that the recent and current population of college faculty has not had its impacts. But before looking further at consequences of the adjunct phenomenon, it will be helpful to look further at some of those 1990s numbers. In spite of conditions in higher education over-all, one-third of full-time faculty in higher education in 1992 had been on the job only seven years or fewer:

> . . . the new entrant cohort in the Fall of 1992 numbered 172,319 full-time faculty. This compares to 342,657 full-time faculty in the senior cohort, or almost precisely twice as many as the new entry faculty. Put another way, these new entrants constituted one-third (33.5 percent) of the 514,976 total full-time faculty. (5)

These were the same years during which older faculty were being replaced with faculty with doctorates. Un-spun, the numbers show that American colleges and universities hired about 172,319 full-time faculty from 1985 to 1992—*total*—in beginning jobs, in all disciplines. This large number could look respectable, but must be placed into perspective by the reminders that it covers seven years; the U.S. has over 3,000 institutions of higher learning; and during the same seven years, total student enrollment in postsecondary education increased by about 2 million. Divide the 172,319 by seven, and then divide the resultant 24,617 by 3,000 (rounding down) for the number of institutions. Result: from 1985 through 1992, institutions of higher learning in the U.S. hired an average *eight* new full-time faculty members, per year, in all disciplines—more in some schools, fewer in others.

It should always be noted that an average is just a snapshot, especially where new branches of burgeoning state systems had to staff whole programs. On the other hand, one must also take into account that not all the new entrants got desirable tenure-track jobs; many full-time lecturers and instructors got appointments of one to three years. And again, as the *New Entrants* publication noted, total faculty in 1992 also included 435,735 part-time faculty. It is reasonable to infer that most part-time faculty were also new entrants, taking part-time work because they were unable to obtain more desirable full-time teaching jobs. To accommodate objections, however, let's hypothesize unrealistically that half of the part-time faculty that year were some combination of research faculty, specialized professionals, and semi-retired senior faculty, voluntarily teaching part-time. This hypothesis is contradicted by the numbers of part-time faculty in the humanities, but let's go with it for argument's sake. Dividing the 1992 part-timers by half leaves a total of 217,867—outnumbering the new full-timers by more than forty-five thousand. This last number (artificially reduced) may look small in comparison to national totals, but it is not small in comparison to the number of years spent getting the master's and doctor's degrees, or to the number of man- or woman-hours spent getting the master's and doctor's degrees. Forty-five thousand unemployed or under-employed people is not a small number by any realistic measure.

Nor is it small in comparison to the total graduate-school tuition paid by students in master's degree and in PhD programs. Nor is it small in comparison to the money saved by institutions which staffed their courses with graduate students as teachers rather than by paying full-time tenured faculty. A full accounting, or even a full estimate, or a full discussion, of the fiscal savings accrued nationwide by using adjunct faculty, other contingent faculty, and graduate students to teach college students, 1970 to now, has yet to be written.

*MICHAEL LEWIS, WHERE ARE YOU?*

## Absence of Blocking Factors

Pursuing the question of causes logically means acknowledging that the over-use of adjunct and contingent faculty came about partly because nothing prevented it. If this sounds like tautology, it is not. One could call this the absence of blocking factors—even from entities or forces one might have expected, or hoped, would operate. In spite of the effects on women and on women's families, for example, the use of thousands of highly educated women as adjuncts never lighted up on the national feminist marquee, in the public discourse. The following is a short list of factors that conceivably might have operated, but did not:

1. no class action lawsuits in graduate programs
2. too little or no effective organizing for adjuncts by labor unions before 2000
3. no action on adjuncts by celebrity feminists or coverage in feminist press
4. no enforcement by the Department of Justice, the Department of Labor, or the EEOC
5. no action by states attorneys general
6. no entity corresponding to the National Association of Law Placement (NALP), for PhD graduates

In summary, while the number of advanced degrees conferred in the U.S. has grown over the years and continues to grow, the number of full-time tenure-track hires in higher education has not grown proportionately. An impact at every level has been growing inequalities *within* institutions of higher learning, mirroring and contributing to the similar inequalities outside the institutions.

## Consequences:

The situation of teaching a university or college course for a semester, for a per-course stipend starting at barely more than $1,000, speaks for itself.

Again, the number of adjunct faculty in the U.S. as of 2018 is more than 740,000, estimating conservatively (Table 315.10; Fig. 1). Multiply that number by the two years usually spent, at minimum, to obtain a master's degree, and you get almost 1.5 million years of graduate-level work. If only one-tenth of adjunct faculty had PhDs, an artificially low estimate, and if each PhD had finished graduate school in four years, another low estimate, you would get more than two and a half million post-graduate years of work. Actual totals are higher.

It is only too apparent that the professional intimidation engendered by 'market forces'—that is, a glut of degrees on the job market, produced by the tenured faculty themselves—has filled the void left by the nominal demise of McCarthyism. Solidarity can be hard-won among junior faculty facing tenure or among senior faculty building estates with their retirement benefits. It can be hard-won between tenured and adjunct faculty. On one hand, tenured faculty may fail to support colleagues who are limited to teaching low-status courses in composition, introductory modern languages, and first-year math. On the other hand, adjuncts who see themselves passed over in every development toward better living conditions for tenure-track faculty may not bear a brief for tenure. Such constraints partly explain why the adjunct situation has not been adequately opposed by the tenure-track or tenured faculty. Too often, tenure-track faculty and contingent faculty perceive themselves as separate and different interest groups.

An anthropological explanation might be that some professors cannot bear to lose their last claim to prestige and status, vis-à-vis the non-tenured, after ceding it hopelessly vis-à-vis better-paid technology managers, physicians, and others. But ethnographic chafes notwithstanding, if professors cannot exert more control over growing production of advanced degrees and hiring of cheap labor in the universities, as faculty they face four certain ills, continuing and already with us:

1) recent doctoral graduates not getting hired, or not for decent tenure-track jobs

2) overburdened graduate students teaching (as "assistants") rather than studying

3) underpaid adjunct "part-timers" filling any teaching void not filled by TAs

4) undergraduates seeing their first- and second-year teachers treated like flunkies

Budget crunches at the state or federal level can always be used to divide and conquer. The ills mentioned continue, however, even in states with budget surpluses. Too few university faculties have organized to save themselves, and too few have substantially improved the treatment of people who teach first- and second-year classes, although some are trying to do so. The consequence for academic freedom is already with us. Institutions vary, and the extent of academic freedom in an institution will depend largely on its leadership. One should always give credit where credit is due. However, other things being equal, generally the only faculty who have something like academic freedom today are the tenured faculty. In my view, this is not academic freedom. From one perspective, it is another form of privilege; from another, it is too much like a bad-conduct prize for acquiescing to the negative conditions around them for six years. And as the #metoo movement has helped to demonstrate, tenured protections at the expense of everyone else are only too liable to degenerate into aggressively inappropriate forms of privilege, i.e., corruption.

The vulnerability of academic freedom is connected to the fragility of shared governance. At present, there are two major problem areas for academic freedom and for faculty shared governance. One is the large number of graduate students teaching undergraduate courses and flooding the academic job market, and the other is the large number of adjunct or "part-time" faculty, also teaching undergraduate courses and flooding the academic job market. Obviously, the two factors are related. These two large groups of people may sometimes find themselves at odds, reluctantly competing for finite resources. But all faculty, or future faculty, share a common interest in not being jockeyed into that situation in the first place.

A large number of part-timers is always a concern for faculty governance. My own university is an exception in forming an adjuncts committee within shared governance, elected by adjuncts. But exceptions do not disprove the general rule. Again, in the most recent survey published by the NCES (Fig. 1), higher education faculty number somewhat more than one and a half million. Of these, nearly half are part-time. Of the full-time faculty, furthermore, 17 percent are non-tenure-track. By any measure, full-time tenured and not-yet-tenured faculty are outnumbered by contingent faculty.[49] And while policies vary somewhat among states and institutions, by and large contingent faculty are the faculty least likely to participate in shared governance.

Even assuming that these tallies are accurate to the last detail, these numbers are not good. At the very least—that is, by even the most conservative, bureaucratic, non-polemic accounting—higher education faculty with relatively secure positions are outnumbered by their most vulnerable colleagues. Put it another way: by even the most official, disengaged accounting, there is at least one faculty member who is temporary, for every person who can (supposedly) count on being kept. Put it still another way: in disciplines where many of the part-timers are reluctantly underemployed to begin with, for every person on the job, there is more than one person seeking that job or the equivalent.

And again, the person more likely to be disadvantaged in this hiring structure, or non-hiring structure, is the female PhD graduate or master's-degree graduate. As many people know by now, part-time faculty fall loosely into two large groups. One group comprises genuine and willing part-timers—retired professionals or professionals with full-time jobs elsewhere, who come onto campus and teach one class of Business Law, etc. This group generally takes no part in faculty governance and makes no motions in the direction of academic freedom. Its members have all the freedom they need—if they can afford to leave any time they feel like it—and they need neither tenure nor a governance role to protect themselves. They're teaching for the stimulation and for the renewed contacts with academe, and their situation is relatively comfortable already.

The other group comprises the unwilling part-timers, often not part-time at all but reluctantly underemployed full-timers in everything but name. Generally, this group has no part in faculty governance either, not because they're happy but because they're not; if they had a role in governance and more voice in the internal workings of the institution, there might be shakeups in hiring, promotion, and employee benefits.

Neither of these groups, by and large, carries any brief for tenure. So, for anyone who still feels that tenure is the best protection for academic freedom, there should be room for concern here; the use of large numbers of either graduate students or adjunct faculty to teach college courses constitutes—as has been pointed out elsewhere—an attack on tenure.

## Further Consequences, or Reciprocal Cause and Effect:

If one effect of replacing thousands of college teaching positions with lower-paid contingent faculty has been to flatten faculty income even for *full-time* faculty, the flattening is surely related to the obvious decline in tenure.

# Figure 7: Table 316.80

Table 316.80. Percentage of degree granting postsecondary institutions with a tenure system and of full time faculty with tenure at these institutions, by control and level of institution and selected characteristics of faculty: Selected years, 1993-94 through 2015 16

| Selected characteristic and academic year | All institutions | Public institutions | | | | | | | Nonprofit institutions | | | | | | For-profit institutions |
|---|---|---|---|---|---|---|---|---|---|---|---|---|---|---|---|
| | | Total | 4 year institutions | | | | 2-year | Total | 4 year institutions | | | | 2-year | |
| | | | Total | Doctoral[1] | Master's[2] | Other | | | Total | Doctoral[1] | Master's[2] | Other | | |
| 1 | 2 | 3 | 4 | 5 | 6 | 7 | 8 | 9 | 10 | 11 | 12 | 13 | 14 | 15 |
| **Percent of institutions with a tenure system** | | | | | | | | | | | | | | |
| 1993-94 | 62.6 | 73.8 | 92.6 | 100.0 | 98.3 | 76.4 | 62.1 | 62.0 | 66.3 | 92.5 | 78.5 | 58.3 | 16.1 | 7.8 |
| 1999-2000 | 55.0 | 72.8 | 96.6 | 100.0 | 95.5 | 86.2 | 50.2 | 55.0 | 63.4 | 81.2 | 72.6 | 54.9 | 14.0 | 4.0 |
| 2003-04 | 57.7 | 71.3 | 90.9 | 100.0 | 98.0 | 70.9 | 59.4 | 57.9 | 61.2 | 86.6 | 71.6 | 49.5 | 14.4 | 3.6 |
| 2005-06 | 52.9 | 71.5 | 90.9 | 99.5 | 98.0 | 71.6 | 59.1 | 56.5 | 59.8 | 85.1 | 67.1 | 49.2 | 11.5 | 2.0 |
| 2007-08 | 49.5 | 70.7 | 91.0 | 100.0 | 98.6 | 71.6 | 57.4 | 57.5 | 60.2 | 87.8 | 66.0 | 49.0 | 13.0 | 1.4 |
| 2009-10 | 47.8 | 71.7 | 90.9 | 99.6 | 98.5 | 71.8 | 57.7 | 57.1 | 59.5 | 87.6 | 64.4 | 44.6 | 12.9 | 1.5 |
| 2011-12 | 45.3 | 71.6 | 90.8 | 99.5 | 98.5 | 70.5 | 57.8 | 56.6 | 58.6 | 79.5 | 61.0 | 42.7 | 8.0 | 1.3 |
| 2013-14 | 45.3 | 74.6 | 95.8 | 99.6 | 98.1 | 86.6 | 58.5 | 59.7 | 61.8 | 78.6 | 63.2 | 49.0 | 12.5 | 1.2 |
| 2015 16 | 51.9 | 74.7 | 95.2 | 99.5 | 97.6 | 85.7 | 58.5 | 57.7 | 60.6 | 79.8 | 62.8 | 47.0 | 7.5 | 1.3 |
| **Faculty with tenure at institutions with a tenure system** | | | | | | | | | | | | | | |
| Percent of all full time faculty[3] | | | | | | | | | | | | | | |
| 1993-94 | 56.2 | 58.8 | 56.3 | 54.5 | 60.5 | 51.1 | 69.5 | 49.5 | 49.5 | 47.6 | 51.8 | 50.4 | 47.9 | 33.8 |
| 1999 2000 | 53.7 | 55.0 | 50.2 | 50.4 | 50.1 | 54.7 | 67.7 | 40.2 | 40.1 | 41.4 | 52.0 | 50.5 | 59.7 | 77.4 |
| 2003-04 | 51.4 | 53.1 | 50.2 | 48.8 | 52.9 | 51.2 | 65.2 | 44.6 | 44.6 | 41.1 | 48.7 | 51.9 | 47.7 | 69.2 |
| 2005 06 | 41.6 | 51.5 | 40.7 | 47.2 | 52.0 | 40.1 | 64.1 | 45.1 | 45.1 | 41.7 | 43.1 | 52.5 | 45.2 | 69.0 |
| 2007-08 | 48.8 | 50.5 | 47.8 | 46.1 | 51.9 | 49.1 | 63.5 | 44.7 | 44.7 | 41.1 | 48.8 | 52.7 | 41.3 | 51.3 |
| 2009-10 | 48.7 | 50.8 | 47.8 | 45.7 | 53.6 | 51.3 | 64.1 | 44.3 | 44.3 | 41.4 | 51.5 | 54.1 | 38.5 | 51.0 |
| 2011 12 | 41.5 | 50.7 | 40.0 | 45.1 | 54.0 | 50.4 | 54.7 | 40.7 | 40.7 | 33.7 | 50.7 | 54.0 | 31.4 | 31.0 |
| 2013-14 | 48.3 | 50.4 | 47.3 | 44.8 | 55.4 | 52.2 | 67.2 | 43.8 | 43.8 | 38.5 | 51.7 | 55.9 | 31.5 | 19.8 |
| 2015 16 | 47.0 | 49.1 | 46.0 | 44.2 | 54.7 | 50.4 | 65.1 | 42.0 | 42.0 | 30.6 | 51.6 | 55.0 | 30.9 | 17.0 |
| Percent of full-time instructional faculty only | | | | | | | | | | | | | | |
| 2013-14 | | | | | | | | | | | | | | |
| Total | 50.7 | 52.8 | 50.0 | 48.1 | 55.6 | 53.5 | 67.2 | 46.3 | 46.4 | 42.9 | 51.7 | 55.9 | 30.5 | 19.8 |
| Male | 56.6 | 58.5 | 56.8 | 55.5 | 61.9 | 56.2 | 69.6 | 52.7 | 52.8 | 49.9 | 57.2 | 61.9 | 36.7 | 21.7 |
| Female | 43.2 | 45.7 | 40.8 | 37.4 | 48.5 | 50.6 | 65.1 | 37.7 | 37.7 | 32.7 | 45.4 | 48.7 | 26.4 | 18.3 |
| Professor | 90.7 | 91.9 | 91.7 | 90.2 | 97.8 | 91.8 | 93.5 | 88.4 | 88.4 | 86.1 | 92.1 | 95.4 | 79.2 | 61.3 |
| Male | 91.1 | 92.3 | 92.1 | 90.8 | 97.9 | 92.6 | 94.4 | 88.8 | 88.8 | 87.0 | 91.8 | 95.4 | 91.7 | 64.4 |
| Female | 89.9 | 91.1 | 90.8 | 88.3 | 97.6 | 90.6 | 92.7 | 87.4 | 87.4 | 83.6 | 92.6 | 95.3 | 66.7 | 55.9 |

| | | | | | | | | | | | | | | |
|---|---|---|---|---|---|---|---|---|---|---|---|---|---|---|
| Associate professor | 77.1 | 80.6 | 80.7 | 77.5 | 90.2 | 85.8 | 79.3 | 70.4 | 70.4 | 63.8 | 78.6 | 86.2 | 42.2 | 22.9 |
| Male | 77.2 | 80.9 | 81.0 | 78.2 | 90.1 | 86.1 | 80.4 | 70.1 | 70.1 | 64.1 | 78.8 | 84.7 | 44.4 | 20.0 |
| Female | 76.8 | 80.1 | 80.3 | 76.6 | 90.3 | 85.4 | 78.4 | 70.7 | 70.8 | 63.4 | 78.5 | 87.9 | 41.7 | 25.0 |
| Assistant professor | 6.8 | 8.7 | 5.2 | 2.0 | 11.6 | 23.9 | 45.2 | 3.4 | 3.4 | 2.1 | 6.7 | 4.5 | 11.1 | ‡ |
| Male | 6.5 | 8.2 | 5.0 | 2.0 | 11.6 | 23.5 | 48.1 | 3.4 | 3.4 | 2.2 | 6.9 | 4.7 | 11.5 | ‡ |
| Female | 7.1 | 9.3 | 5.4 | 2.1 | 11.6 | 24.3 | 43.0 | 3.3 | 3.3 | 1.9 | 6.6 | 4.3 | 10.8 | † |
| Instructor | 28.4 | 34.4 | 2.1 | 0.9 | 1.8 | 11.6 | 61.7 | 0.5 | 0.5 | 0.4 | 0.4 | 1.6 | 9.1 | 66.7 |
| Lecturer | 1.6 | 2.0 | 1.3 | 0.7 | 2.9 | 4.6 | 20.9 | 0.3 | 0.3 | 0.1 | 1.0 | 1.4 | † | † |
| No academic rank | 32.3 | 41.1 | 20.4 | 1.0 | 7.5 | 64.0 | 69.1 | 9.6 | 9.5 | 1.2 | 19.7 | 42.3 | 37.1 | 11.7 |
| 2015-16 | | | | | | | | | | | | | | |
| Total | 49.6 | 51.7 | 49.2 | 47.4 | 54.8 | 54.3 | 65.1 | 45.3 | 45.3 | 41.8 | 51.6 | 55.6 | 33.9 | 17.0 |
| Male | 55.5 | 57.4 | 55.9 | 54.6 | 60.7 | 57.3 | 67.5 | 51.7 | 51.7 | 48.8 | 57.3 | 61.4 | 46.1 | 18.9 |
| Female | 42.4 | 44.9 | 40.6 | 37.4 | 48.2 | 51.4 | 63.1 | 37.0 | 37.0 | 32.2 | 45.2 | 49.1 | 25.6 | 15.5 |
| Professor | 90.3 | 91.5 | 91.6 | 90.0 | 97.9 | 92.2 | 90.7 | 88.1 | 88.1 | 85.6 | 92.9 | 95.8 | 80.6 | 61.6 |
| Male | 90.8 | 92.0 | 92.0 | 90.7 | 97.9 | 93.2 | 91.7 | 88.5 | 88.5 | 86.6 | 92.8 | 95.8 | 88.9 | 66.0 |
| Female | 89.3 | 90.4 | 90.5 | 88.1 | 97.9 | 90.8 | 89.8 | 87.1 | 87.1 | 83.1 | 93.0 | 95.8 | 69.2 | 55.6 |
| Associate professor | 76.4 | 80.0 | 80.3 | 77.3 | 90.2 | 87.0 | 77.0 | 69.6 | 69.6 | 63.3 | 78.2 | 86.7 | 53.7 | 34.8 |
| Male | 76.7 | 80.5 | 80.6 | 77.8 | 90.5 | 86.9 | 78.4 | 69.5 | 69.5 | 63.6 | 78.3 | 86.0 | 81.3 | 29.7 |
| Female | 76.1 | 79.4 | 79.8 | 76.5 | 89.8 | 87.2 | 75.8 | 69.7 | 69.8 | 62.7 | 78.1 | 87.5 | 42.1 | 38.5 |
| Assistant professor | 6.0 | 7.7 | 4.5 | 1.7 | 10.1 | 25.2 | 43.5 | 2.8 | 2.8 | 1.8 | 5.6 | 3.9 | 11.1 | 4.9 |
| Male | 5.8 | 7.3 | 4.3 | 1.7 | 10.1 | 25.0 | 47.0 | 2.9 | 2.9 | 1.8 | 6.0 | 4.5 | 13.0 | 4.9 |
| Female | 6.2 | 8.2 | 4.7 | 1.7 | 10.1 | 25.3 | 41.0 | 2.6 | 2.6 | 1.7 | 5.3 | 3.3 | 9.7 | 4.9 |
| Instructor | 27.4 | 33.6 | 3.5 | 0.5 | 2.4 | 23.5 | 59.5 | 0.3 | 0.3 | 0.1 | 0.4 | 1.2 | ‡ | 3.1 |
| Lecturer | 1.8 | 2.4 | 1.8 | 1.0 | 3.7 | 4.3 | 22.5 | 0.2 | 0.2 | 0.1 | ‡ | 1.2 | † | † |
| No academic rank | 31.9 | 39.8 | 23.1 | 7.3 | 5.1 | 60.1 | 67.9 | 10.4 | 10.3 | 1.4 | 21.0 | 43.0 | 40.6 | † |

†Not applicable.

‡Reporting standards not met (too few cases).

[1] Institutions that awarded 20 or more doctor's degrees during the previous academic year.

[2] Institutions that awarded 20 or more master's degrees, but less than 20 doctor's degrees, during the previous academic year.

[3] Includes instructional, research, and public service faculty.

NOTE: Degree-granting institutions grant associate's or higher degrees and participate in Title IV federal financial aid programs. Data include imputations for nonrespondent institutions. Some data have been revised from previously published figures.

SOURCE: U.S. Department of Education, National Center for Education Statistics, Integrated Postsecondary Education Data System (IPEDS), "Fall Staff Survey" (IPEDS-S:93-99); and IPEDS Winter 2003-04 through Winter 2011-12 and Spring 2013 through Spring 2016, Human Resources component, Fall Staff section. (This table was prepared December 2016.)

As Table 316.80 shows, from 1994 to 2016, the percentage of institutions with tenure systems has dropped in the U.S. Within those institutions that still have tenure systems, the percentage of full-time faculty with tenure dropped in the same years. As might be expected from conditions discussed already, in schools which still have tenure systems, the percentage of men with tenure is greater than the percentage of women with tenure.

In general, wherever there are problematic conditions for postsecondary faculty—such as flattened pay and lack of tenure or other protections—those conditions tend to be worse for women faculty. As indicated in Table 316.80, among all full-time faculty, women make on average better than men only at for-profit institutions (scroll down), regardless of rank. And again, women continue to be disproportionately represented in the ranks of contingent faculty. Gender becomes, again, one of the signals.

Trends often come to feed on themselves. In the 1970s, the rising divorce rate undermined confidence in marriage, contributing to further divorce and more cohabitation of partners. In a more positive light, the success of hundreds of thousands of young women as college students contributed to continued rising enrollment by women as undergraduates. The use of adjunct faculty, once begun—and not stopped—in the 1970s, became customary and accepted if not appropriate.

The same holds true for 'personal' matters such as child care and childbirth. It has been customary if not appropriate for the lack of reliable child care in the U.S. to be dealt with individually. In most workplaces, parents have to cobble together an *ad hoc* combination of babysitters, relatives, and sometimes day-care facilities. In universities, such is often the condition of full-time and tenured faculty, let alone of adjuncts and other contingent faculty. The negligible benefits for adjuncts and graduate students are unlikely to include child care support or even child care facilities on-site. (Universities typically do not step onto terrain that might open them up to litigation, outside big-time athletics programs.) The fact that lower-paid employees and graduate students on financial aid can less likely afford child care does not mandate that universities provide them with more support for child care, even if child care is a necessity for the employee to work.

It should be clear by now that underemployed contingent faculty teach many classes; they do research, present papers and publish articles—as they must, if they wish to advance in the profession—and they serve on committees regarding classes and curriculum. They perform largely the same functions as other faculty, and where they do not perform the same functions, it's often because they are prohibited from doing so. The choice is more often up to the employer—the university—than to the adjunct. Contractually, however, adjuncts are defined as "part-time." And there's the rub. When you get into contracts and "part-time" nomenclature, you get into areas of state law. The laws on state institutions vary from state to state; my own adjunct experience is in Maryland—neither the best nor the worst among the fifty states and the District of Columbia.

When my child was born, I was teaching English 'part-time' at the University of Maryland, College Park. I was teaching three classes each semester, six classes per year, I also participated in other faculty work as feasible. But categorized as part-time, I had no maternity leave. Fortunately, I had my baby in summer. But that fall term afterward, I was up at night to breast-feed three to five times before dawn, again just at dawn, then back down for a half-hour to an hour of rest, before dressing, packing up the beautiful baby and his paraphernalia, and dropping him off at the home of a graduate-student wife, near campus, just before class. The baby had spent two weeks in the Neonatal Intensive Care Unit with a life-threatening infection. I was so drained that my teaching evaluations that fall dropped from excellent to not. My evaluations were summarized harshly by a tenured faculty member with a weak teaching record himself. The department was not so cruel as to fire me; my small family's health coverage depended on my adjunct teaching. But the following semester I was transferred, so to speak, from teaching literature and classes in my field (Shakespeare) to teaching freshman composition. I was never allowed to teach Shakespeare classes at the University of Maryland again, although I did teach them later at the UMD-connected night school. (I had to drop that night teaching gig after a couple of years, because the cost of child care offset the value of the part-time job.)

Later, I was told that some percentage of leave *might* have been available, perhaps for a few weeks at the beginning of the semester, had I known to apply for it, but the policy was never clarified, and in any case I did not know about it at the time. If I had been defined as "full-time," I could have had maternity leave even if I had been teaching fewer than three classes, as many tenured faculty do. Basically, better-paid faculty are eligible for better maternity support and better family leave, and less-paid aspirants to a profession, or dedicated but underemployed college teachers, are eligible for less or worse or none. In academia as elsewhere, the economic trend is too often toward disparity.

# 4. Possible Courses of Action

Sunlight is the best disinfectant.

We are writing this book to acquaint more people in the general public with some recent history and with one of the causes behind today's gross national wealth disparities—that higher education itself is structured, regrettably, in a way that entrenches gross inequalities of distribution. The entrenched inequalities have already harmed hundreds of thousands of highly-educated Americans since the 1970s.

We also are writing to tell more people inside universities their own numbers. Freely communicating and sharing valid information is a course of action.

The section below will sketch some feasible ways to improve the condition of adjunct faculty. To clarify: when my co-authors and I work on behalf of adjunct faculty, we are working on behalf of all faculty in higher education. To divide an entire profession into haves and have-nots is not a sustainable model. Nor does it reinforce any good lesson for students. Our goal is modest—to do what we can to help save college teaching.

The following recommendations are not an exhaustive list. They are a start.

## Re-establishing university fundamentals

It must be remembered that some principles are essential and valid and apply to all faculty, regardless of rank or employment status (full- or part-time). Some of the fundamental principles in academia are those which govern intellectual property and those which govern teacher-student interaction. They apply, or should apply, to all faculty and to all students, regardless of faculty rank, discipline, or employment status. (Recent sports headlines are a reminder that they should apply to faculty in athletics programs.) They should apply across the board for all faculty, unbiased and undiminished by TT versus NTT. A basic substratum of fairness underlies academic and educational principles in the university as workplace. On behalf of all faculty and on behalf of all students, every institution should recognize the following.

1) The principles of intellectual property and of academic integrity apply to all faculty.

The most serious paper offenses in academia are the same as in other professions that emphasize writing, research, and creating. Call them white-collar offenses, although a better term would be intellectual property offenses. They include plagiarism, piracy, fabrication, defamation, and falsifying credentials in a *curriculum vitae* or elsewhere. The principles apply to all faculty; otherwise they are not principles. Offenses should be addressed without undue regard to the rank or employment status of the faculty member.

To that end, it is essential to state university policy and university system policy clearly, in writing; to make sure that the statement is equally accessible to all faculty; and to make sure that all faculty are cognizant of it.

2) Standards for hiring, staffing, and fulfillment of position apply to all faculty.

Part-time faculty should be hired with as much care as full-time faculty. Departments have it in their power to avoid problems like falsified credentials at the outset. Most problems I have observed in regard to adjunct faculty, aside from the problems with the condition itself, stemmed from careless hiring in the first place. Careless hiring typically happens when supervisors slide into a logical fallacy based on a mystified or unanalyzed concept of status—something along the lines of, 'These positions are not important; therefore whom we hire to fill them is not important . . .' But the students of one faculty member are as important as the students of any faculty member.

The same principle applies to abuse of position. Any position, however minor, can be abused. Often, the supervisors tasked with handling adjunct matters and adjunct employment in their programs are low-level supervisors. When adjunct faculty are distanced from their department or from the institution, a low-level supervisor can have an unfettered power of hiring, firing, and staffing (assigning courses) exceeding that of some department chairs. Abuse of position is such, regardless of the employment status of either the offending party or the injured party or parties.

That said, abuse of position by someone higher up is liable to have more grave or more widespread consequences. The more people an administrator has under his/her responsibility, the wider the harm. A department chair who bargains for raises for tenured professors by low-balling on adjunct pay harms every adjunct in the department. A chair who engages in cronyism, favoritism, or targeting ultimately harms the entire department. (Word always gets out.) A dean who lets individual department chairs run rampant on staffing or pay harms the entire college. Generally, adjunct faculty benefit when some at-least-minimum standards are upheld across departments, for all departments, like some policies being adopted where I work—a minimum stipend per credit hour, year-long academic contracts, regularized standards for adjunct promotions.

3) The principles of freedom of expression and of the free exchange of ideas and information apply to all faculty.

Americans typically give up some corner of their First Amendment rights when they go to work in the morning. This occurrence is so ordinary that it does not necessarily arise in the public discourse. The First Amendment protects off-color, negative, and provocative utterances up to a point, but not necessarily on the job. If an employer has guidelines in place limiting some forms of expression, generally the employer has the last word. The rationale is that colleagues, customers, or clients may not respond well to, or may not be comfortable with, unlimited expression.

The same general practice also characterizes universities, with some differences. The students have an equal right and a civil right to the education they are there for; it includes exchange of ideas and information unbarred by intimidation. By the same token, they themselves have a right not to face intimidation and harassment. So do the faculty. These principles apply across the board. Sometimes a balancing act is necessary, in listening and in speaking. But the balancing act of freedom of expression versus the equal contractual right to an education should not be warped by extraneous factors of status. As students of adjuncts have the same rights as students of other faculty, adjunct faculty have the same speech rights as tenured faculty. Whatever privileges tenure does confer, it does not outweigh the First Amendment.

Some related considerations:

Standing to report a problem. If any faculty members are enabled to report an infraction of university policy or other offense by faculty, staff, or students, then all faculty members should have the same standing. This includes sexual assault. If any faculty member learns of a sexual assault on campus or in a university activity, then that faculty member should be able to report same, and should be responsible for reporting same, equally with other faculty members.

Confidentiality in a conversation with administrators. Individual faculty members sometimes have occasion to talk with a department chair, a dean, or another member of the university administration on matters requiring confidentiality. An instructor of lower rank or more tenuous employment status should have the protection of confidentiality, where another faculty member would have such protection.

Confidentiality in a grievance process or in filing a complaint related to the workplace. Individual faculty members sometimes have occasion to file a grievance or to forward a complaint or concern, including a concern about a supervisor. An instructor of lower rank or more tenuous employment status should be able to file a grievance or convey a concern with the understanding that confidentiality will be preserved as it would be for any other faculty member.

Standing to file a professional complaint. If any faculty members are enabled to file a professional complaint related to the university workplace, then all faculty members should have the same standing.

Religious observance, access for people with disabilities, special support circumstances. Such principles of academic administration as permitting days for religious observance, modifying the physical plant for personnel with disabilities, and arranging workplace coverage or leave time for personnel with family emergencies should not be unduly affected by faculty rank or employment status.

4) The principle of academic integrity and the role of the teacher must be supported for all faculty.

The teacher in a classroom, regardless of faculty rank, is still the teacher. Every institution has a policy supporting academic integrity. Students are taught not to cheat and not to plagiarize. If a tenured professor has the right and the responsibility to discipline a student for infraction of academic integrity, then an adjunct professor has the same right and the same responsibility. Adjuncts and tenure-track faculty should be consistently supported if and when they have the unhappy task of addressing infractions. If the principle of academic integrity is not consistently enforced, it is not a principle. To fail to support an adjunct faculty member who tried to address a student's cheating would be disaster. When a problem of academic discipline arises, the faculty member should be supported consistently, as appropriate to the case, without regard to rank or to employment status.

Current information from adjuncts in the U.S. often reflects material difficulties or lacks, and rightly so. Lack of office space, phones, and technology harms both the faculty member and the students. These are not bagatelles, any more than the lack of pay, stable employment, and health and disability coverage are bagatelles. But along with the material conditions, a basic harm is done when adjunct faculty are not consistently or fairly supported in painful matters having to do with students. It is scary to think that a vague concept of status could outweigh a fundamental like academic integrity, and it is scary when fear of retaliation (of not being hired again) interferes with a faculty member's teaching in any way.

Student academic integrity. All faculty members, regardless of rank or employment status, are responsible for upholding the university's standards of academic integrity for students. If any faculty members are expected to report infractions of academic integrity, then all faculty members should be expected to report them. No faculty members should be denied the support of supervisors or of the administration, in matters of student academic integrity. No faculty members should be under more pressure than others to report integrity matters. No faculty members should be under a quota system for such reporting; faculty should understand that all faculty are equally required to report infractions according to university policy.

By the same token, students of adjuncts have the same rights as other students, and have an equal right to clear and consistent standards of behavior, grading standards, and confidentiality. A violation or an abuse of position by the teacher is such, regardless of rank or employment status. Every classroom teacher is equally a teacher in the classroom and should be treated consistently as such.

Grading standards. All faculty members should understand that they are equally connected to the university's policy on grades, grading, and grading standards. TT and NTT faculty members have the same responsibility to grade fairly and rigorously. TT and NTT faculty have the same responsibility to help students where possible.

Student-teacher confidentiality. Federal and state laws mandate confidentiality between student and faculty member, regarding the individual student's academic performance. That principle should apply regardless of rank. In matters where confidentiality is protected for the student, it should be protected regardless of whether the instructor is a full professor or an adjunct. No instructor of lower rank or more tenuous employment status should be under pressure to violate a principle of confidentiality, where another faculty member would not be under such pressure. Conversely, no NTT faculty member should be considered exempt from a professional standard of confidentiality, where another faculty member would not be.

Given the goals of higher learning, it is regrettable to have to face negatives like plagiarizing or fabrication, petty theft or vandalism, harassment or intimidation, let alone worse offenses. But in any large number of people, some people will violate standards held in common. The pain, harm, and loss are lessened when there are clear and consistent policies to deal with the exceptions.

5) The facilities in use affect all faculty. Some considerations:

Workplace safety. All faculty members should expect that they will be protected by university security and other workplace safeguards, regardless of faculty rank or employment status.

Access to health facilities. All faculty members should expect that they will have access to the institution's health and medical facilities, regardless of faculty rank or employment status.

Communications. All faculty members should expect to have access to institutional communications and/or correspondence regarding matters of concern or interest to the entire university, regardless of faculty rank or employment status.

## National and State Policy

If physical infrastructure in the U.S. presents a challenge to be addressed, so does America's intellectual infrastructure. The nationwide downsizing of college faculty is a national problem, and the harms damage the public. Not every challenge can be addressed by an institution alone or addressed only within the institution. Several measures can be supported at the federal or state level.

Since the public good is better served by shoring up the floor than by cracking the ceiling, I will begin with worst-first:

- *Bring hiring and staffing at community colleges into better alignment with practices at other institutions.* Two-year public community colleges in the U.S. are important. Unfortunately, teaching conditions for adjunct faculty in community colleges are often the worst. Pay, workload, job stability, and responsible supervision should not be worse for faculty teaching in community colleges than for faculty teaching elsewhere. The fact that the community colleges so often are snake-bit, now, means that they haplessly drag down faculty pay across the board. Nor should the proportion of faculty hired part-time at community colleges exceed that elsewhere.

- *Define "full-time" teaching appropriately.* The term "full-time" should be defined clearly and consistently in a way that reflects the actualities of college teaching. Regardless of rank, employment status, or type of institution, a four-four teaching load is enough (four courses per semester). Neither community college faculty, nor 'freeway flyers' teaching piecemeal as adjuncts, nor full-time lecturers/instructors, nor tenured faculty at poor institutions should carry a course load of more than four classes per regular semester.

- *Define "part-time" appropriately, with pro rata pay and benefits.* If "full-time" is four courses, then "half-time" is two courses. If pay for a full-time lecturer is $40,000 per academic year, then pay for a half-time faculty member should be $20,000. The same principle applies to benefits. If a faculty member teaching eight courses per year gets X in health coverage and retirement options, then a faculty member teaching half that number should get half X.

Two main ills can be and should be addressed: both graduate-school debt and for-profit schools need to be reined in.

Let's take graduate debt first. Going into debt to go through medical school is one thing; most doctors still get jobs (although they seem to be at the mercy of malpractice insurers once they do). Going into debt to go to graduate school is quite another, depending on program. Much as I love the humanities, it is unconscionable for humanities programs today to admit graduate students UNLESS they can award full fellowships. Does this proposition sound radical? —Fine; then test it, textbook-style:

Do administrators or public officials in your state use market forces to explain lower pay for faculty in some fields?

—If so, they are declaring what they know: their own advanced-degree grads in some fields have lower (according to them) earning power in the job market. Thus there is no pretext for allowing their graduate students to incur sizeable debt while getting these degrees. Q.E.D.

On a related point, the for-profit schools badly need to be reined in. They have worse records on educating, they have poor records on job placement—contrary to some of their advertising—and they have less oversight and accountability than public or private not-for-profit institutions. But they drive their students into debt with the best of them. The national load of education debt in the U.S. has begun to draw media attention. The fact that some students incur massive debt to get a for-profit degree has also begun to get some media coverage. A glut of lawyers on the market, beset with both problems, has also begun to surface in media. (As with insurance industry abuses in earlier decades, the heightened attention comes not just from journalism but also from popular fiction like John Grisham's recent novel *Rooster Bar*.)

## State Policy and University System Policy

At the flagship institution of the University System of Maryland, the University of Maryland, College Park, use of adjunct faculty grew to such proportions that in 2012 the university established the Task Force on Non-Tenure Track Faculty to study it and to recommend policy.[50] On a very large campus at one of the largest state schools in the U.S., adjuncts were two-thirds of the faculty, teaching under the negative conditions typical for adjuncts except that they had health coverage. (Previously, I taught for seven years as an adjunct at UMD and had every form of coverage known to humanity, for a few dollars per paycheck.) To its credit, the task force did two years of very honest work and issued a report which recommended substantive improvements. Most were implemented by the university. To improve the condition of long-time adjunct faculty and of researchers living from semester to semester, UMD created a new category of faculty, "Professional Track Faculty."[51] The new category provides a regular path for many people who had worked semester to semester, for years, as adjuncts. For research categories, it supports research. For all faculty who fall into the new category, it makes for a living wage and stable employment and offers other protections.

Since the University System of Maryland operates under the principle of "institutional autonomy," other institutions in the state university system are under no obligation to do a similar overhaul. However, the principle of shared governance is state policy, supported in written expression by the Board of Regents,

## Year-long Contracts

Among more limited reforms, there is one specific action that improves conditions for everyone involved: hire adjunct faculty on academic-year contracts rather than semester by semester. The move improves employment stability for the adjuncts. It also saves time and bookkeeping labor for staff (who otherwise have to enter and re-enter the adjunct faculty members into payroll every semester or every term, rather than once at the outset of the academic year), and therefore saves money for the university. It also spares supervisors some of the complexities of staffing classes. My own school has begun to use academic-year contracts, starting with a limited pilot program; the provost has already referred to it as "a win-win-win."

In an institution where enrollment fluctuates, the number of courses to be offered will not be 100 percent predictable. But improvement does not depend on 100 percent predictability. Any institution that hires a large number of adjuncts knows roughly the number of courses or sections of a given course it will be offering, in both fall and spring semesters. That's why the school has been hiring squads of adjuncts, semester after semester, year after year, to teach the same courses—often, though not always, basic courses and required courses. Thus some *minimum* number of classes will be predictable. What is the minimum number of sections your school has offered, over the past five years, in—for example—freshman composition, beginning math, beginning modern languages, intro to computer science, and intro to information technology? Those, if they are taught by adjuncts, can be staffed by adjuncts teaching on contracts for the full academic year. If there are deviations from the norm, presumably some additional appointments could be more temporary. New hires could also be temporary (although this reasonable modification can be abused, if the department decides to avoid improving the condition of adjuncts by using high turnover instead—the other side of 'market forces').

The abuse is that "flexibility" is sometimes used as the rationale for temporary hiring, even where the faculty have the same classes or have taught in the same institution for years. A state government or a university system that truly wants to support professionalism in its institutions will address anomalies like re-naming arbitrariness "flexibility." Better hiring means less arbitrariness, less internal politicking, and fewer unnecessarily transactional or hierarchical behaviors by individuals in responsible positions. There is no good reason for not hiring faculty by contract for the entire year, including adjunct faculty, once you ascertain that the courses will be offered and that the faculty member will be available.

A premise of the last statement is that administrators are responsible, or should be responsible, for ascertaining what courses will be offered and what faculty will be available. Last-minute, seat-of-the-pants hiring does not bolster the institution. Speaking of state governments and of university systems, the principles of transparency and accountability should mean that routine abuses are at some point addressed. High faculty turnover and last-minute hiring are not pluses, any more than high staff turnover or last-minute hiring of staff would be considered pluses. The general principles of transparency and accountability should be recognized for adjunct faculty as well as for staff.

## University and Department Policy

Some policies may have to be implemented within the institution. One recommendation is already implemented in some departments – to have each faculty member teach courses at different levels, rather than teaching the same two or three courses over and over, year after year. By and large, departments which implement this policy also tend to treat their adjunct faculty better in other ways, treating adjunct faculty as colleagues and as professionals. From my observation, to have all college faculty teaching courses at all levels, or at as many different levels as possible, benefits the health of the department and of the discipline. Seated at my office desk one day, I overheard one tenured faculty member saying to a visitor, just outside my door, that our department tries not to let (tenure-track) faculty get too stale by having them teach the same course too often. This is a good practice, and one that self-evidently applies across ranks. If you can get stale as a full prof, then you can get stale as an adjunct. Conversely, if you can be enriched by variety as a full prof, then you can also be enriched by professional extension as an adjunct. Pursuing the principle to its logical conclusion, it would seem healthful for full professors and for associate professors to teach first- and second-year courses as part of the mix.

It is also healthful for adjuncts and contingent faculty to teach courses in their own fields of expertise. My doctorate was in Early Modern/ Shakespeare, but I teach only composition, first-year or third-year classes. I am a professional writer, and I love teaching the writing classes. They are interdisciplinary, including a range of student backgrounds, aptitudes, and interests. They challenge me to stay grounded and clear. But no faculty should be required to teach only one course over and over. Back when I was tenure-track, I enjoyed the experience of having some of my freshman students take sophomore-level and then upper-level classes of mine, moving with former composition students into literature classes, even as I still also taught first-year classes each semester. Now, I cannot have that experience.

Instead, the converse practice holds; teachers of first-year courses are being segregated more intensely all the time. The intense separation has led to some ironic and presumably unintended consequences. Take the 'foundational' aspect of Freshman Composition. I fully support the idea that first-year writing should be a foundation for future courses besides English. Writing is essential everywhere, and anyway writing and reading should not be only for English classes, any more than art should be exclusively for museums or science exclusively for laboratories or an understanding of law only for lawyers. Skills developed and improved in English class are valuable throughout college and beyond. But allowing first-year English only as a 'service' course has impoverished English departments. It prevents first-year English from being a farm team to grow future English majors. Quite the opposite; the more routine-ized the class, the less likely to appeal to a student seeking a major that engages him or her. As a consequence, many or most English majors are students who entered college planning to major in English—many of whom skipped first-year writing via Advanced Placement, or tried to do so. As a further consequence, without the freshman course as a farm team, sophomore courses have also taken a hard hit. Sophomore-level literature survey courses and other introductory courses end up being de-emphasized rather than being developed energetically to attract majors and minors—all of this when the decline of the humanities is bemoaned in every organizational statement from the profession.

The result is not good for the academic job market, of course. A paucity of upper-level classes taught by a handful of tenure-track faculty on one hand; scores of sections of first-year writing classes taught be a raft of adjuncts on the other. The inevitable outcome?—the number of tenure lines shrinks predictably every four or five years. Meanwhile, even as freshman English classes are prescribed as foundation, or service, for courses in other disciplines, they are taught by contingent faculty—often the faculty least likely to know professors in other disciplines. (Not all adjunct faculty meet even the senior faculty in their own departments; fewer adjunct faculty rub shoulders with senior faculty in other divisions.) Having all ranks of faculty teach all levels of students, where possible, would improve the academic job market for PhDs and would benefit the intellectual atmosphere in higher education. College faculty would look better and would sound better. Staffing a course would depend on qualifications, not on rank. In fact, this one simple wave of the magic wand would do away with most of the anomalous two-tier system entrenched today. All faculty or most faculty would teach senior courses, junior courses, sophomore courses, and freshman courses. Their teaching a share of the first-year courses would in turn open upper-level classes for other faculty to teach, such as adjuncts.

This is in fact the model implemented by many departments in the social sciences, for example, sometimes in the arts, and in some of the humanities. The rigid two-tier model tends to characterize mostly English (writing programs) and modern languages. Therefore, with an unhappy irony, the courses most affected are some of the first courses an entering student takes. Sometimes it may be difficult for senior faculty to remember that sizzle of excitement at being in college—*college!*—for the first time. Routine-ized, de-skilled, and over-controlled first-year courses—in writing, for example—where faculty creativeness, strong preparation, and strong credentials are discouraged as poaching on tenure-track turf, drain away that sizzle. So do too many of the textbooks used in programs that can be soft ripe prey for well-hyped but less than interesting corporate products.

## Actions by Adjunct Faculty

All of the foregoing are recommended actions, to be supported where feasible by adjunct faculty members. If it is feasible to move for action at the state or legislative level, adjuncts should be involved, on their own behalf. If it is feasible to move for action within the institution or at the level of the university or college system, adjuncts should be involved.

That said, the authors of this book recognize that asking adjuncts to work for themselves is asking for yet more unpaid work—sometimes from people already spread too thin. With all recommendations, we proceed under that understanding.

For adjuncts themselves, acting on their own behalf, three broad strategies have potential to help, singly and in combination:

1) do what-you-can-when-you-can-where-you-can, the *ad hoc* model

2) collective bargaining, the organized labor model

3) create a separate professional track for long-time adjunct faculty who have shown continuing commitment to the institution, the UMD model

Probably the first of the three strategies—what I have called the *ad hoc* model—has to be implemented regardless of whether any other strategies are implemented. Given the conditions of adjunct employment, doing what you can toward improving the conditions, when you can and where you can, is not desultory. It is necessary.

Needless to say, it also involves a balancing act, or more than one balancing act. Obviously each individual has to try to find a work-life balance—and each person has to keep adjusting the balance, going on. In a group effort, one must balance time spent coordinating with others in the larger interest with time spent on one's individual studies. Balancing acts are part of life. As good parents find, one must balance the interests of one's own offspring, helping them grow up as well equipped as possible to deal with the world, with the consideration that they also have to have a world to grow up in. Dog-eat-dog, as under the old sudden-death master's degree that Johns Hopkins University used years ago, takes you only so far.

For the individual faculty member, the balancing act involves a series of choices. Regardless of age or employment status, there are decisions to be made. Do you go ahead and pursue a doctorate? If so, do you stay in the field you're in, or do you switch disciplines? (While adjunct hiring was rife mostly in the humanities early on, now even 'hard sciences' like physics are being taught by adjuncts. At least a couple of friends of mine with well-respected degrees in science switched into computer technology, at some point, to make a living.) Where do you apply? Can you relocate, or do you have to consider only schools near where you currently live? If you are admitted, can you afford the program?

> WARNING:
> If you apply to graduate school in
> any of the traditional disciplines, do not enter unless they
> GIVE YOU MONEY.

Every institution has an obligation to its students. Any institution that admits graduate students has an obligation to keep a close eye on two things—the quality of the education, and the prospects of getting a job afterward. This is especially so in the traditional disciplines, whose main reason for being is the life of the mind and where a rewarding job is the traditional tenure-track position in a university. Given the academic job market in the humanities, a graduate program should make every effort to support its post-graduate students as directly as possible. One route is fellowships, rather than teaching assistantships. Another route is waiving tuition for graduate courses. (Harvard and a few other Ivy League institutions have recently begun to admit undergraduates tuition-free. They should consider doing the same for graduate students, at least in some disciplines.)

Another possibility—neglected for quite a few years, now—is tuition remission. Along with the other material benefits for tenured faculty that I listed on page 19, many schools allowed tuition remission for dependents of their faculty. The extent of the waiver or of the discount varied from school to school, and sometimes between programs in the same college, but in some places, faculty could be hired with the additional perk of tuition remission. When they signed on the dotted line, it was the additional inducement that their dependents could attend the university, if admitted, paying no tuition or a discounted tuition. This perk still exists to some extent—but not, as a rule, for adjunct faculty, and not for graduate students. If a graduate student or an adjunct had the same benefit, its value would likely exceed the amount of his/her teaching assistantship or stipend. That's a good reason for offering it. After decades of a declined academic job market, nationally we have many older adjuncts and older grad students—old enough to be parents, and often old enough to be facing the quandary of how to put their offspring through college.

This brief discussion is not to be construed as despairing, cynical, or excessively discouraging. The bottom line is that graduate students, especially in the humanities, face an academic job market that the schools they attend either know about or should know about. A childless person in his/her twenties may be able to afford graduate school, eking out a living as a teaching assistant or on a (rare) fellowship while studying, for a few years, especially if he or she can live with relatives or split rent with housemates. The time spent learning in one's twenties is time well spent,

- IF the learning has the good qualities of genuine depth, breadth, and rigor, opening a window onto a bigger world and helping the graduate student enjoy and benefit from a life of the mind
- IF the graduate student is not prevented from learning by an overload of teaching for financial aid
- IF the graduate student is able to complete the degree

Even under these conditions, the time spent in graduate school and the credentials conferred by post-graduate work do not guarantee a tenure-track job in academia, and that fact should be faced clearly and should be taken into account when one makes decisions.

The same concerns apply at least as much to anyone, inside or outside academia, trying to decide whether to teach as an adjunct. For a childless twenty-something able to split rent with housemates, the situation may be viable for a while. For anyone with dependents, the picture is more mixed (even more mixed). This may seem like an obvious point to belabor, given the low pay most adjuncts receive, but it needs making. What universities offer especially is a flexible work schedule. The work-life balance, or seeming balance, is particularly appealing to women who are parents or who may become parents. I myself began teaching as an adjunct a couple of years before I became a parent, and partly because the institution offered two inducements—the flexible schedule sometimes allowed by academia, and the full insurance coverage seldom offered. The health coverage plan did indeed cover my pregnancy and my baby's birth, the broken leg my then-husband suffered halfway through my pregnancy, and my baby's severe illness and stay in the Neonatal Intensive Care Unit. Most importantly, my child's serious infection was cured, and he came out well and wealthy. I provided my small family's health coverage by teaching as an adjunct, I brought in one-third of our family income (by teaching six courses per year), and the trade-off of low pay for health coverage, in combination with flexible 'part-time' teaching hours, was worth it.

Without that priceless health coverage, the trade-offs in teaching as an adjunct would not have been feasible. The Affordable Care Act of 2010 should shore up contingent faculty and other contingent workers.

But an intense propaganda campaign against it has not helped. One of the false claims in my state (Maryland) is that the ACA forces universities and colleges to limit the number of credit hours or courses an adjunct can be hired to teach. A similar story was put around that the ACA made things harder on part-timers, because institutions were allegedly using it as an excuse to cut back classes for individual part-timers. The accurate statement is that if the adjunct teaches thirty hours per week, then s/he is eligible for coverage under the ACA. The IRS itself has clarified that "thirty hours" is not to be construed only as time spent in the classroom but is to include class preparation.[52] In practice, adjunct faculty are eligible for coverage under the ACA as long as they teach a certain number of credit hours per semester, usually equivalent to three three-credit courses. The coverage applies to all schools the faculty member teaches in. For example, someone teaching one three-credit course at one institution and two courses at another can add both workloads together, and meet the minimum required. Nothing in the ACA requires an institution to limit the number of courses an adjunct can teach.

Individual action is hardest to prescribe, so this discussion has perforce to be summary. But some other ways to take action are suggested by the list on page 56, of factors that should have operated to benefit university faculty. If there has been too little collective bargaining on behalf of contingent faculty in the past, then organizing for collective bargaining is one way forward. More of it has begun to happen in the past decade, and the trend seems to be taking hold in some large metropolitan areas—including even the Washington, D.C., region which was almost impervious to unions in the 1980s and the 1990s. If the justice system has taken too little notice of gender discrimination and workplace violations, then enforcement through any viable entity may be a way forward. If states attorneys general have taken no action in the past—as in Maryland—then they should be alerted to the issues involved.

In particular, the seeming opacity of the job numbers needs to be addressed. If PhD graduates in a field are getting tenure jobs, all well and good. If not, the public has a right to know that before paying graduate-program tuition for the advanced degree. It would surely be a good idea for the college teaching profession to have some entities in place like the National Association of Law Placement (NALP) in law, for PhD graduates.

For additional information, and to aid in individual or broader action and for additional information, below is a very short list of relevant professional associations and resources.

## Professional Organizations

American Association of University Professors

American Political Science Association Committee on the Status of Women in the Profession

Conference on College Composition and Communication (National Council of Teachers of English) Committee on the Status of Women in the Profession

MLA Committee on Contingent Labor in the Profession

Modern Language Association (MLA) Committee on the Status of Women in the Profession

## Professional Resources

"Annual Report on the Economic Status of the Profession." Published by the American Association of University Professors.

*Digest of Education Statistics*. Published by the National Center for Education Statistics, U.S. Department of Education.

## WORKS CITED

"American Association of University Professors Annual Report on the Economic Status of the Profession." *Academe* 104: 2 (Mar/Apr 2018), 4-10.

Belisle, Mary, and Prudence Brown. *Humanities Doctorates in the United States: 1987 Profile*. Office of Scientific and Engineering Personnel, National Research Council. Washington, D.C.: National Academy Press, 1989.

Burns, Margie. "It's Time to End Random 'Politically Correct' Accusations," *Thought & Action: The NEA Higher Education Journal* 10: 1 (Spring 1994), 31-55. (Repr. in *Business Ethics for the 21st Century*. Eds. David M. Adams and Edward L. Maine. California State University – Pomona, 1998)

________. "Service Courses: Doing Women a Disservice." *Academe* 79: 3 (May/June 1993), 18-21

________. "'Women in Literature' versus Women in Writing." *Forum: Issues about Part-time and Contingent Faculty* (CCCC) 2 (1991), 5-7, and 3: 1 (1991), 1-5.

________. "Women, Part-Time Faculty, and Illusion." *Thought & Action* 8: 1 (Spring 1992), 13-28

Card, David and Thomas Lemieux. "Going to College to Avoid the Draft: The Unintended Legacy of the Vietnam War." *American Economic Review* 91: 2 (May 2001), 97-102.

_______. "Dropout and Enrollment Trends in the Post-war Period: What Went Wrong in the 1970s?" *Risky Behavior among Youths: An Economic Analysis.* Ed. Jonathan Gruber. Chicago: U Chicago Press, 2001. 439-482.

"College Enrollment Linked to Vietnam War," *New York Times* 2 September 1984. National edition. 1001024. https://www.nytimes.com/1984/09/02/us/college-enrollment-linked-to-vietnam-war.html

*Digest of Education Statistics: 2016.* National Center for Education Statistics, U.S. Department of Education. NCES 2017-094, February, 2018.

Donahue, Christiane. "50th Anniversary Dartmouth Institute and Conference: A Brief History (From the US Perspective)." https://dartmouthwritinginstitute.wordpress.com/1966-seminar/a-brief-history/

_______. "Impact of the 1966 Seminar." https://dartmouthwritinginstitute.wordpress.com/1966-seminar/impact/

Gubar, Susan. "Our Brilliant Career: Women in English, 1973-2010." *College English* 76: 1 (September 2013), 12-28.

Malamud, Ofer and Abigail Wozniak. "Impact of College on Migration: Evidence from the Vietnam Generation." https://awozniak.nd.edu/assets/210448/viet_mobility_dec2011.pdf

New Entrants to the Full-Time Faculty of Higher Education Institutions. National Center for Education Statistics, U. S. Department of Education. Statistical Analysis Report, 1993 National Study of Postsecondary Faculty. NSOPF-93, October 1998.

Peterson, Wallace C. *Silent Depression: Twenty-Five Years of Wage Squeeze and Middle-Class Decline.* New York, London: W. W. Norton, 1994.

Quart, Alissa. *Squeezed: Why Our Families Can't Afford America.* New York: Ecco, 2018.

Vietnam Veterans Memorial Fund. "What Was the Makeup of the US Military in Vietnam?" What was the makeup of the US military in Vietnam? Discussion Guide. Vietnam Veterans Memorial Fund. www.vvmf.org

# Notes

[1] https://nces.ed.gov/programs/coe/indicator_csc.asp

[2] *Digest of Education Statistics*, 2016, Table 315.10. "Number of faculty in degree-granting postsecondary institutions, by employment status, sex, control, and level of institution: Selected years, fall 1970 through fall 2015." At https://nces.ed.gov/programs/digest/d16/tables/dt16_315.10.asp. (Fig. 1)

[3] Ibid. This number may be an undercount; part-time appointments are harder to count than full-time tenure lines.

[4] Some of the peer-reviewed articles on literature are referenced at https://www.worldshakesbib.org. Some are posted under author's profile at www.academia.edu.

[5] In 19[89?] *The Nation* magazine awarded me an Honorable Mention in its annual Discover/The Nation poetry contest. I still have the postcard they bestowed on me.

[6] Belisle and Brown, 36.

[7] *Seinfeld* pilot. At https://www.youtube.com/watch?v=am_xK41HYYs.

[8] For example, "Women, Part-time Faculty, and Illusion," 1992; "Service Courses," 1993; "'Politically Correct' Accusations," 1994.

[9] On the Dartmouth Seminar, see Donahue, "Brief History," "Impact."

[10] Veblen, *The Higher Learning in America: A Memorandum on the Conduct of Universities by Business Men*. New York. B. W. Huebsch, 1918. "[T]he professional and technical schools are now in fact rated as adjuncts rather than as integral constituents of the university corporation" (40).

[11] Rice University was not alone in this regard, and the size of the program was not the only determinant. The large and well-respected Department of English at the University of Virginia, with its large graduate program, also did not hire a woman faculty member (post-World War II) until the 1970s.

[12] See for example *Harvard Crimson*, November 15, 1968, "Yale Will Admit Women in 1969." At https://www.thecrimson.com/article/1968/11/15/yale-will-admit-women-in-1969/.

[13] Among recent articles, see Gillian Thomas, "Women Were Included in the Civil Rights Act as a Joke." At https://longreads.com/2016/07/07/women-were-included-in-the-civil-rights-act-as-a-joke.

[14] See Reid Orvedahl, "PrimeTime: Marrying to Avoid Draft." ABC News broadcast February 1, 2009. At https://abcnews.go.com/Primetime/story?id=132298.

[15] *Digest of Education Statistics*, 2016, Table 318.10, "Degrees conferred by postsecondary institutions, by level of degree and sex of student: Selected years, 1869-70 through 2026-27." At https://nces.ed.gov/programs/digest/d16/tables/dt16_318.10.asp.

[16] For example, full-time hotel workers can have their health benefits cut during some months of the year. David Struett, "Thousands of hotel workers begin strike in downtown Chicago," *Chicago Sun-Times* September 7, 2018. At https://chicago.suntimes.com/news/hotel-workers-strike-downtown-chicago-unite-here-local-1.

[17] Morris Zapp is a fictional English professor who figures in David Lodge's three excellent novels set in academia—*Changing Places*, *Small World*, and *Nice Work*. The character, who teaches at the University of California and insists

on being paid better than anyone else in the profession, has been suspected of paying gently satirical homage to Stanley Fish.

[18] From Pew Research Center; see http://www.pewresearch.org/fact-tank/2016/05/11/are-you-in-the-american-middle-class. The definition of middle-class income is a range. Size of family and cost of living by area affect the amounts.

[19] *New Entrants*, 1.

[20] The AAUP Annual Report on the Economic Status of the Profession, 2017-2018, has clear data . At https://www.aaup.org/report/annual-report-economic-status-profession-2017-18. See especially Academe 104.2 (2018), 4-10.

[21] *Digest of Education Statistics*, 2016, "Characteristics of postsecondary faculty," 3.

[22] The death of Professor Vojtko aroused outrage. See among others http://www.post-gazette.com/opinion/Op-Ed/2013/09/18/Death-of-an-adjunct/stories/201309180224; https://www.insidehighered.com/news/2013/09/19/newspaper-column-death-adjunct-prompts-debate; and https://www.npr.org/2013/09/22/224946206/adjunct-professor-dies-destitute-then-sparks-debate.

[23] For a partly similar look at the same decades, see Gubar's retrospective.

[24] See https://www.politico.com/story/2012/01/us-military-draft-ends-jan-27-1973-072085.

[25] Vietnam Veterans Memorial Fund, at What was the makeup of the US military in Vietnam? Discussion Guide.

[26] Card and Lemieux; Malamud and Wozniak. Also see https://www.nytimes.com/1984/09/02/us/college-enrollment-linked-to-vietnam-war.html. See *Digest*, 2016, at https://nces.ed.gov/programs/digest/d17/tables/dt17_302.10.asp?current=yes (Table 302.10) "Recent high school completers and their enrollment in college, by sex and level of institution: 1960 through 2016."

[27] See for example enrollment in English letters and literature, which had been majority-female in 1950 but became much more so when male enrollment dropped in the 1970s. *Digest*, 2016 (Table 325.50), at https://nces.ed.gov/programs/digest/d17/tables/dt17_325.50.asp?current=yes.

[28] *Silent Depression*, 17, 20, 26, 30, 35, etc.

[29] *Digest*, 2016 (Table 317.10), "Degree-granting institutions, by control and level of institution," at https://nces.ed.gov/programs/digest/d17/tables/dt17_317.10.asp.

[30] James Sledd, "Disciplinarity and Exploitation: Compositionists as Professionals," *Workplace: A Journal for Academic Labor* 7 (June 2001): 31-39. http://ices.library.ubc.ca/index.php/workplace/article/viewFile/184511/184146.

[31] Another view of the growth in part-time faculty is published by the AAUP. At https://www.aaup.org/sites/default/files/Academic_Labor_Force_Trends_1975-2015_0.pdf.

[32] *Digest*, 2016. At https://nces.ed.gov/programs/digest/d16/tables/dt16_314.30.asp (Table 314.30) "Employees in degree-granting postsecondary institutions, by employment status, sex, control and level of institution, and primary occupation: Fall 2015"

[33] https://nces.ed.gov/programs/digest/d16/tables/dt16_303.45.asp "Table 303.45. Total fall enrollment in degree-granting postsecondary institutions, by

level of enrollment, sex, attendance status, and age of student: 2011, 2013, and 2015"

[34] https://nces.ed.gov/programs/digest/d16/tables/dt16_318.10.asp "Table 318.10. Degrees conferred by postsecondary institutions, by level of degree and sex of student: Selected years, 1869-70 through 2026-27." See also https://nces.ed.gov/programs/digest/d16/tables/dt16_318.30.asp "Table 318.30. Bachelor's, master's, and doctor's degrees conferred by postsecondary institutions, by sex of student and discipline division: 2014-15."

[35] https://nces.ed.gov/programs/digest/d16/tables/dt16_315.70.asp "Table 315.70. Full-time and part-time faculty and instructional staff in degree-granting postsecondary institutions, by field and faculty characteristics: Fall 1992, fall 1998, and fall 2003."

[36] Ibid.

[37] Some first-hand accounts of this experience have been posted on Facebook at "Con Job: Stories of Adjunct and Contingent Faculty. See https://www.facebook.com/groups/conjobdoc/

[38] The expression "real job" can also be used with self-deprecating irony to refer to a job outside academia. See Quart, 43.

[39] In Maryland, state compensation of state employees is published online by the *Baltimore Sun* newspaper. At https://salaries.news.baltimoresun.com. Search by name, organization, etc.

[40] https://nces.ed.gov/programs/digest/d16/tables/dt16_318.30.asp "Table 318.30. Bachelor's, master's, and doctor's degrees conferred by postsecondary institutions, by sex of student and discipline division: 2014-15."

[41] Ibid.

[42] Susan B. Barnes, "Expand Your Horizons," *Southwest: The Magazine* (August 2018), 70.

[43] https://nces.ed.gov/programs/digest/d16/tables/dt16_318.20.asp "Table 318.20. Bachelor's, master's, and doctor's degrees conferred by postsecondary institutions, by field of study: Selected years, 1970-71 through 2014-15."

[44] *Digest of Education Statistics*, 1995, 289 (Table 262).

[45] *New Entrants to the Full-Time Faculty of Higher Education Institutions*, National Center for Education Statistics (NSOPF-93, Oct 98), v; 1-3; 5-6 (and tables).

[46] *Digest*, 1995, 309 (Table 297).

[47] *New Entrants*, 1998, 8 (Table 2.2).

[48] *Digest*, 1995, 307 (Table 294); 308 (Table 295).

[49] It should be noted that the numbers most liable to be undercounts are those of the contingent faculty, who do not have tenure lines specified in budget documents. Part-time faculty have been the most difficult to count accurately and the most liable to be under-surveyed, either from lack of institutional reporting and self-study, or because the numbers fluctuate somewhat, because of anomalies in the nomenclature of part-time status, or because they predominate most in two-year institutions most liable to be under-surveyed.

[50] University of Maryland Faculty Handbook, "Professional Track Faculty at UMD." See at https://www.faculty.umd.edu/policies/ptk_changes.html.

[51] UMD Faculty Handbook, "New Professional Track Faculty Titles." At https://www.faculty.umd.edu/appointment/new-titles.html.

[52] American Association of University Professors (AAUP), "Statement on the Affordable Care Act and Part-time Faculty Positions," April, 2013. At https://www.aaup.org/news/affordable-care-act-and-part-time-faculty#.W40OfOhKiM8.

# Requiem for Meritocracy

# Requiem for Meritocracy: The Academic Female Precariat in the Margins

RACHELANN LOPP COPLAND

- Introduction
- Section 1: Defining the Academic Precariat
- Section 2: Academics as Martyrs: Extra Unpaid Work Does Not Equal Caring about Students
- Section 3: Money Talk: Culture of Silence
- Section 4: An American Problem: Definitions of Work, Class and Labor and Gendered Implications
- Section 4 Part 2: Securities out of Reach
- Section 5: Blue Precarity
- Section 6: Precariat Motherhood
- Section 7: Precarious Mental Health
- Section 8: Academic Precariat Problems-Lack of Solidarity
- Section 9: Activism, Empowerment, Conclusions

## Introduction

Under a plague of anxiety, lack of vacation or leisure, a heavy workload of three precarious contracted jobs, and unreliable benefits, I attended the 2017 Northeastern Modern Language Association's (NeMLA) annual conference in Baltimore, MD with my family. It was a welcome relief to mingle with other academics, specifically women, who were experiencing similar employment woes and to have some leisure time with my family (even if that meant 10 hours round trip in the car). Additionally, the roundtable on which I participated included mothers who balance a career in higher education with being awesome moms ("Reports from Academic Moms on Life-hacking the Ph.D-Career-Kid Matrix," chaired by Dr. Amy L. Friedman, Temple University). Their powerful stories and activist mindsets inspired me.

I networked and got to know members of The Women's and Gender Studies Caucus, which led to my participation in the WGSC annual meeting held at that 2017 conference. WGSC sponsors a panel at NeMLA every year and proposed the topic of the "academic precariat" for the following year's (2018) conference. I wasn't even sure exactly what that meant, but I knew I wanted to participate in whatever the WGSC sponsored. After details were briefly explained, the committee encouraged me to develop a panel, given the nature of my 2017 NeMLA roundtable paper, "Interiors on the Exterior: I Wear my Motherhood on my Sleeve," which addressed the difficulties of balancing adjunct life with not only motherhood, but fertility matters as well. My work for that paper narratively explored the boundaries of professionalism and personal life—how the idea of "oversharing" is yet another way to silence women and make them feel guilty about sharing "too much information." I realized while working on that paper that my (lack of) career and the precarious nature of my job(s) was something that I needed to address, and most importantly, that I was far from alone.

As a new voice in this field of work on precarity and women in the workplace, my hopes are that this project will help other contingents in academia find their unique voice and use it for progress and education. Part of that journey requires building meaning around membership in the academic precariat. How is this accomplished? What is my place in the precariat and what do I truly *know* about that place—my rights, my access to benefits, my line of bureaucratic authority figures, etc…? How do I advocate for change and progress within our ranks, meanwhile avoiding burnout? How am I processing my employment status mentally and emotionally? What do I do now with the probable energy generated from this pondering, this research, and this reflection?

I recognize that I am not an economist, an expert in higher education hiring practices, unions, etc. I put this work in front of my readership knowing that it would be impossible to address fully all of my topics and explain the intricacies of their web in a short chapter. I invite my readers to experience this exploratory chapter, as I have: wading through and trying to grapple with the difficulties of precarious work in higher education, of gender equity matters, labor activism, self-reflection and of work-life balance.

The nature and exploration of my precarious work situation begins with defining my various identities as a woman, a mother, a wife, a scholar, a first generation college graduate and a teacher. I found myself in the precariat after romanticizing it in graduate school. Adjuncting seemed so attractive in conjunction with mothering (and of course a spouse's "stable" income and financial security), but it progressed so quickly into something stressful and unmanageable. My reliance on my spouse's income and my blue-collarbackground clouded my vision of our future. Currently, I am still an adjunct, trying to "build" my academic teaching career, but I also now balance a full-time administrative job as our family's primary income, in addition to adjunct teaching, research projects, activism and personal life.

Complicated conclusions emerge when I reflect on the blue collar community in which I was raised, my gender and my role as a mother and spouse, as related to my current status in the academic precariat—a status that negatively affects my mental health, but lends itself to creating a new activist identity. Why did I romanticize the adjunct job? Why did I think working hard and building my CV would naturally lead to more stable employment, or at least higher payment and benefits? Could my Protestant blue-collar community upbringing have something to do with my unwavering belief in the myth of meritocracy? What is my work identity now, as a more informed member of the precariat?

My experiences reflect much larger systemic and social issues related to each of my individual identities. These conclusions combined reveal an urgent need for re-defining American definitions of work, class and labor. Promoting academic precariat and full-time colleague solidarity and my own activism at the possible cost of losing my contingent employment seems a requirement for progress. My story and research are meant to empower women, especially in crafting their own work-life narrative and finding their own activist voice and solidarity with their fellow colleagues.

British economist Guy Standing expresses these notions about the precariat that resonate with me:

> The precariat wants freedom and basic security. As the theologian Kierkegaard put it, anxiety is part of freedom. It is the price we pay for liberty and can be a sign that we have it. However, unless the anxiety is moderated, anchored in security, stability and control, it risks veering into irrational fears and incapacity to function rationally or to develop a coherent narrative for living and working. This is where the precariat is today, wanting control over life, a revival of social solidarity and a sustainable autonomy, while rejecting old labourist forms of security and state paternalism. (*The Precariat* 155)

This chapter explores these fears, encourages creating our own "narrative for living and working," proposes what the "revival" Standing speaks of might look like and describes the necessary break with laborism through a discussion of blue collar Protestant work ethic implications.

## Section 1: Defining the Academic Precariat

> *"One theme [of the neo-liberal model of market competitiveness derived by economists and politicians in the 1970s] was that countries should increase labour market flexibility, which came to mean an agenda for transferring risks and insecurity onto workers and their families. The result has been the creation of a global 'precariat', consisting of many millions around the world without an anchor of stability"* (The Precariat *1*).

Let's narrow down Standing's all-encompassing definition: The precariat includes a burgeoning class of people and is often divided by type of labor, and often includes certain community identities as signifiers. In the case of this chapter, "adjunct," "contingent," "female," "mother" are signifiers discussed, among others. Standing defines the precariat class as a "new mass class" that has been "denied so-called 'labour rights' and social entitlements that went with twentieth century industrial citizenship" and claims that:

> the growing precariat needs new systems of regulation, social protection and redistribution...[and] will require new forms of collective action and representation, and should seek to redistribute the key assets of twenty-first century tertiary societies, including income security, control of time, financial capital and the commons. ("Understanding the Precariat" 963)

Preach it.

Let's first investigate what exactly the academic precariat faces on a consistent basis. One reliable aspect of the academic precariat is that our employment remains unreliable, semester after semester. The academic precariat must face and embrace the ugliness of constant, inflexible flexibility—meaning the required flexibility that we must maintain if we want the best chances for the contracts we desire. We have to be "yes" people to course times, class size, load amounts, types of courses and class location, and don't forget! Last minute changes to *everything*. When I spoke up to my department about my continually over-capped class sizes, I was told that enough students would eventually drop the course. That's encouraging. What a way to have confidence in students.

While full-time colleagues often are subject to these same inflexibilities, they obviously have the benefit of stable income and benefit security. If their classes are scheduled across campus or only an hour apart, they have options for office repose, planning ahead, beginning the trek to classes at a leisurely pace. For the precariat, and more specifically, those with care work responsibilities, we do not have the luxury of a leisurely walk to our classes. We are often calculating our commute minutes, our power-walking abilities, and the least amount of time we will have to pay a substitute care worker. Our contracts are often bogus times—perhaps a morning class at 9am and an afternoon class at 3pm. We often languish in student computer labs, campus coffee shops, in our shared offices so far out of students' reach that they never come, etc…, watching unpaid hours slip away. For me, the hope of building my CV and gaining experience has been worth it, but when I think of my adjunct colleagues and what I have sacrificed for this precarious job, I truly wonder why so many of us do it. And why so many of us are voiceless and powerless over our career trajectory, our involvement in the institution, our income.

The inflexible flexibility of course type is another layer of anxiety and work that requires the precariat to always be ready to create a syllabus for a course they have never taught, which thus, if we want the best chances to be offered such luxurious predicaments, we must pursue professional development and show ourselves as eternally able to multitask and balance significant last-minute change. I have been offered courses I've never taught and had to develop a new syllabus, including choosing textbooks, organizing Blackboard, creating new rubrics and assignment descriptions, within two days of the semester start date. I've also had courses changed at the last minute (courses for which I spent hours planning—for nothing! In all "fairness," I *was* given the option to simply not accept the change and forfeit the class, thus losing the course and the benefits associated with a two-course assignment completely). A final anecdote—I began a class that later cancelled for low enrollment, after being promised by the Dean in person and via email that my class would NOT be cancelled. The school tried to pay me for one measly class instead of the proper ⅕ payment I was entitled to via the union contract. When I complained about the Dean's incorrect promises and lack of competency, the department simply said "oops, the Dean is new" and paid me only after the union stepped in on my behalf. This last minute change-frenzy is fair neither to me nor to the students.

## Section 2: Academics as Martyrs: Extra Unpaid Work Does Not Equal Caring about Students

Education has morphed into quite a beast for many reasons (many that I will not get into here) in the United States. Too often, teachers must constantly defend to the public their "summers off" and how easy their jobs must be, especially if they have union support. (And by the way, a lot of us work during the summer anyway: I personally don't know any instructors k-higher-ed who do not take on some sort of summer work, including scholarly and family care work.) Time away from the classroom RARELY means vacation time. We plan, research, collaborate—often doing work not compensated.

I constantly hear the phrase, "I do it for the students," particularly from women who are teachers. I will admit—I've said it many times. "Teaching for the students" almost always refers to unpaid labor, although that labor is never outrightly identified as such. This phrase indicates that unpaid work is/should be done in the name of personal sacrifice for students. The teaching profession seems to have no boundaries for the workday: we have classroom responsibilities, grading, planning, administrative duties, professional development... but also, try googling "teacher quotes." The results suggest that in order to be a "good" teacher, we must inspire, create, show, care, imagine—countless abstract notions that encourage a suffocating amount of emotional labor (we also have to look attractive). In America, "labor increasingly is viewed as a mere commodity, a resource open to control (every bit as much as land and capital) by the ownership class" (Fink 100). To become more valuable in our economy, we must constantly prove ourselves worthy both by merit and abstract notions, especially in a position of authority and educational leadership.

For women, the constant pressure to present ourselves as nurturing, caring and maternal, magnifies exponentially in the teaching profession. Making ourselves more available, spending more emotional labor on students, being more creative and engaging with assignments and classroom activities, attending more student events, etc... become par for the course of being a woman and being a teacher. Try a Google Image search of "teacher": the results include mostly females, with huge smiles at the front of the classroom. Do teachers always need to be happy? Wearing a pearly white smile? Then do a Google Image search for "professor": the results show mostly white men, not necessarily smiling happily, but looking more "scholarly" and serious. Women too often wear the hat of maternal teacher while trying to create space in a patriarchal system that still projects maleness, whiteness, and unemotional scowls as the only option for "professor." We need to stop complacency with these contradictory gendered cultural expectations and become more comfortable drawing boundaries that reflect more accurately our actual contractual obligations.

But in the case of precariat instructors, this pressure, this drawing of boundaries around contractual obligation can be enough for us to lose our jobs. For example, my contract does not require me to hold office hours, yet the chair and the dean often communicate the fact that adjuncts are strongly encouraged to hold physical office hours. What are the implications here? That if we don't, we won't be re-hired? I used to hold physical office hours in my shared-with-three-instructors office in a totally inconspicuous space that students never pass by. This required me to pay for childcare, even though I made nothing for the hours I held. I also held office hours in the interim time between classes, because what else was I supposed to do? Go home for twenty minutes and return to campus? I cannot bring myself to eliminate office hours because it is truly unfair to students, yet the responsibility of mediating that unfairness falls to me, not the real entity responsible. I now hold hours by appointment and email, which probably ends up being more time than the physical hours anyway, but I can at least respond to emails from home where I can be with my family.

The risk of negative judgement permeates the academic precariat's work narrative—we must not care about the students if we refuse to hold unpaid office hours. How could we be so inconsiderate? So irresponsible and careless? Perhaps the fear that the less we are present on campus, the fewer chances we have of being consistently re-hired every semester keeps us, unpaid, on campus. The idea that the teaching profession is a sacrificial type of employment, where we over-expend ourselves to benefit students is one that needs laid to rest. It encourages people to work beyond their contractual obligations and to invest overly in emotional labor. Often, teachers are judged negatively if they make it known that they will not work beyond contracts. One of my co-authors, Margie Burns, discusses teachers teaching for dedication to teaching. The truth of this idea has become so ingrained in the profession—if teachers care about students, they will do whatever it takes to contribute to retention initiatives, student engagement, across-curriculum collaboration and research and more. While some of these responsibilities may be part of a full-time instructor's required paid work, the academic precariat typically earns for none of these, yet we are to care for students equally to other instructors. It's never explained to students that their professors have different work requirements, so when my students learn that I don't hold physical office hours, their surprise indicates feelings of unfairness. If I do not attend their collegiate events, spend time advising them or emotionally investing in their lives, write extensive notes on their graded papers, I must not be as "good" or as committed as their other professors.

Grading, especially in composition courses, robs instructors of even more time outside of work. Or course, grading is part of the job, but I have heard colleagues say things like, "I probably shouldn't, but I write a lot of comments on my students' papers and spend way too much time grading them." The conversation always ends with the idea that this practice is "for the students." Let's imagine an adjunct instructor has three classes at one institution and two at another. It is probable that each class has 20-30 students. One hundred student papers at five pages each totals 500-750 pages of reading for one class, for one assignment, not counting time for comments or filling out rubrics. What should our responsibility to students be in this scenario? Many administrators and other privileged workers may say that our responsibility is to reduce our workload—not take on so many classes. Obviously, not our first solution, and not a viable one either for the precariat. Also, not a collaborative or supportive solution.

Assessment is a complicated part of our jobs, and when the stresses of precarious employment pile on top of this tiresome time requirement, adjuncts must be creative and fair when developing grading systems that work for them and for students. Looking for support in other colleague's practices or asking for advice benefits our practices. The more advice and collaboration I seek, the better suited to work-life balance my work becomes. For example, investing time in creating rubrics that function for a variety of writing assignments, organizing Blackboard courses that can be copied over into the next semester, using Open Education Resources, and collaborating with other faculty on assignments.

Associated with the culture of martyrdom that instructors face is the culture of silence surrounding money, which harms progress for the precariat and efforts at solidarity.

## Section 3: Money Talk: Culture of Silence

As American education becomes an increasingly capitalistic, commodified beast, so does the system of low-paid educators. I've chosen to discuss money in this chapter because I believe that if students and colleagues realized the position of adjuncts, they may be more inclined to pursue solidarity and activism. Guy Standing not only describes and defines the global precariat, he also criticizes how the education system churns out degrees that are more and more expensive and bring less return (*The Precariat* 68). The less money institutions can get away with paying their instructors, the larger the mass of contingent instructors becomes. Yet this mass believes it is powerless, and seems comfortable with the minimal rights, money and benefits conveyed. Why open a single tenure line, when re-hiring a few adjuncts and denying them benefits is more financially savvy? As American universities embrace the free market business model, instructors and students suffer. Let's be real about what higher education has become in America: a neo-liberal system that cares primarily for money and has commodified the abstract idea of "education." Standing describes perfectly what the "neo-liberal state" has done to school systems:

> The neo-liberal state has been transforming school systems to make them a consistent part of the market society, pushing education in the direction of 'human capital' formation and job preparation. It has become one of the ugliest aspects of globalisation. Through the ages education has been regarded as a liberating, questioning, subversive process by which the mind is helped to develop nascent capacities. The essence of the Enlightenment was that the human being could shape the world and refine himself or herself through learning and deliberation. In a market society, that role is pushed into the margins. The education system is being globalised. It is brashly depicted as an industry, as a source of profits and export earnings, a zone of competitiveness, with countries, universities and schools ranked by performance indicators. It is hard to parody what is happening. Administrators have taken over schools and universities, imposing a 'business model' geared to the market. Although its standards have plunged abysmally, the leader of the global 'industry' is the United States. The idea is to process commodities, called 'certificates' and 'graduates.' Universities tend to compete not by better teaching but by offering a 'luxury model'—nice dormitories, fancy sports and dancing facilities, and the appeal of celebrity academics, celebrated for non-teaching achievements. (*The Precariat* 68)

In my experience touring campuses, and accompanying students on many campus tours, I hear and see primarily about exactly what Standing describes. I have often had to request a meeting with a professor to meet a real-live professor on these tours. I never have to request to see the fanciest dining facility or the new activity building with the rock wall. Instructors are no longer part of the attractiveness, as universities try to sell their campuses to bright-eyed students who live in a culture of comfort and luxury. Of course, adjuncts are completely left out of the tour, the campus PowerPoint—campuses pride themselves on courses taught by "real" professors with PhDs, not TAs or contingents. Think about what these statistics imply, often published on campus websites, and highlighted on tours: TAs and contingents are less-thans and students should not desire to be taught by them (even though the TAs probably have fresh and innovative ideas and the contingents definitely love what they do if they agree to be paid so minimally).

As mentioned before, students are uneducated about the varying levels of contractual obligation their professors have, even though students pay the same amount of money, whether they have a PhD full professor or a brand-new adjunct with a master's degree. Although exact numbers are not easy to come by, as the data constantly changes and metrics vary, a study by Paul J. Yakoboski, a senior economist with TIAA Institute estimates that, "50% [of college and university faculty] are part-time non-tenure track," while "71% are either non-tenure track full-time or non-tenure track part-time" (53-55). According to the AFT Higher Education Data Center, in 2013, tenured or tenure track faculty make up less than one-third of faculty positions (54); the National Center for Education Statistics reports that in 2015, 52% of faculty were full-time, but does not sparse out non-tenure track full-time. Either way, institutions clearly rely on adjuncts to function, at the cost of the adjunct's quality of life, financial stability and work load. While rank and contractual status may not seem important to students, when my students discover the actual amount of money adjuncts earn, their reactions are confused, angry, shocked. Consider the price they pay for college. Then consider that my contract, for example, pays me $75 per class—if I only divide the money by class. If grading, planning, email, staying after class is taken into consideration, the amount becomes embarrassingly minimal per task. Work outside of the classroom permeates instructor life. Students often have no clue what their professors make, but since they are paying the price, I think it is their business to know.

Obviously, adjunct pay varies from state to state and from institution to institution, but let's take a generalized look: $29,420 is the 2018 Federal Poverty Guideline for a family of five, which my family recently became. As an adjunct, I would never have the luxury of being assigned a full teaching load, equivalent to the prestige of a tenure-track faculty member's schedule; BUT, if assigned a full course load at my current adjunct pay, I would be paid a gross salary of $24,500 for five classes per semester, resulting in approximately $17,000 in yearly net pay. Far from luxury. My husband and I currently work five contracts in higher education between us. Luckily, one of mine is salaried. It is important to note here that Yakoboski's study recognizes that adjunct pay typically falls at or below the poverty line, but he argues: "Financial wellness is best considered in a household context, and the data indicate that a large share of adjunct faculty have a spouse or other household member who is earning a relatively high income" (56). This explanation glosses over the true plight of adjuncts as individuals, and keeps adjuncts in the margins of academia, simply as contributors, as a part of the whole. A 2017 Pew Research Center study found that although women's financial contributions to family are on the rise, men still earn more than women in roughly two-thirds of cohabiting couples (Parker & Stepler). This finding, combined with Yakoboski's explanations about financial wellness, undermine the female academic precariat. Our choice is to remain silent or stand up and expose the glossing explanations of higher education's treatment of adjuncts. And that's far from easy to do.

The cultural silence associated with discussing salaries keeps the academic precariat on the margins. I often discuss the reality of adjunct pay to my colleagues, and not one has shared their salary amount with me; and in my opinion, it is not out of embarrassment that they make so much more than me, it is out of pride and secrecy. How can we act on the unfairness, if we don't know what it is? John W. Curtis, Director of Research and Public Policy for the American Association of University Professors claims, "It's vital that faculty members take an active leadership role on equity, rather than waiting passively for administrators to solve the problem" (10). Any higher education job I've held reflects a lack of active solidarity with the precariat, except from overarching unions who at least try to consider the precariat in negotiations. Curtis continues, "Change does require commitment and shared activism" (10). Most full-time faculty colleagues are appalled by the details of my blunt descriptions of my contract, and lack of rights and pay, and it's often because they don't know and don't consider it important to know. Many know about their own rights and are too busy to engage with solidarity and activist efforts that support the lower ranks. They picket for the union for their raise and paid family leave rights, most of them not knowing that concepts like "leave" are foreign to adjuncts. I understand that unfortunately, there is probably not a lot of energy left over for supporting those outside of one's own experiences, but equity will remain out of reach if full-timers do not advocate for it along with us. We take on too much risk when we speak out too loudly and don't have tenure to protect us.

Before solidarity happens with full-time colleagues, part-timers must make an effort to be informed. They must advocate for change. Part of the unique aspect of the academic precariat is the false prestige associated with employment in instructional academia. While instructors may receive equal respect from students as their full-time colleagues, that respect becomes meaningless. Ego may get in the way of an adjuncts' ability to have perspective, recognize injustice and act on it. A first step would be to *start talking about the money*.

We never talked about money figures in my household. I never knew and still do not know how much money my parents or siblings make or save—this is private information. My parents were experts at "making do." Hard work, thrift and putting money away for the future were the American ways of financial education in my home, which was situated in a small, blue-collar community in South Central Pennsylvania. My father says, "I have been both a blue collar worker and a white collar worker. It did not matter to me if I was performing blue collar work or white collar work, the goals, work ethic and desire to see a job well done should be the same for either type of work." Definitely an ethical practice for a career. However, the desire to see a job well done often means beating out your competition by working unnecessary hours and committing to too much. It also can mean suffering in a hated job to maintain the benefits that came with laborism and the rise of unions. These benefits trapped blue-collar workers in long careers with which they were not necessarily satisfied. To combat this dissatisfaction, Protestant ideologies merged with blue-collar work ethics. If someone looks at his or her job in purely religious or spiritual terms, the job seems more acceptable.

Protestant work ethic ideology permeated my view of work and labor. I talked work ethics and history with my parents for this chapter—my father explains his work ethic: "I obtained my work ethic in large part from my belief that 'in all you do, do it as unto the Lord.'" So many Americans continue on doing work they don't necessarily like or enjoy because of this ideology. So many times, I've heard "it's just a job" from people in my hometown, meaning that suffering in a job you don't like is acceptable. It also encourages compartmentalizing and building identity completely outside of career.

Both of my parents value the Protestant work ethic. My mother obtained her work ethic through "family upbringing [Presbyterian], school [blue collar community], husband, and [the] experience of working different jobs." During my childhood, my father worked a blue-collar job that transformed into a stressful white-collar job at a now-defunct company, while my mother stayed home doing care work raising my siblings and me. He eventually moved on, but for years, the promise of benefits for his family and stable income kept him trapped. Mom babysat for extra money, took us to volunteer opportunities at nursing homes, gardened and canned, mended clothes, made a hot meal every night. I developed meanings of "work" that completely divided gender and place: I believed my dad went off to "work" every day with his briefcase, and my mom did not work, she stayed home. I also did not consider my dad's efforts at home, fixing things, gardening, mowing, and cleaning as "work." I understood all of these tasks as one lump of responsibility, especially because anything we did was done for the Lord. For me, religious ideology on top of stressful work just wasn't working.

It took me a long time to realize that work and life were interconnected and that life identity included work as well. Being in the home did not mean leisure or not working. Because I never labelled anything WORK outside of leaving home and going to a place of work that issues a paycheck, I overworked myself in everything I took on. Minimizing what it truly means to do care work or labor at home harmed my idea of career, family, labor and leisure. Standing describes this cultural misstep in creating a definition for what labor truly involves:

> Throughout the twentieth century, labour—work having exchange value—was put on a pedestal, while all work that was not labour was disregarded. So work done for its intrinsic usefulness does not appear in labour statistics or in political rhetoric. Beyond its sexism, this is indefensible for other reasons as well. It degrades and devalues some of the most valuable and necessary activities—the reproduction of our own capacities as well as those of the future generation and activities preserving our social existence. We need to escape from the labourist trap. No group needs that to happen more than the precariat. (*The Precariat* 117)

We need to recognize that our responsibilities to future generations include responsibility outside of "work having [monetary] exchange value"—we have to commit to social health, equity and progress in other ways. This consideration didn't occur to me for a long time. My prioritization of financial wellness took over other areas of wellness, especially the idea of leisure time.

America embraces the dualism boundaries of work and leisure, influenced by capitalistic values that plague our ideas of work and time. Standing explains the problem of time dualism:

> Consider time from the perspective of the demands placed on it. The standard presentation in economics textbooks, government reports, mass media and legislation is dualistic, dividing time between 'work' and 'leisure.' When they say work they mean labour, that part of work that is contracted or directly remunerated. This is misleading as a means of measuring the time devoted to work, even the work required to earn income, let alone the forms that have no direct connection to labour. The other side of the dualism, leisure, is equally misleading. (*The Precariat* 119)

As I formulated my own ideas about work and work ethic, entered college and the paid working world, I realized that not only was I doing myself a disservice by overworking, but that I needed to develop a defined voice that could address many factors lending themselves to my current place in precarious academic work, while balancing my other top priorities of being a mother, wife and scholar.

## Section 4: An American Problem: Definitions of Work, Class and Labor and Gendered Implications

As America continues to embrace neo-liberalism and competition in every nook and cranny of daily life, its citizens will struggle to narrate healthy work-life balance. Labor infiltrates the home and crosses boundaries of workplace. Work-life balance boundaries blur, especially for women, who take on the majority of care and home work.

Percent of population who did household activities on an average day

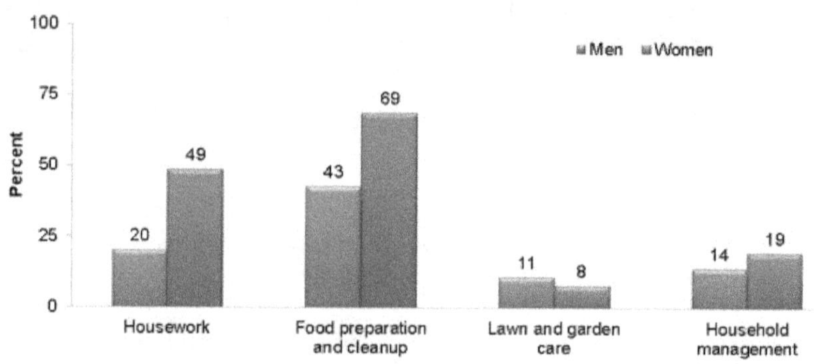


NOTE: Data include all noninstitutionalized persons age 15 and over. Data include all days of the week and are annual averages for 2014. Travel related to these activities is not included in these estimates.

SOURCE: Bureau of Labor Statistics, American Time Use Survey

*Figure 1*

As women enter the American workforce, they continue to take more and more onto their plates and struggle to maintain healthy work-life balance. Based on Figure 1 above, the lack of gender balance continues to lag behind, specifically with mothers. The labor force continues to include more and more mothers:

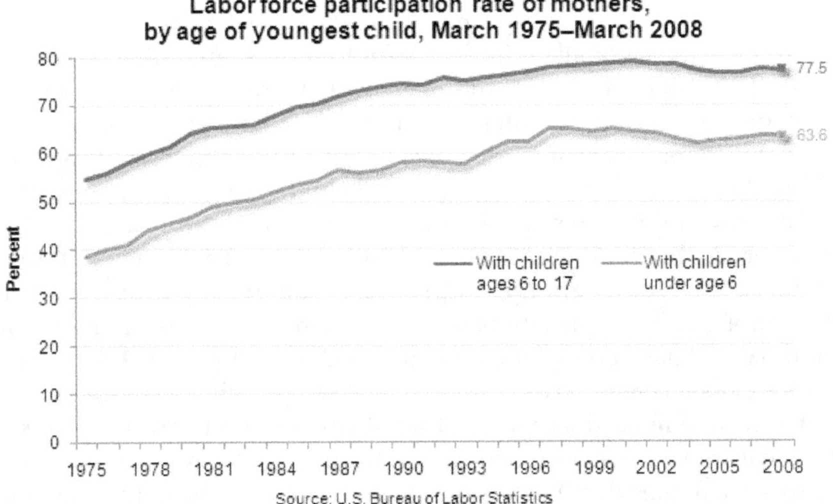


*Figure 2*

While these graphics show a larger perspective of work and employment than the realm of academia, I chose to reference them to show the disparity in what men and women consider "work." Women experience more of an ingrained ideology that necessitates work in the home, part of their gendered responsibility; yet now too, as women embrace careers or have no choice but to take on work because of economic situations, workloads become unbearably varied and large for them. If mothers in the ***Figure 2*** are primary caregivers for their children, they must find substitutes for the time they work. This process in itself tasks women with additional emotional and mental labor: posting the care work job, interviewing applicants, deciding what to ask/require, and facing the task of trusting others with their children. Partner support obviously eases these labors.

For the precariat, childcare costs force parents to make difficult decisions about the "worth" of their career. The financial question of: *is it worth the money I spend on childcare to spend the time at work, away from my children?* Not only do such questions stress parents, the probable judgment from others awaits women who work. How could I pay more for childcare than the income I make? According to Stanford sociologist Shelley Correll, "there is a cultural perception that if you're a good mother, you're so dedicated to your children that you couldn't possibly be that dedicated to your career" (Kitroeff & Silver-Greenberg). Too often, society's conclusion is that I must value my career more than my children if I am making little to no profit from my career. Let's talk numbers for a clearer picture: If I teach two concurrent classes, two days per week (a rare timing luxury in the precariat), I would have to put my two children under school age in daycare for at least half day. The center I would use does not allow half days for infants, so my infant would be in care two days per week at $125 per week. I would then have to make the choice of putting my other daughter in for two half days, which is allowable in her age group. That means two different pick-up times and adding the time for my school-age third child getting off the bus. Two half days would be $70 per week for my older daughter. That's a total of $195 per week in the most minimal childcare scenario, where I am not holding office hours, grading or planning. I am simply dropping them off, running to class, picking one up, and then picking the other up four hours later. That allows for minimal profit when I am paid $2,425 per course, per semester. All of my adjunct colleagues who are mothers have been forced to make decisions that sacrifice contracts because it just isn't "worth it" or because the scheduling is terrible. In my experience, almost always, if a female declines a contract offer, a male ends up teaching that course.

## Section 4 Part 2: Securities out of Reach

So many aspects of the female precariat order us into the margins of our institutions. Besides confused definitions of work and the ethics associated with work, labor-as-paid-work has many protection facets that are unavailable to the precariat. Let's look at various forms of security that developed during and after industrialization for laborers as defined by Guy Standing (*The Precariat* 10):

| **Forms of labor security under industrial citizenship** | **Explanation** |
|---|---|
| Labor market security | Adequate income-earning opportunities; at the macro-level, this is epitomized by a government commitment to 'full employment.' |
| Employment security | Protection against arbitrary dismissal, regulations on hiring and firing, imposition of costs on employers for failing to adhere to rules and so on. |
| Job security | Ability and opportunity to retain a niche in employment, plus barriers to skill dilution, and opportunities for 'upward' mobility in terms of status and income. |
| Work security | Protection against accidents and illness at work, through, for example, safety and health regulations, limits on working time, unsociable hours, night work for women, as well as compensation for mishaps. |

| Skill reproduction security | Opportunity to gain skills, through apprenticeships, employment training and so on, as well as opportunity to make use of competencies. |
|---|---|
| Income security | Assurance of an adequate stable income, protected through, for example, minimum wage machinery, wage indexation, comprehensive social security, progressive taxation to reduce inequality and to supplement low incomes. |
| Representation security | Possessing a collective voice in the labor market, through, for example, independent trade unions, with a right to strike. |

*Figure 3*

These securities accompany full-time salaries while academics in the lower ranks lack access to these luxuries. I do not hear people talking about these aspects of career. It's no surprise to me though—when I have had full-time, salaried work, I definitely took for granted these aspects of my job. Now I look at those securities as basic rights denied to a majority of contracted workers in higher education. Isn't America embarrassed by this paradox? The highly educated, reduced to poverty within the confines of educational institutional employ.

We invent "skill reproduction security" opportunities ourselves, believing in meritocracy but chained to "keeping up with" educational developments. We also know that if we do not pursue additional skills that increase our hireability and uniqueness, we may quickly become obsolete, especially in technology innovation. Part of our unpaid labor includes a constant refreshing of skills such as new technologies and pedagogies. Standing describes this paradox perfectly:

> Insecurity is greater with certain occupational skills. One may spend years acquiring qualifications and then find they have become obsolescent or insufficient. An acceleration of occupational obsolescence affects many in the precariat. There is a paradox. The more skilled the work, the more likely it is that refinements will take place, requiring 'retraining.' Another way of putting it is as follows: The more trained you

> are, the more likely you are to become unskilled in your sphere of competence. Perhaps deskilled would be a way to describe what happens. This gives a strange time dimension to the idea of skill. It is not just a case of being as good as you were yesterday but of being as good as you should be tomorrow. The behavioural reaction to skill insecurity may be a frenzy of time-using investment in upgrading or it may be a paralysis of the will, inactivity due to a belief that any course would have a very uncertain return. Commentators who endlessly call for more training and bewail a lack of skills merely contribute to an existential crisis. This is not a social climate conducive to capability development; it is one of constant dissatisfaction and stress." (*The Precariat* 123-24)

The academic precariat constantly has to make themselves unique, bring new ideas to the profession and strain to be noticed, with no expectation of monetary award.

The precariat's access to the securities in ***Figure 3*** varies by state and institution. For example, I do have access to a strong union that advocates for adjuncts—a very lucky aspect of my employment indeed. But of course, more can always be done and the union does not offer tangible security or protection to adjuncts. Every semester, I hold a one-semester contract with no hope of renewal. My union advocates particularly for access to benefits and minimum pay thresholds, among other things. BUT the recent JANUS decision by the Supreme Court severely jeopardizes unions by reducing the potential for funding ("Janus v. American Federation").

Too often, the belief that hard work will "get us somewhere" allows us to work to the point of burnout. To believe that we can possibly build merit for ourselves. A good reputation perhaps, but how often will that respect amount to $$$ or a more stable offer of employment? If we are lucky, academic merit may amount to a head-nod of an important campus figure during a meeting, or perhaps we will see our name highlighted in a campus newsletter. I receive generic semesterly letters from my dean thanking me for my service to the students and the college, letters from University Faculty Senate, thanking me for my committee participation, recognition in faculty meetings; however, this is a false sense of esteem. Is there compensation associated with these recognitions? Ability to "move up"? Not so far.

When I gave a presentation at a conference held at Harvard University, my campus did a newsletter piece on it and so did the local town paper. It felt great to hear congratulations from colleagues and see that at least the community cared, but some colleagues tried to reduce my sense of accomplishment through mockery. Colleagues had the audacity to make fun of the PR I received, trying to make me feel like I desired too much attention, like I was making their jobs harder by doing this work, or making them look bad. These comments angered me, but perhaps they were partially right; all of that work surely amounted to experience, development, networking—yet I couldn't help but feel that the nods from the campus and community amounted to nothing. Did my supervisors consider this work when re-hiring me or assigning me classes? Absolutely not. I had been convinced that I was doing all of that hard work for something tangible and not simply unpaid work. It brings back childhood memories of swimming in the exhibition lane during competitions and earning participation ribbons (no matter what true "place" I finished) that meant nothing except *great job for existing.*

Even when I have the promise of employment, unemployment seeps in: Payroll removes me during the winter break between semesters and only keeps me on through summer if I teach courses. During these periods of unemployment, we are not NOT working. Standing describes aspects of this extra work that the precariat often faces even in times of unemployment:

> They [the unemployed] have multiple 'workplaces'—employment exchanges, benefit offices, job-search training offices—and have to indulge in a lot of work-for-labour—filling in forms, queuing, commuting to employment exchanges, commuting in search of jobs, commuting to job training and so on. It can be a full-time job being unemployed, and it involves flexibility, since people must be on call almost all the time. (*The Precariat* 48)

I check my email constantly during breaks of unemployment to see what my next semester may look like, what syllabi I need to develop, what rushed childcare I need to arrange. This anxious activity on top of any individual scholarly work and my home and care work obligations. And I've given up on pursuing welfare system benefits. Either our income just tops the income qualifying requirements or the massive amount of work I would have to put into it, attaining the benefits for each period of unemployment simply isn't worth it. Standing explains this difficulty for the precariat:

> It is not as if labour is all the work that people do. To function well in a tertiary flexible-labour society, much time must be used in 'work-for-labour,' work that does not have exchange value but which is necessary or advisable. One form of work-

> for-labour done by the precariat to a greater extent than others is in the labour market. Someone who exists through temporary jobs must spend a lot of time searching for jobs and dealing with the state bureaucracy or, increasingly, its private commercial surrogates. As welfare systems are restructured in ways that force claimants to go through ever more complex procedures to gain and to retain entitlement to modest benefits, the demands on the time of the precariat are large and fraught with tension. Queuing, commuting to queue, form filling, answering questions, answering more questions, obtaining certificates to prove something or other, all these are painfully time consuming yet are usually ignored. (*The Precariat* 120)

The precariat must invest astronomical amounts of time in working outside of labor, and beyond required work-outside-of-labor; we often do it in the name of merit, believing that our hard work will be rewarded with at least some sort of security. The securities with which I grew up seeing in my community now fade, as I weigh the (non)choice of my work in the academic precariat. I also question what those securities were worth and what it cost to maintain them.

The connections between my complacency with precarious work and an upbringing in a blue-collar community reveal larger systemic gender inequities that I previously ignored. My emergent voice requires reflection on my level of confidence in the paid working world, my reliance on someone else to bring in income, and my initial silence over inequity.

## Section 5: Blue Precarity

> *The unions saw the answer to precarious labour in a return to the 'labourist' model they had been so instrumental in cementing in the mid-twentieth century – more stable jobs with long-term employment security and the benefit trappings that went with that. But many of the young demonstrators had seen their parents' generation conform to the Fordist pattern of drab full-time jobs and subordination to industrial management and the dictates of capital. Though lacking a cohesive alternative agenda, they showed no desire to resurrect labourism.* (The Precariat 2)

Standing references young precariats who value their work, but refuse to subject themselves to the same dreary "it's just a job" mentality of their parents' generation. As Americans embraced industrialization and monetary definitions of wealth and happiness, the rise of unions and worker protections and regulations, work ethics remained rooted in Protestantism, especially in blue-collar communities.

The dualism (mentioned previously) of work and leisure tangled with the progressive idea that paid-for-labor workers deserved basic rights like health care, retirement, safety regulations and so on. Jeffrey Sklansky, Associate Professor of History at University of Illinois at Chicago, furthers Standing's definition of dualisms in capitalist society:

> The two-dimensional perspective underlies a further set of closely linked dualisms including those of market and state (the former supposedly natural, the latter artificial), country and town (the former imagined as the primary scene of production, the latter as the central arena of exchange), and home and work (whose separation symbolizes the ascendance of paid labor and market relations). (26)

Boundaries based on monetary exchange crop up because of this perspective, especially between home and work. Wherever one gains money, that place gains more and more value; thus, the home and work outside of paid-for-labor is devalued. The dualism reaches further, as religious ideology piles on top of economics: work is *good* or *right* and leisure is *indulgent* and *sinful.*

The more one was committed to his/her salaried job, the more his/her hard work could be looked on with approval. The rise of positive thinking and self-help drove people to the point of convincing themselves to remain committed and to an empty satisfaction in their jobs, which results in complacency. Standing references Barbara Ehrenreich's connections between "positive thinking" and the marginalized:

> In *Smile or Die*, Barbara Ehrenreich (2009) attacked the modern cult of positive thinking. She recalled how in the United States in the 1860s two quacks (Phineas Quimby and Mary Eddy) set up the New Thought Movement, based on Calvinism and the view that belief in God and positive thinking would lead to positive outcomes in life. Ehrenreich traced this through into modern business and finance. She described how motivational conferences had speakers telling short-term contract workers who had been made redundant to be good team players, defined as 'a positive person' who 'smiles frequently, does not complain and gratefully submits to whatever the boss demands.' (*The Precariat* 20)

Salaries and protections, formulated in a man's working world, kept workers silent and doing extra work, whether self-assigned or assigned by the big boss. The more approval one gained increased the chances at secure employment. To combat disapproval or lack of merit recognition, religious ideology and positive thinking stepped in to pick up the pieces. If one's reward were not earthly, surely it would be heavenly. I often reflect on a picture of heaven I drew as a child: me, crowned, jeweled and bedecked in a beautiful gown, on a balcony in my mansion made of gold that sat atop the clouds, with the white-male-bearded God beside me. Capitalism poisoned my outlook and my values, as I skipped over my earthly life to focus on a monetarily rich afterlife that rewarded hard work, *especially* hard work that went unrecognized on earth. Thus, working outside of required hours, extra labor and skills development became acceptable as ancillary requirements to paid work because reward would be extended if not on earth, then in heaven.

Thrift, positive thinking and hard work, no matter the costs to one's family or value of time, continue to drive workers towards a capitalistic mentality of what wealth means. Pepper religious ideology onto those tenets of working life and *not working* or voicing discontent at over-assignment becomes sinful. Time management and work-life balance disappear as salaried careers chain people to their jobs. While some view the twentieth century as progressive, the ideologies that kept workers in union-protected jobs also often kept them doing work they didn't particularly like. For my community, the idea that a career could 1. Change and 2. Be something to enjoy and create an identity around, still shocks. Standing highlights the frustration that drives workers to emerge from victimhood by recognizing means of liberation and looking for more than capitalistic wealth in:

> There is a lot of anger out there and a lot of anxiety. But although this book highlights the victim side of the precariat more than the liberating side, it is worth stating at the outset that it is wrong to see the precariat in purely suffering terms. Many drawn into it are looking for something better than what was offered in industrial society and by twentieth century labourism. (*The Precariat* vii)

Although I recently acquired a salaried job (not in my field), my passion for teaching and my content area keeps me tied to the precariat and wanting more for us. Many precariats turn away from their passions to embrace the salaried job outside of their field because existing in the precariat becomes impossible.

My journey into the precariat began in my first grad class, a course on the Romantics. My professor asked students why we were pursuing the Master's of English. My answer was, "I can be a mom and an adjunct with a flexible schedule!" My naiveté sprung from many places including a working class upbringing, excitement about being a new, first time mother, a reliance on a spouse's stable employment and financial support, and an ingrained self-doubt about my own goals. I actually never pictured myself being capable of creating more of a stable employment future for myself, of being financially independent, or attaining a full-time job as a professor. Adjuncting was my true ceiling; that was my true vision of ultimate success.

For me, my precariat problem originates in the educational and social ideologies that consumed the small blue-collar town where I grew up, including exclusionary definitions of labor and work, as I've mentioned before. Discussions of activism and rights rarely occurred in my schooling. Boundaries around types of work blared red, with no option for challenge. According to Standing, labor *needs* divided and credited into types of work so that we don't "lose the capacity to understand patterns of exploitation and control, as well as the patterns of political consciousness that they generate or encourage. . . . 'Labour' is done for a wage" and when all types of work are categorized as 'labour,' "different forms of exploitation and oppression" surface ("Understanding the Precariat" 964-65). My journey to these understandings developed through the identification of exploitation and control, and the realization of my own political consciousness.

My town reflects this issue of gendered boundaries in labor and work. A snapshot:

The median total household income in my town is $40,417, with males earning 1.2 times higher salary than females ("Newville, PA"). This statistic is for those in the workforce and does not take into account those who stay at home for what Standing calls "care work (done mainly by women looking after children, the home and so on)" ("Understanding the

Precariat" 964). If the statistic counted women working in the home, the ratio would be vastly higher than 1.2 times. The largest labor industry is wholesale trade and primarily male: transportation, warehousing and manufacturing. The poverty statistic: 14.3% of the population in Newville, PA (1,347 people) live below the poverty line, a number that is a bit lower than the national average of 14.7%. The largest demographic living in poverty in Newville is Female 25-34, followed by Female < 5 and then Female 55-64 ("Newville, PA"). National data reflects this gendered problem. Women and children account for 70% of the nation's poor (*Legal Momentum*). Not a great outlook for women. Or, clearly, females have a harder row to hoe when it comes to making money.

Many blue-collar towns promote the community industries' skills to the next generation to maintain their unique cultured economy. Often, a lack of education about higher education harms opportunistic outlooks, especially for women in blue-collar towns. While America continued to see a dramatic rise in white-collar jobs throughout the 20th century, the educational roots of blue-collar ideologies remain embedded in much of American education. High school in a blue-collar town often doesn't see as many college recruiters, and may lack funding to disperse to academic track classes like AP, ACT and SAT preparation. Even when the recruiters come, the push to attend seems to fall on those who can afford it. What parent is going to encourage their child to accrue $100,000 debt? My parents did not push me to consider college, nor did they support me moving away to a college when I could have lived at home and commuted to schools nearby. When my high school had college-preparation information meetings, it did not occur to me to go. Why would I do something neither my parents nor I had the money for? My father reflects the anxieties any parent has, but especially those parents who cannot afford to pay for their children's college:

> I was very concerned about the field of education and expense. Knowing and seeing downsizing of corporations and people losing jobs in various fields I tried to steer them [his children] towards vocations that would always be needed in the future. This would not be a guarantee but it would put them into a field less likely to go out of business or downsize. Only being able to help out my children on a limited basis, by sharing some of the expense of college, I knew the debt was something that many would not get out from under until maybe into their 40's.

The primary vocations in my town did not interest me. Nor did the well-established and reputable vocational training alternative my high school provided. I was torn between the idea of a career I enjoyed, but suffering from debt, or suffering my entire life in an identity-less job that was "just a job."

Research shows that blue-collar communities push students towards community economy: according to a study on the relationship between blue-collar communities and their high schools by Cornell University's April Sutton et al., gendered, spatial inequalities often emerge from a tight connection between high school training and local work economy (721). Sutton's assessment of case studies revealed that often, "the major goal of the district was to offer vocational courses that align with local economic demands. Thus, school decision-makers' curricular investments may be circumscribed by the realities of local economic opportunities" (725). So, while women currently earn more college degrees than men, women in blue collar communities that focus their funding on blue collar training and not on academic preparation are at a disadvantage.

Even when women are trained in the blue-collar jobs, they are making less money than their male counterparts, and are less likely to be employed. Women fare better in the job market after earning a college degree. Sutton et al.'s study "found that high school training is stratified along a spatial axis of inequality, and the link between schools and communities in places with prevalent blue-collar jobs disproportionately penalizes women" (739). Their findings "highlight the labor market costs of a less academically rigorous curriculum for women" in schools that "emphasize blue-collar training for young men but deemphasize academic coursework that encourages four-year college completion" (740). When my high school counselor asked if I was considering college and I said no, she pushed me to consider a two-year degree, but nothing more, although my academic interests were leaning towards high achievement—I was in the Honors Society, on the swim team, volunteering and making Dean's List every semester. I was the perfect recipe for a college candidate, but no one told me that until my senior year AP English teacher, Jon Tarrant. He was also a private college counselor, whose services were more than my family could afford or would ever consider. But he met with me privately one day about my AP paper which laid out my future, and argued that a two-year degree in Paralegal Studies would suffice enough until I got married and could stay home with my children, similarly to my mother's choice of career. The ignorance in the paper was rampant—dependent on early marriage, successful fertility, a committed partner, a partner who made money, happiness in domestic labor. It never occurred to me that those things might not be guaranteed or what I would even like. Mr. Tarrant pushed me to consider college and consider a career I actually enjoyed, but what could I possibly do with an English degree? In my mind, higher education caused conflictions: a dream, unattainable, too costly and somewhat useless—a notion I know now developed from cultural aspects of blue-collar thinking. My hometown neighbor always takes a dig at my "hot-shot" professorial career, as if I think I am better than everyone else. (An irony since I actually earn below poverty level wages from my precarious work.)

Finally, I decided that if I pursued the English teaching degree, I would earn my parents' support ("vocation always necessary"), but be able to indulge in creative writing and reading all of the books I could! My problem was that none of my hard work in high school amounted to scholarship (I didn't even know how to apply). I considered that work a part of my education (which it was of course); it was not doing anything out-of-the-ordinary and extra. I faced undergrad and then, later, precarious work, with the notion that part of the job included hard extra work. I also faced the working world with student debt, as my parents feared. At least I had found something to do for money that I enjoyed. Now, the obstacles of thought I faced became relying on a spouse's income as I pursued my dreams, recognizing inequity, discrimination and the unarguable need for activism and advocacy not only for myself, but for my colleagues. Add motherhood and mental health struggles to my journey and the creation of a new, empowered voice emerges.

## Section 6: Precariat Motherhood

*Doing research for this chapter*
***Figure 4***

Motherhood made my work-for-pay precarious. I was a secondary charter schoolteacher in a stable job, who was told two days after returning from maternity leave that my contract had "ended." It conveniently went to the single, white male who covered my maternity leave and was new to the profession. They hired him at the first salary level and only had to pay single benefits. I was too costly, too experienced, but most of all, too inconvenient. Because of the ethics and privilege in which I grew up believing, I had never really considered that my career could so easily become precarious. I was working hard, had a great resume, had a college degree, and found myself unemployed with a newborn baby.

I entered graduate school as a part-time student while my spouse worked at a job he loathed to support our family. My glass ceiling in graduate school was being a mom and an adjunct who did not have to worry about income. I did not picture myself being capable of moving beyond the precariat—again, like college, going beyond the adjunct position did not occur to me. It also did not occur to me how difficult it would be to maintain a consistent grasp on my employment (or my selfhood for that matter) after earning my master's degree. When my spouse's employment became unstable and miserable, I committed myself to doing everything I could to build a career again—one that could support my family and my husband's return to graduate school to pursue his dreams. This time, my career path was in higher education, in guaranteed-precarious work, and I had no clue about the struggles I would face.

At my first adjunct job at a private for-profit institution, I was required to use my breast pumping time to call students who did not show up to class, document our conversations, all while my pump ran loudly in the background. Holding two pumps and a phone is really difficult. There were no women in leadership to turn to. I just did what I was told—put the pump on my breast, picked up the phone, and wrote down the useless notes about who was absent and why. I didn't realize there were other options of support, voice or activism in the workplace; I was too afraid to lose what I had worked so hard towards, so I never questioned authority.

One co-worker with whom I connected through our common subject matter seemed interested in my family, my work, and me. We became workplace friends. One day, when he offered to "help me out" in front of male colleagues at a happy hour gathering, you would think I would have been grateful or relieved that someone wanted to help me. But his offer to "help me out" was to "help me out" with pumping breast milk. I mentioned I had to get home to nurse my daughter, and he laughed and said, "We can help you out with that so you don't have to go." I froze—my chest constricted and instead of the angry reaction I have dreamed of repeatedly since then, I mustered a laugh and left in the midst of other males uncomfortably laughing as well, including the Dean. This male coworker continued to make comments about my appearance "improving" since having a baby, inviting me to happy hours, scheduling his office hours to coincide with mine. Still, I said and reported nothing. How could I? When the supervisory Dean had laughed along with everyone else, as if yes, he agreed—he could help me out too with my milk-bulging breasts. I did not want to risk my precarious job, so I remained silent at the expense of my Self. The work I would put into documenting these transgressions was more emotional labor than I could handle, especially after the work I put into legal action during the charter-school-job-loss fiasco. The American Association of University Women recommends the following in cases of pregnancy discrimination, which also applies to gender discrimination:

**What to do if you think you've been discriminated against based on pregnancy or pregnancy related condition:**

1. **Write down what happened.** Write down the date, time, and place of the incident as soon as possible. Include what was said and who was there. Keep a copy of these notes at home. They will be useful if you decide to file a complaint with your company or to take legal action.
2. **Talk to your union representative.** Union rules often allow you to file a grievance. If you don't have a union, call a women's or civil rights group for help.
3. **Talk to your employer.** Your company may have an Equal Employment Opportunity Officer or a way for you to file a complaint. For instance, some companies have new ways to resolve problems, like mediation. Check your employee handbook for procedures.
4. **Keep doing a good job and keep a record of your work.** Keep copies at home of your job evaluations and any letters or memos that show that you do a good job at work. Your boss may criticize your job performance later on in order to defend his or her discrimination.
5. **Seek support from friends and family.** Discrimination at work is a difficult thing to face alone, and the process of fighting discrimination can be very stressful.

*Figure 5*

In my case, no union represented us and talking to my employer was talking to my supervisor Dean who had laughed at the breast milk joke. This entire institution is now defunct, and I wish I could have been at its funeral. At the time, I didn't know about the support and legal services available for free (more time-cost researching). The exhausting work to simply stand up for oneself, report discrimination and find avenues of support all too often snuffs out women's voices.

Thankfully, I moved on from that part-time job to a combination of tutor and adjunct positions at more legitimate, established institutions, but continued to suffer the precarious world of this life, this lack of institutional and colleague support, this lonely trajectory. I had a rush of success—landing adjuncting and tutoring jobs that filled my schedule and allowed my spouse to begin a transition out of the dead-end, stressful job into graduate school.

But three semesters into this precarious success, I experienced two consecutive miscarriages (the first, the day before the semester began). Of course, I started the semester, limping and bleeding, but professional, half-smiling, going over my syllabus as a distraction. I feared losing the entire semester's contracts if I did not show up or called in sick.

I also faced the option of being elusive about the miscarriages or frank about it with both my students and my supervisors, and learned a lot about my Self and the workplace in that process. I faced twice-weekly blood draws, doctor's appointments and sonograms that—no matter how hard I tried to avoid it—had to be scheduled during work hours. I was advised by most people that I know—friends, parents, colleagues, etc., male and female—to "not make anyone uncomfortable;" "no one needs to know specifics" when sharing the news. When I told two of my supervisors, both male, one was sympathetic, yet clearly uncomfortable, pushing his office chair back from his desk (I must have some disease, or perhaps the presence of my female reproductive system caused this reaction) and breaking eye contact. He offered the "support" of the department and to let him know if I needed anything, although, when I asked for coverage, no one responded. I think "support" meant: we won't fire you if you need to cancel a class or two.

The other supervisor didn't even respond to my email requesting a meeting to discuss my absence for having a miscarriage. The anxieties associated with sharing such news suffocated me. Add these to a post-miscarriage diagnosis of depression and anxiety. Would my supervisors hold these absences against me? Consider the fact that I may get pregnant next semester when re-hiring me? I became paranoid that I would not be offered Spring employment, which meant my entire family would be cut from all benefits. I had blown my cover; now, my employers could guess that I was still family planning and could possibly need maternity leave, if I ended up with a viable pregnancy.

In precarious work, maternity leave is typically a foreign idea. If I was contracted, and had to leave, my benefits would immediately be revoked during a spring or fall semester. I would only be paid for sick time accrued, which accrues at a measly half day per month. The only semester that it was safe to be due with a child was summer. Restrictions on my reproduction and body made this all the more difficult. And I wouldn't accrue vacation time, so paid maternity leave is a joke and

FMLA is almost a guaranteed unattainable protection for the precariat. There is no way to meet the conditions of FMLA in my type of work. I would have to log 24 hours of work per week, which I often do ("Need Time?"). But my adjunct contract only pays me for class time, not for planning, grading, emailing and all of the other trappings of adjunct work.

After I had the miscarriages, I investigated further about my rights and job security. I went to my union representatives and asked: What should I do to avoid discrimination if pregnant? Their answer: Avoid my supervisors until I get a contract and oh yeah, also, wear loose clothes to hide the pregnancy. Also, I was warned that the Union doesn't provide much protection to adjuncts. The most pathetic part of the advice is that it's true. I considered digging a hole on campus labelled "where to go if pregnant" and wearing a burlap sack. That's pretty much the only way to ensure a pregnancy isn't considered when being offering classes in my opinion. It's illegal to discriminate! Everyone says, but of course, what boss is going to say "I didn't give these classes to her because I know she's pregnant!" My pregnancy would mean more work for the department. New York Times reporters Natalie Kitroeff and Jessica Silver-Greenberg argue that "managers often regard women who are visibly pregnant as less committed, less dependable, less authoritative and more irrational than other women," referencing a study by Stanford sociologist, Shelley Correll. Correll "presented hundreds of real-world hiring managers with two resumes from equally qualified women. Half of them signaled that the candidate had a child. The managers were twice as likely to call the apparently childless woman for an interview. Ms. Correll called it a 'motherhood penalty.'" Would I suffer the "motherhood penalty?" University of California Hastings College of Law professor Joan C. Williams explains in the same NY Times article, "There are 20 years of lab studies that show the bias exists and that, once triggered, it's very strong" (Kitroeff & Silver-Greenberg). My bosses do not need to provide an explanation for hiring, and there is no system for hiring and re-hiring adjuncts at the institutions for whom I work(ed). The lack of hiring transparency allows significant room for this type of silent discrimination that I would not be able to fight.

That year, spring offers of classes were sent out, and confirmed my fears—after being offered the necessary amount of classes to qualify for insurance for five semesters in a row, I was offered only one section for the spring, kicking my family off health benefits. I immediately went to the union, and the Women's Rights and Concerns committee. We looked at the schedule and saw that several adjuncts were offered one spring class, including only one other woman and the rest were men, including two men who were new hires. I guess my Master's degree, impeccable teaching record, and vagina did not stand a chance against a penis with an MFA. I told my Union that I would be filing a grievance if things didn't change. Two days later, my supervisor, who never calls my cell phone and had originally promised to "do all he could in his power to ensure I got two sections," called and said a section had opened and would I take it? And of course he reiterated how he was doing the best he could to make sure I had those two classes. What a valiant effort. Of course, I thanked him profusely and got off the phone feeling vindicated, yet knowing that the truth was that I wasn't. I had to present a humble, meek disposition—SO grateful for this "break." My career was in the hands of men who valued convenience. I am not convenient.

The 2017 Women's March on DC brought such ignition to everything I had been feeling since I began working after undergraduate school. I went to the Women's March with other women and men from our campus and the surrounding areas. I started my journey at 12:30 a.m.; a colleague I had not known before met me at my house, then we picked up another colleague I didn't know very well, and drove an hour for the 2 a.m. bus to DC. We didn't know each other, were totally different ages, and had very different higher-ed jobs from one another—yet we all had similar stories of struggle, of sexual harassment, of losing jobs when male ego was hurt. We chatted about politics, sexual harassment (we had a slew of anecdotes), feminism, age, motherhood, wifehood, sisterhood.

By the time we arrived at the bus, I was already feeling the excitement, the rage, the need for change. As soon as I boarded the bus, I felt a surge of energy and sisterhood. I could not sleep, I was so excited. Our stop in Pennsylvania coincidentally was very close to my best friend's house, so she boarded our bus and we continued our journey to D.C. Our 9 a.m. arrival had similar sisterhood vibes—the streets were filled with men and women in pussy hats, holding signs, wearing homemade shirts, waving and encouraging each other. We stood through six hours of speakers and artists, our legs sore, our backs aching, our bladders full, with little food to eat. I saw children standing like this, grandmas and grandpas, entire families. I heard a woman talking about her sore legs from her recent double-knee replacements, yet she continued to stand and participate in chants and roars of support, encouraged by her husband. As the march began, so did group songs, chanting, fists in the air, hands holding hands, tears, laughter. The most memorable speaker for me was 6-year-old Sophie Cruz, the daughter of undocumented immigrants, who was born in the U.S. She gave her speech in English, then in Spanish, and then started a roaring chant of "Si se puede!" It was the most powerful wave of inspiration I have ever been a part of.

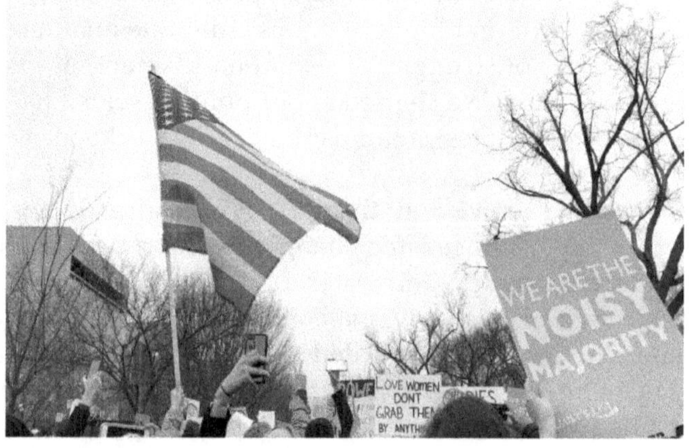


*Rachelann Lopp Copland and Destiny Beck participate in the Women's March on Washington, January 21, 2017*
***Figure 6***

After the march, when my friend and I finally were able to eat, the bars were overflowing with happiness and cheer, as the televisions broadcasted us, our national sister marches, our global sister marches. I have never felt more connected to the world.

Upon return, something changed in me. I stopped needing to please everyone. I started speaking up. Defending myself. Apologizing less. Looking into what I could do to continue this iron energy.

This March led into my NeMLA 2017 presentation, referenced in the introduction to this chapter. I presented on the roundtable about the difficulties of being a mom in higher education at NeMLA 2017, I drafted a resolution demanding menstrual equity across our state system campuses that was voted on and passed; I am working on another resolution demanding lactation spaces on our campuses. I continue my participation in the Women's Rights and Concerns Committee on our campus and was recently appointed Co-Chair, and am voicing my discontent with the lack of support adjuncts receive.

Fast-forward to 2018—I am pregnant, having to fight for offers of two courses each semester yet again. When I met with my supervisor about potential offers of courses for the semester in which I was due, he asked many inappropriate questions about the pregnancy: How much sick time did I already have? Was I planning to use it? What would it look like for me to work part of the semester? When was my due date? He went as far as to ask, "Wait, is it legal for me to be asking you these things?" As if I were the Head of Human Resources or responsible for working out such a huge inconvenience. I understand that yes, work planning is necessary when a pregnancy occurs, but these questions were asked before a contract was even offered, and unsurprisingly, I ended up with only one course offered.

The mental and emotional work the academic precariat invests in simply attaining contracts exhausts us. We often look for work outside of our field, need psychological support that we can't afford, take on too many contracts when we can get them, and the list goes on. Standing explains:

> The precariat knows there is no shadow of the future, as there is no future in what they are doing. To be 'out' tomorrow would come as no surprise, and to leave might not be bad, if another job or burst of activity beckoned. (*The Precariat* 12)

The most dangerous part is that academics often hold out hope for more, believing their merit and hard work may "pay off" with more stable employment at the institution that precariously employs them. For example, Yakoboski's research indicates that "31% of adjuncts report research as a job responsibility" and goes on to say that this response may "indicate a 'self-requirement' that enables securing a tenure-track position or attaining an adjunct promotion" (58). The academic precariat carries with it the shadow of prestige—thus, the "outing of tomorrow" that Standing references, may indeed come as a surprise to us as we reflect on our merits and hard work. Or at least a huge disappointment.

## Section 7: Precarious Mental Health

A union researcher recently asked me, "Would you recommend your job to the next generation?" Yakoboski's study shows that 42% of adjuncts are likely to recommend their career to a promising student, signaling "an inherent optimism among adjuncts about the future of college and university faculty..." (59). This inherent optimism reflects the meritocracy beliefs of the precariat and the myth of prestige surrounding our positions. Would the adjuncts studied actually recommend low wages, instability, lack of benefits, and lack of power over one's time and career to the next generation? Is it the pure enjoyment of the profession that they recommend? I love teaching—it gives my life a sense of purpose; however, I could never wish this brand of instability, low wages, and work load to my children's generation. The unhealthiness of precarious academic work cannot seep down into the next generation.

For me, on top of all of the mental and emotional changes that accompany motherhood, the precarious nature of my employment lends itself to additional anxiety. According to Watson and Osberg's Canadian study of the relationship between mental health and precarious employment, current scholarship finds negative implications of economic insecurity for mental health, especially in North America where precarious employment has seen a significant rise. This is no surprise! This field of research finds that the "threat of unemployment can be just as detrimental" as unemployment itself (Watson & Osberg pars. 1-3). Thus, there is a resulting "scaring effect" associated with the probability of future unemployment. The scaring effect of future unemployment becomes even more detrimental than the actual occurrence of job loss (par. 7). My contingent contract will always be semester-by-semester—every few months, wondering whether I will have: #1. My job; #2. My benefits. Psychological distress about future employment increases significantly for the academic precariat, who suffer from the repetition of semester-by-semester contracts. We languish in what Standing calls a "leisure deficit" and lack time in which we are not distracted, nervous from insecurity or spent from labour and work, or by the sleeplessness induced by it... The time is perceived as unavailable. Or those in the precariat feel guilty about devoting time to such activities, thinking they should be using their time in networking or in constantly upgrading their "'human capital'" (*The Precariat* 128). Another study by Andrew Abeyta, Clay Routledge,

Michael Kersten and Cathy R. Cox found that financial insecurity, as opposed to income amount, led to reduced ability to maintain meaning in life (Abeyta et al 696). The uncertainty of semesterly contracts harms the precariat's ability to maintain a sense of meaning in life: Abeyta et al's research found that "financial security threats undermined meaning" for people and that the threat of insecurity as opposed to the actual loss of employment created deficits in meaning of life (699). It seems the "scaring effect" more than generically negatively affects psychological health. In the words of Watson and Osberg: "while it is reasonable to expect a person to heal from past one-time spells of economic insecurity, repeated bouts may cause this same individual to break" (par. 4). Not a great outlook for adjuncts.

## Section 8: Academic Precariat Problems—Lack of Solidarity

A general lack of consistency and transparency in hiring practices at any institution, including the lack of administrative support and oversight on adjunct hiring practices, explains the need for solidarity. Inability to connect to colleagues except by engaging in unpaid labor prevents the precariat from having a voice. We miss forming work relationships, unless we invest more time in showing our faces on campus or at department meetings and happy hours.

The problem arises for those in the academic precariat of respecting the authority of those offering them contingent employment versus questioning anything related to that contingent employment. My experience with a rampant lack of hiring practices transparency harms any campus. One immediate supervisor claimed to me that he just "does what he is told" when making decisions about teaching assignments, instead of standing up to *his* supervisor who holds students' professor evaluations and his own teaching evaluations hostage in a locked filing cabinet in his office. This supervisor of mine has used phrases like "bottom of the barrel," "embarrassing," "totally incompetent" to describe those instructors he repeatedly rehires but then claims he cannot do anything to help me maintain any consistency in my contracts. So I am competing for a job against these so-called "bottom of the barrel" instructors. The [lack of] policies are considered "fair" hiring, although my Dean told me in my interview that benefits would not be an option because he makes sure to offer minimal classes to adjuncts in the spring, which prevents them from qualifying for benefits. Department administration cannot seem to figure out rehiring practices that balance credentials, colleague and student observations, commitment and longevity. And service and research are not considered in the least when re-hiring time comes around. Adjuncts are not expected to serve or research or attend professional development, so those that do, do so without recognition.

Fortunately for me, I have access to union support. Unfortunately, many institutions lack unions. While unions have strong bargaining power in states like New York, the rights and negotiation details often leave precariat workers with grossly less than their full-time, stably employed counterparts. The precariat often stands alone: Leon Fink argues, "The uncoupling of work relations from collective bargaining and/or enforced workplace welfare, safety, and other regulations leaves the industrial worker more exposed than ever to a competitive free-for-all..." (101). Although the academic precariat isn't necessarily "industrial," the same idea applies. The resulting "competitive free-for-all" Fink references makes it impossible for adjuncts to maintain any sense of stability or reliability. The recent Janus vs. AFSCME Supreme Court case ruling against unions may significantly weaken unions that are already unable to support the basic human needs of the precariat workers behind whom they stand.

## Section 9: Activism, Empowerment, Conclusions

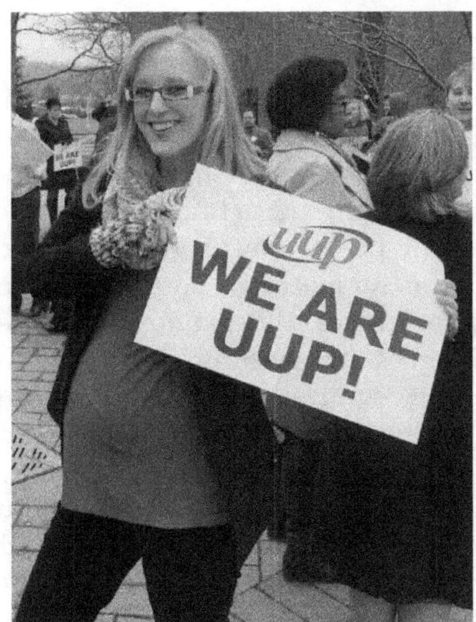


*Pregnant Picketing Spring 2018*
***Figure 7***

So why remain in the precariat if it is so horrible? My current employment situation fits my family needs for now and of course includes a full-time salaried position outside of my field. I have resigned myself to the fact that full-time employment in my field will not be a climb-the-ladder situation or a reward for campus-work and scholarly merit. I convince myself that hours of job searching will eventually pay off. Standing recognizes the tiresome aspect of job searching and proving oneself: "Working on those manufactured CVs, in the dispiriting effort to impress, to sell oneself and to cover as many bases as possible, takes up a huge amount of time. It is dehumanising, trying to demonstrate individuality while conforming to a standardised routine and way of behaving. When will the precariat protest?" (*The Precariat* 122). I will have to pour hours into applications, cover letters, research on the job market, and be willing to move anywhere if I want a full-time instructor position. So, for now, my voice is loudest here in the precariat, trying to stir up protest and solidarity.

Higher ed will leave the precariat behind if it lets itself be left behind. The labor involved with "keeping up" with the academy's rules, hierarchies, unions is a necessary ancillary if the precariat is to become an informed class for change. Standing points out that to be a "citizen in a society governed by complex laws and regulations, we need to know the laws and be able to access reliable sources of knowledge and advice" (*The Precariat* 125). Our rank is not as equals to our full-time colleagues, and even our full-time contingents. The hierarchy of the academy patronizes its members and encourages such a heavy focus on rank and division, that instructors are no longer a group unto their own. Those in the lower ranks are not required to participate in shared governance, and often not individually encouraged or invited. Lack of participation keeps a large portion of the academy in the dark. Leadership hides behind the reason of academic freedom that does not want to infringe upon a lower ranked employee's labor requirement. I often am surprised to find out that I am "allowed" to participate in many meetings, larger institutional systems and other governance opportunities. When I do participate, colleagues express shock at my willingness to work for free, to be involved even though my contract does not require it and I am not paid for it. While I do not want to model working for free, the systems in academia will only change and listen if I am invested and informed. Thus, to maintain being informed, one must work outside of the labor requirements of their contract. The precariat is often too tired, too busy with other jobs, caring for family members, too frustrated, to invest in these exclusionary systems. Academia might argue that the systems are not exclusionary because many times, they are open to contingent participation—yet the reality is, there is no inclusionary environment that welcomes that participation or pays for it.

My growing involvement in union participation led to the union president asking me to be a "go-to" on campus for other contingents, which I declined. Then, he encouraged me to run for the contingent representative slot in the next term. What a relief! That my efforts are noticed. Yet, I couldn't help but to add up the amount of work and emotional labor involved with representation. All in the name of progress—no extra pay or benefit. These are the decisions the academic precariat must face: work beyond an already minimally paying contract and try for non-guaranteed progress or languish in that minimally paid contract, semester after semester.

My ingrained blue-collar Protestant work ethic has perhaps had its returns in some cases, but it is time to wake up and realize that those "wholesome" American work values no longer catapult the masses into economic stability and security. It is time to actually take vacation days that we work hard to earn instead of martyring ourselves, believing it will be "good" for us. It is time to stay home from work when we are sick. If we do not have those vacation days or sick time, we should fight for them.

So far, the reward of empowerment, networking, and progress has satisfied the lack of pay. I also have access to benefits (depending on course assignments) and union support; but then again, I have only been in this game for a few years. I also recently had my third child and have to choose what to cut from my too-full plate. Unfortunately, I have to make these cuts based on income. If my time lacks monetary reward, I have to step back. My committee work, scholarly work and activist work slide to backburners. This situation only adds to the anxieties of precarious employment. If I let go of the things that empower me, that I believe are working for change on campus, I feel powerless and downtrodden when I receive my offers, wait endlessly for my offers, wait for my offers to be taken away or changed at the last minute, etc. The unpaid work that I do associated with my precarious employment allows me to continue in it and often helps reduce the anxieties. It is a complicated dichotomy that lends itself to feelings of being trapped, stagnant, and useless. Therefore, projects like this one provide purpose and keep my mind engaged outside of the classroom.

Reflecting on the evolution of my work-life narrative empowers me and will, I hope, others. Although activism and empowerment come at a cost and are unpaid labor, I find that my values have shifted. My activism was born out of setting store by rights and values in my profession, not the pursuance of wealth and money. The academic precariat will never be monetarily "rich," but we must pursue riches in values, control of time and leisure, and mental and emotional health. We must press our superiors in accountability and fair hiring practices. As for me, my children inspire me to refuse unfairness. Our children, our students, the next generation, are watching and learning. An inheritance of passivity simply is not an option.

## Works Cited

Abeyta, Andrew A. et al. "The Existential Cost of Economic Insecurity: Threatened Financial Security Undercuts Meaning." *The Journal of Social Psychology* 157: 6 (2017): 692-702. DOI: 10.1080/00224545.2016.1270892

Curtis, John W. "Persistent Inequity: Gender and Academic Employment." *New Voices in Pay Equity EVENT.* 11 April 2011. https://www.aaup.org/NR/rdonlyres/08E023AB-E6D8-4DBD-99A0-24E5EB73A760/0/persistent_inequity.pdf

Fink, Leon. "The First Precariat?" *International Labor and Working-Class History* 91 (Spring 2017): 99-108. DOI: 10.1017/S014754791600034X

"Higher Education Data Center." *American Federation of Teachers.* https://www.aft.org/higher-education-data-center.

Janus v. American Federation of State, County, and Municipal Employees, 31, ET AL. No. 16-1466. Supreme Court of the United States. 2018. 1-83. https://www.supremecourt.gov/opinions/17pdf/16-1466_2b3j.pdf

Jorgensen, Martin Bak. "Precariat—What it Is and Isn't—Towards an Understanding of What it *Does.*" *Critical Sociology* 42: 7-8 (2016): 959-974. DOI: 10.1177/0896920515608925.

Kitroff, Natalie and Jessica Silver-Greenberg. "Pregnancy Discrimination is Rampant in America's Biggest Companies." *The New York Times.* 15 June 2018, https://www.nytimes.com/interactive/2018/06/15/business/pregnancy-discrimination.html. Accessed 30 July 2018.

"Know Your Rights: The Pregnancy Discrimination Act." *AAUW (American Association of University Women),* 2018, https://www.aauw.org/what-we-do/legal-resources/know-your-rights-at-work/pregnancy-discrimination-act/. Accessed 17 Aug. 2018.

*Legal Momentum.* "Women and Poverty in America." Legal Momentum, 2009-2017, https://www.legalmomentum.org/women-and-poverty-america. Accessed 15 Aug. 2018.

Lopp, John. Personal interview. 2 Feb. 2018.

Lopp, Terry. Personal interview. 2 Feb. 2018.

"Need Time? The Employee's Guide to the Family and Medical Leave Act." *Department of Labor: Wage and Hour Division,* https://www.dol.gov/whd/fmla/employeeguide.pdf. Accessed 2 Feb. 2018.

"Newville, PA." *Data USA.* https://datausa.io/profile/geo/newville-pa/ Accessed 1 March 2018.

Parker, Kim and Renee Stepler. "Americans See Men as the Financial Providers, Even as Women's Contributions Grow." *Pew Research Center,* Sept. 2017, http://www.pewresearch.org/fact-tank/2017/09/20/americans-see-men-as-the-financial-providers-even-as-womens-contributions-grow/ . Accessed 29 Aug. 2018.

"Poverty Guidelines." *U.S. Department of Health and Human Services,* ASPE, https://aspe.hhs.gov/poverty-guidelines. Accessed 10 Mar. 2018.

Sklansky, Jeffrey. "Labor, Money, and the Financial Turn in the History of Capitalism." *Labor: Studies in Working-Class History of the Americas* 11: 1 (2014): 23-46. DOI: 10.1215/15476715-2385381.

Standing, Guy. *The Precariat: The New Dangerous Class.* London: Bloomsbury Academic, 2011.

Standing, Guy. "Understanding the Precariat through Labour and Work." *Development and Change* 45: 5 (2014): 963-980. DOI: 10.1111/dech.12120.

Sutton, April and Amanda Bosky and Chandra Muller. "Manufacturing Gender Inequality in the New Economy: High School Training for Work in Blue-Collar Communities." *American Sociological Review* 81: 4 (2016): 720-748. DOI: 10.1177/0003122416648189

Watson, B. and L. Osberg. "Healing and/or Breaking? The Mental Health Implications of Repeated Economic Insecurity." *Soc Sci Med* 188 (Sept 2017): 119-127. DOI: 10.1016/j.socscimed2017.06.042.

Yakoboski, Paul J. "Adjunct Views of Adjunct Positions." *Change* 48: 3 (May/June 2016): 54-59. DOI: 10.1080/00091383.2016.1170553

## Figures

Figure 1: "Percent of Population Who did Household Activities on an Average Day." *United States Department of Labor Bureau of Labor Statistics,* 2014. https://www.bls.gov/tus/, Accessed 2 Feb. 2018.

Figure 2: "Labor Force Participation Rate of Mothers, by Age of Youngest Child, March 1975-March 2008." 2008. *United States Department of Labor Bureau of Labor Statistics,* https://www.bls.gov/tus/ Accessed 2 Feb. 2018.

Figure 3: Standing, Guy. *The Precariat: The New Dangerous Class.* London: Bloomsbury Academic, 2011.

Figure 4: Personal Photo

Figure 5: "Know Your Rights: The Pregnancy Discrimination Act." *AAUW (American Association of University Women),* 2018, https://www.aauw.org/what-we-do/legal-resources/know-your-rights-at-work/pregnancy-discrimination-act/. Accessed 17 Aug. 2018.

Figure 6: Personal Photos

Figure 7: Personal Photo

# The Feminization of Digital Work

# The Feminization of Digital Work: The Invisible Appropriation of Un(Der)Paid Female Labor

TAMARA IONKOVA HAMMOND

## Introduction

This chapter examines a prevalent aspect of digital work—the exploited unpaid work that is perceived as an investment in future employment and is a result of neoliberal policies of outsourcing/crowdsourcing. In the case of outsourcing, the business capital is moved abroad to cheaper labor markets, whereas crowdsourcing is specific to digital labor and describes multiple volunteers' individual work performing partial tasks of larger projects paid by the lowest bid. The fluid capital, as opposed to the inflexible work forces, compels the employees to compete against each other globally, while the capital owners are exempt from the competition. My focus on the precarious status of women and minorities in the digital market is determined by their continued exclusion from technical and leadership positions and the mediation of new media in the process. To illustrate this discriminatory policy, it suffices to underline the ratio of female employees in technology, maintained at below 20 percent and minorities at 2-5 percent (Kang). According to social and cultural analyst Andrew Ross, the Internet economy is a reflection of the "feminization of work" not only because the majority of women are doing unpaid work, but because when the boundaries between duty and opportunity are blurred, women are affected more than men (Ross 24). Admittedly, there is plenty of material written on the merging of work and play and the digital exploitation by scholars such as Tiziana Terranova, who popularized the term "social factory" (33),[1] Maurizio Lazzarato, who coined the term "immaterial work" (133), and Trebor Scholz, who conducted a conference on the topic, titled *The Internet as Playground and Factory*, to name a few (Scholz 1). However, the free aspect of digital work that is performed disproportionately by women, remains overlooked and insufficiently covered, therefore I am motivated to make a contribution to this specific area of scholarship. I analyze the relationship between unpaid digital labor and various aspects of intersectional feminism including racism, classism, sexism, homophobia, xenophobia, ageism, and ableism in the workplace. I draw on the works of scholars such as Dorothy Sue Cobble, Linda Gordon, Astrid Henry, Chimananda Adichie, and bell hooks, who emphasize class struggle and racism in their works, as well as Dawn Foster, Rebecca Solnit, and Brooke Erin Duffy, who elaborate on sexism, ageism, ableism, and other forms of oppression.

In analyzing the digital market and its implications for women and minorities, it is important to introduce the new class that they belong to—the precariat, a term coined by political economist Guy Standing in his 2011 book *The Precariat: The New Dangerous Class.* One of the most devastating effects of the neoliberal policies is the creation of this new class whose members sustain economically precarious, unstable lives. According to Standing, unlike the proletariat, which succeeds in becoming organized in unions during the industrial era and identifies itself as a homogenous class with distinct characteristics, the precariat is heterogeneous, disorganized, and has no class consciousness, therefore, it becomes an easy prey for exploitation (11). Furthermore, explains Standing, while trade unions, labor parties, and social democrats fight to implement some forms of labor-related security for the industrial proletariat, the precariat lacks representation and fares worse in all aspects of job security (11). For example, long-term contracts, protection against loss of employment, health insurance and other benefits are not provided for the precariat by its employers (11). Standing explicates the historic foundation of women becoming part of the precariat, "It is because women have always done most of the care work that it has been neglected in economic statistics and social policy. This was brought to its absurd worst in the twentieth century, when doing care work did not count as work at all" (71). Conditioned throughout a long history of unpaid domestic work, childbirth, and childcare, women transitioned to the digital market with little change in their subordinate positions.

The notion that the precariat is disproportionally composed by the most vulnerable social groups—women and minorities, is imperative for understanding that gender, racial, and class discrimination are inherent in patriarchal capitalism. The shift from unpaid care to unpaid or low paid digital work is viewed as liberation; however, it is yet another way of oppression through unequal participation in the labor market. In his chapter, "Who Enters the Precariat?" Standing explains that, "Gender inequality is a cultural legacy that has fed into a gendered precariat, in which women are concentrated in temporary, low-productivity jobs, resulting in one of the highest male-female wage differentials in the industrialized world" (71). Furthermore, the author explains that the shifting of labor market to service where manual strength is not required makes women preferable to employers who do not provide benefits or other forms of security (70). Standing concludes that, "Women have taken disproportionate a share of precarious jobs, being far more likely to have short-term contracts or no contracts at all" (71). In examining the political and economic implications for the growing female precariat, it is important to consider the role of new media. In the digital labor market, new media both amplify and undermine women's exploitation and discrimination. The phenomenon of female presence on new media is indicative of their access to public forums that wasn't possible prior to the Internet. Women and minorities can now create their own blogs, publish articles on any social media network such as Facebook, Twitter, Instagram and LinkedIn, and voice their opinions in group discussions or chat rooms on the Internet. However, this presence is also associated with two negative repercussions: unpaid digital labor that contributes to the precarious economic status of women, and becoming a target of harassment and physical threats against them. In the context of the neoliberal concentration of capital, corporate owned new media both maintain the status quo and facilitate the disrupting of power structures. Furthermore, the owners could control the visibility of overtly dissident content through carefully chosen algorithms that determine the newsfeed (Rader and Gray). Despite this manipulation, women and minorities are capable of publishing any critical material they want, and although it could be drowned in a sea of opposing writings pushed by the algorithms, it is still available to those who are interested in reading it.

The official policies in technological companies demonstrate support of diversity expressed in superficial acts of concern for discrimination and harassment of the minorities. For example, Facebook advertises their diversity training online, showing false demographics that contradict the real ratio of employees in the company (Facebook). Even though Facebook doesn't break down the number of employees showing their positions for obvious reasons, according to their global director of diversity, in 2017, the numbers were around the normative for Silicon Valley—women at 19 percent, Hispanics at 5 percent, and black employees at 3 percent, reducing black women to barely non-existing (Williams). Thus diversity rhetoric is copious and well developed, but it only serves to camouflage racism, sexism, ageism, homophobia, xenophobia, among other discriminations, evident in the company's demographics. Similarly, Google participates in this rhetoric as well. The company's year diversity statement begins with the opening sentence, "Google should be a place where people from different backgrounds and experiences come to do their best work—a place where every Googler feels they belong" (Google Diversity). It continues with commitment to fight bias and efforts to look for bias "at Google, in the industry, and in society" (Google). These claims are in blunt contradiction with Google's demographics, which, according to a *Forbes* article, are far from diverse. Despite the misleading title, "Google's 2017 Diversity Report Shows Progress Hiring Women, Little Change for Minority Workers," the demographics show a decrease in hiring minorities. According to the same article, women in Google are 20 percent, Blacks are 1 percent, down from 2 percent in 2016, and Hispanics are 4 percent, down from 5 percent the previous year (Donnelly). The statistics demonstrate that the tech companies' employers don't really care about diversity; they just craft a politically correct strategy to prevent lawsuits. When facing such lawsuits, the companies can show evidence of diversity training and blame the lack of minorities on the pipeline (Thomas).

In my analysis of the feminization of digital work in this chapter, I will use Elissa Shevinsky's anthology *Lean Out*, and the professional social network, LinkedIn, to support my claim for discrimination of women and minorities in the digital market. I chose the works of multiple authors using different media to demonstrate the disadvantage of being female or minority in technology. Analyzing a popular book and a new media network, I present various angles of ambient policies of discrimination. Furthermore, these media express unpopular critical views against these policies and more importantly, refute the notion that recruiting employees in technology is based on merit. Therefore, I will use these authors' works organized in two case studies for explaining the female precariat in the digital market.

## Professional Women in Silicon Valley: Debunking The Myth of Meritocracy in Technology

This case study is based on the work of Elissa Shevinsky, an author, entrepreneur, and cybersecurity expert. Her 2015 edited collection *Lean Out: The Struggle for Gender Equality in Tech and Start-Up Culture* contains the accounts of nineteen female entrepreneurs representing various minorities such as people of color, LGBTQ communities, transgender groups, and genderqueer individuals, among others. Based on the analyses of the nineteen authors from the anthology, who are consistent in their emphasis on sexism, they could be divided thematically into several additional categories: focus on exploitation, marginalizing of LGBTQ individuals, racism, and sexual harassment. As Shevinsky succinctly put it, her book *Lean Out* matters because "we are part of a movement to tell the untold stories" (13). The editor refutes the myth of the white male heterosexual genius who single-handedly created giant digital companies such as Apple, Google, or Facebook, and adduces facts of the erasure of numerous women who contributed to these creations and were omitted from history including Radia Perlman, known as the "Mother of the Internet" (Rosen). Elisa Shevinsky underlines some prominent women including Judith Estrin, a key designer of Transmission Control Protocol/ Internet Protocol (*Tech Target*); Radia Perlman mentioned above, who invented Spanning Tree Protocol; Glenda Schroeder, who created the electronic mail; Sandra Lerner, the co-founder of Cisco Systems; Nicola Pellow, who wrote the first platform web-browser; and 19th-century Ada Lovelace, who was the very first programmer in the world.

Furthermore, Shevinsky maintains that her book explores the question of whether technology deserves women and minorities (14). In suggesting that women and minorities should lean out because they are not treated adequately by the industry, Shevinsky opposes the popular recruiting slogan for "leaning in" promoted by Facebook CEO Sheryl Sandberg and supported by many. In her bestselling book *Lean In,* Sandberg blames women for not being hired in leadership positions and urges them to be more aggressive and fight their innate passivity (Sandberg 24). By rejecting the idea of leaning in, Shevinsky is resisting corporate efforts to recruit women and minorities as cheap labor in order to exploit them. More importantly, Shevinsky voices the opinions of multiple representatives of women and minorities who choose to lean out and refuse to facilitate their own exploitation by greedy corporations. Sandberg's idea of leaning in shifts the burden of work discrimination to the victims, and condones the system that exploits them. In contrast, the opposite concept of "leaning out" puts the blame back to the institutions and calls for boycotting the system. By publicizing the latter platform, Shevinsky refutes the common narrative and false excuses blaming the pipeline, women's choices, and even female aptitude in science for hiring so few women in technology. An ensuing challenge confronted by the author is how to create specific cultures, in which women and minorities lead and not follow, and in which they belong (Shevinsky 14). According to one of the authors, female founders of startups acquire only 7 percent of the venture capital funding, and as a result, found just 11 percent of tech companies, because they are facing enormous difficulties and discrimination (128). They need public awareness and support, and they need to be acknowledged and rewarded for their bravery and dedication to a field that constantly rejects and opposes them. This situation is described by multiple authors such as venture capital intern Erica Swallow, whose project to investigate the lack of women in technology was rejected, or Katherine Cross who claims that women's and minorities' partial acceptance is contingent on their willingness not to challenge the fictional myth of meritocracy in the digital economy (Shevinsky 80). In an interview with *The Mercury News,* Shevinsky contends that justifying the lack of women in technology with platitudes such as "women aren't smart enough," or "there aren't women interested," is laziness that is counterproductive (Fancher).

According to Shevinsky, the tech industry narrative has done substantial damage to women and minorities, because "'the pattern of recognition' in favor of young white male nerds is deeply ingrained" (10). From Bill Gates to Steve Jobs to Mark Zuckerberg to current investors in startup companies at Silicon Valley, white male dominance is omnipresent. This is evident in the fact that women in technology are over 18 percent below the national average for all other private industries, while minorities are almost 50 percent below the average for the rest of the country (USEEOC 2014). Moreover, the exceptional roles of women in the process of building the giant digital companies "have been carefully erased by men like Zuckerberg and Jobs who are both widely acknowledged to be masterful story-tellers" (Shevinsky 11). The neo-liberal policies of focusing on unrestrained corporate profit and governments with limited regulations make it possible for individuals to privatize the profit resulted from decades of government-funded research in state universities such as MIT or Stanford, among other prestigious institutions. Everything from microchips to Apple digital products to social networks was the final product of publicly funded years of scholarship, recently appropriated by businessmen whose only goal is profit. This contributes to the current economy of inequality and exploitation because founders such as Mark Zuckerberg or Bill Gates are privatizing the gains resulting from public funding without giving back to society the deserving right to own the social network publicly instead of privately. Social networks such as Facebook, Microsoft, or LinkedIn should be public, not private based on the years of federal funding that led to their development. Furthermore, because of their massive public participation, these networks function as utilities, therefore, should subscribe to constitutional protections such as freedom of speech, non-discrimination, and so on. Finally, the financial gap between digital moguls and the employees in the industry deepens with gender, race and ethnicity, as emphasized earlier.

According to one of the early employees of Facebook, Zuckerberg's ghostwriter Kate Losse, there are nameless women shown in photographs and documentary records of the early days of the companies exposing their critical roles in performing many digital and social tasks without recognition. These female associates have never been compensated for their work, or even acknowledged as contributors (Losse). Only a few are credited or included in Wikipedia and other internet information sources—the ones who are either wealthy or have decades of seniority in technology—and can, therefore, be found through search engines. For example, a quick Google search leads to the 2017 *Forbes* magazine's list of the richest women in tech, composed by only six women internationally, two of them American, among a hundred male billionaires (Au-Yeung). Moreover, none of the female inventors in technology mentioned earlier are wealthy enough to be included in the *Forbes* classification, and none of them make claims to be single-handedly responsible for their important inventions. On the contrary, some of them, most notably Perlman, maintain that the Internet was not created by any individual but rather was the final result of deliberate, long collective work (Shevinsky 11).

Perlman's determination to not waste time contesting for credit for her work, or monetizing her creativity, explains the fact that she is not on the *Forbes* list. Like most talented people, she is genuinely interested in the creative process, the results of her research, and the advancement of technology. However, the imposed neoliberal evaluation of everyone based on wealth and ranking profit beyond all other values keeps women, minorities, and individuals who deviate in their priorities in subordinate positions in technology.

Moreover, Perlman explains that in the late 1960s and 1970s when she went to college studying math, she rarely saw other women: according to Perlman, there were approximately 50 women in a class of 1,000 students, that is, only five percent (Rosen). When asked if there is a difference now, in the 21st century, Perlman summarizes as follows:

> Honestly, not much has changed. Obviously it was possible to have a job in the industry long ago (like my mother did in the 1950s). People's assumptions these days are that companies are desperate to hire and promote women, and that being female must be a big advantage. Companies do spend money on sponsoring events for women's groups, but actual hiring decisions are based on subjective feelings, and I think there is often an unconscious bias where the hiring manager doesn't really see a 'true engineer' if the candidate doesn't fulfill some preconceived vision (for instance, a younger version of himself). None of this is intentional, and it's very difficult to do anything about it. (Rosen)

The pattern of employing younger versions of the hiring management in digital companies is problematic, because it perpetuates the exclusion of women and minorities. Even for a senior engineer such as Perlman, who has more than forty years of experience in technology, it is difficult to fit in the culture, and it is obvious to her that the bias still exists after decades of proof that women are both capable and inclined to work in the field (Rosen). As a result, Perlman's words of advice to young graduates in a commencement speech at Rochester Institute of Technology are resonant with these insights (Rosen). According to Perlman, she remembers three of the recommendations from her commencement speech, "Ten Things I Wish I Knew When I Was Your Age." They are remarkably simple. The first one states that life is not fair, but we must strive to correct this flux by giving people credit for their work. The second reveals that everyone is insecure; however, "Really smart people are actually sweet and generous." Finally, Perlman encourages young graduates to ask for help as well as be happy to help others, and especially, to be generous with credit (Rosen). More remarkably, the famous line "Life is not fair" wrongly attributed to Bill Gates, is in fact coined by Perlman in the same commencement speech (Rosen). While Gates's alleged phrase is "Life is not fair, get used to it," Perlman's suggestion at the commencement is the opposite of accepting this injustice (Rosen). As the *Forbes* magazine demonstrates, women are at a disadvantage when it comes to receiving credit because popularity is proportional to the individual's corresponding wealth. Consequently, based on a single criterion, wealth, as a prerequisite to be promoted by the media, women are overlooked by the press and become invisible in history. In my view, women were erased from public records for both economic and political reasons: economic, because they have been exploited, harassed and undermined and thus, had failed to acquire the massive amounts of wealth of their male counterparts; political, because women in technology have no adequate power and are not able to monopolize the market and rewrite history like the male digital moguls. Kept in the ranks of the precariat through discrimination and exploitation, women and minorities are in a perpetual vicious circle: as the precariat, they cannot accumulate money, and as the poor, they cannot access political power and change the system. Thus, Shevinsky's anthology is important, because it offers the accounts of women in technology, otherwise unavailable in the mainstream media. It is very unlikely that information such as the unpopular viewpoints of women or minorities exposing their discrimination and exploitation would be reported adequately by a press sponsored by the ruling class that oppresses them. Ironically, the owners of new media such as Gates, Bezos, Zuckerberg, and so on, resemble the old ruling class: rich, white, male, and straight. Thus, neoliberalism is an extension of the capitalist patriarchy. The way white rich men dominated societies when women weren't allowed to have property or vote in the 19th century, or the way women and minorities were prohibited to study science, law or business in the early to mid-20th century, the 21st century's women and minorities are obstructed and prevented from entering technology.

Two of the analyzed essays of Shevinsky's anthology are written by an anonymous, genderless fictional author named FAKEGRIMLOCK. It is not a coincidence that Shevinsky starts and ends the collection with a symbolic androgynous author FAKEGRIMLOCK, whose two essays are titled "You Belong in Tech," and "You Must Start Up." The essays are supposedly written by a "Robot Start up Dinosaur," and according to Shevinsky, "could be male, female, or neither" (14). The essays include messages in succinct imitation of AI language lacking auxiliary verbs, infinite and definite particles, and other parts of speech, and are written in capital letters resembling code language. The significance of this symbolic language is multifaceted: it represents coding in technology, as well as erases the difference between gender, race, class, and sexual orientation, age and health condition. This should be the epitome of meritocracy: to evaluate one's work without knowing this person's demographic data. Thus in a patriarchal culture, anonymous procedures for hiring and evaluating one's work could be the only measure for eliminating the discrimination of certain social groups. Furthermore, the message conveyed by FAKEGRIMLOCK is a warning not to use technology to further enhance inequality; therefore, promoting egalitarian society. The caution about the future of technology is chilling and empowering at the same time. One effective foresight describes in very few lines what happened in the last four decades—the use of technology for achieving neoliberal goals, and even predicts a future development. The author maintains that the control imposed on the Internet users through ownership of the networks by a handful of billionaires is even more concentrated than before and could be easily reduced to just one single owner. In the author's own words:

> WITH TECH,
> YOUR LIFE, YOUR JOB, YOUR RIGHTS, EVERY DAY
> CHANGED BY TECH, EVERY DAY FUTURE ARRIVE
> FASTER AND FASTER, EVERY DAY IT BUILT BY FEWER AND FEWER.
> UNTIL ONE DAY ONE PERSON CHANGE
> ENTIRE WORLD WITH LINE OF CODE. (Shevinsky 21)

These lines reflect the concentration of capital in the hands of a few oligarchs and the tendency to use money to influence politics and to use politics to enhance personal wealth. The process is completed because of the interconnection between the government and the financial monopoly, and it is made possible with the help of technology. Because the same tendency of interdependence between executive policies and financial power exists in technology, digital companies become more and more concentrated in the hands of a few multibillionaires such as the owners of Amazon, Microsoft, and Facebook, among others. Every one of these magnates sells his customers' data to both private corporations and government agencies such as the CIA, the FBI, the NSA, and so on (Fang). As exposed in 2013 by former NSA engineer and dissident Eduard Snowden, the largest Internet companies such as Microsoft, Google, Apple, and Facebook, among others, were recruited by the government security agencies as early as 2007, and continued in current times (Greenwald 108). Furthermore, these giant companies are lobbying in Washington and working relentlessly to protect their billions by removing more and more regulations, resulting in a plutocracy. For example, according to business journalist Nitasha Tiku, Google spent $5.4 billion in lobbying between April and June of 2016 alone (Tiku). In the same effort to influence policies such as privacy, net neutrality, and tax reform, corporations in technology have been funding think tanks, academics, and non-profits (Tiku). This is what FAKEGRIMLOCK means when It says, "UNTIL ONE DAY ONE PERSON CHANGE ENTIRE

WORLD WITH LINE OF CODE" (Shevinsky 21). The author is referring to the concentration of power in technology that is wielded by fewer and fewer owners. For example, according to their website, professional network LinkedIn was bought by Microsoft in 2016, in addition to Skype, bought in 2011; Instagram and Whatsapp were bought by Facebook respectively in 2012 and 2014, and so on. The digital companies are getting bigger and fewer. The final essay in the anthology, "You Must Start Up," prescribes a proactive attitude, especially taking matters into the hands of women and minorities through self-education in technology. The act of starting independent digital companies in order to avoid exploitation and playing by the rules of plutocracy is the idea behind leaning out and refusing to support an exploitive system that maintains gendered and racial inequality, among others.

Elissa Shevinsky's anthology aims at dismantling these abusive practices and creating a safer, more egalitarian environment in technology. Shevinsky's labor of searching, collecting, and interviewing these authors as well as publishing their points of view consists of free work associated with any kind of activism. The efforts of contemplating, analyzing, and writing the stories by the nineteen female authors could also be considered unpaid work since they have no guaranteed return on their intellectual investment. The editor has contacted and met with every author in order to familiarize herself with their work in technology. After interviewing them, she describes all of the authors in her introduction, and briefly presents them before each essay. Shevinsky's own contribution to the anthology consists of two essays titled respectively "That's It—I'm Finished Defending Sexism in Tech," and "The Pipeline Isn't the Problem." Both explore the fact that so few women still exist as professionals in the field of technology and that the environment is overtly hostile and discriminative towards women and minorities. The first essay warns that shifting the responsibility to women in dealing with the problem is not a viable solution: "It's wrong to invite women to come in and be the fix—because women are not the problem. We also need men to step up and to welcome us" (Shevinsky 69). In the second essay, Shevinsky refutes another erroneous myth: that technology has a pipeline problem. Having well over ten thousand hours of experience building web applications used by millions, Shevinsky and many of her colleagues are qualified and actively searching for jobs; however, they are consistently rejected by major companies such as Google and Facebook. Based on these facts, the author's illuminating suggestion is: "So let's stop saying that women aren't here, or that they aren't skilled. Let's instead look at why we are not seeing/bringing/promoting/funding/respecting the women who are" (210).

The two main fallacious reasons given as an excuse by the tech companies when confronted by critics are well articulated by Shevinsky—on the one hand, shifting the burden of resolving the problem to the victims, and on the other, the excuse of the pipeline. There are many women and minorities that are qualified, experienced and available; however, they are invisible to the hiring agents, as Perlman noted earlier. The culture of exclusion, discrimination, and elitism that characterizes technology undoubtedly resembles a fraternity, and as such, continues to appropriate the entire industry and to apply principles of white male supremacy (140). This bias is confirmed by the US Equal Employment Opportunity Committee, reporting that high technology industries demonstrate higher gaps in employment between men compared to women and minorities than any other industry. In technology, 83.3 percent of employees holding executive positions are white, whereas in all other industries the ratio is 68 percent white to 32 percent minorities. Furthermore, in technology there are 64 percent men, 36 percent women, 7.4 Black, and 8 percent Hispanic, compared to 52 percent men, 48 percent women, 14.4 percent Black, and 13.9 percent Hispanic in all other industries (US EEOC 2014). Since technology hires almost 50 percent fewer minorities than other industries, and over 18 percent fewer women, this practice reflects the retrograde mentality in technology, and the uncomfortable work experience women and minorities describe in Shevinsky's anthology.

The first common theme emphasizing exploitation is represented by several authors who suggest leaning out in response to their discrimination. Although it may seem to some a strategy of surrender, leaning out could be interpreted as boycotting the industry that could result in improvement, as similar forms of opposition proved effective in the past. For example, in 2016, the Communications Workers of America reported a victory for the employees against a major digital corporation, Verizon, after a 45-day strike of 40,000 workers (CWA). The gains for the workers include the opening of 1,300 new call centers on the East Coast, 11 percent raise of wages, bonuses, pension increase, minimum profit share, and the first employee contract for retail store employees, among others (CWA). In the age of rampant outsourcing policies, these gains are encouraging and prove that leaning out could achieve far better results for the majority than leaning in, which only benefits a selected minority of token employees.

Another form of exploitation is the widespread practice of internship, a form of unpaid digital labor that epitomizes both feminization of work and discrimination. Interns fit perfectly well in the definition of precariat—they work for little or no money, have no guarantee of being hired, and see their labor as an investment in the future. Erica Swallow, an entrepreneur, technology journalist, and international speaker, shares her internship experience in her essay, "On Being a Female in Venture Capital." In Swallow's own words, "Throughout my summer internship as an associate at Boston-based venture capital firm General Catalyst, I was consistently reminded of my place as a woman in man's world"

(Shevinsky 126). According to Swallow, women in venture capital do not exist "beyond the high-heel-studded secretaries and assistants" — a mere 4.2 percent at partner-level decision-makers (126). Even worse for Swallow, her proposal for research project, "Female Founders," was rejected by her project lead based on the premise that the project couldn't continue without her, therefore had no future (127). Swallow's interest in female scarcity in venture capital was sparked by a study conducted by Harvard/Wharton/MIT, showing that men are more likely to be funded than women by 60-70 percent (128). Since Swallow was the only woman working in General Catalyst temporarily, the issue was considered to be of no interest to men. Similarly, when Swallow turned to an investor for support, the answer was, "Not specialized enough, not important to focus on, and not where the money's at." (128). Swallow's topic, conveniently rejected by the male leaders, demonstrates their intention to maintain the status quo, evident in their refusal to investigate the reasons for women's scarcity in technology. Ironically, internship is a form of exploitation, because it is rarely paid or paid extremely low. Viewed as an investment in someone's career, in the case of women and minorities, it seldom materializes in jobs as noted earlier. Furthermore, according to the Intern Bridge report of 2010, women are engaged in unpaid internship at 77 percent of all participants. This pattern of feminization of unpaid work continues to persist. For example, in 2017, computer games company Blizzard increased its female employment from 12 to 32 percent simply by hiring exclusively female interns (Louis). Therefore, as most forms of exploitation, the practice of internship proves to be gendered.

The next author who discusses exploitation in the workplace, is a celebrated "30 under 30" entrepreneur Sunny Allen. She describes the price she paid for her success in her essay, "What We Don't Say." Among some of the ordeals Allen had to endure was the fact that she was homeless for two years in San Francisco, commuting three hours each direction from the shelter to the Coding Bootcamp, and she was also hospitalized because of health issues during this time. According to Allen, she didn't have the image that venture capitalists and hiring managers looked for, and in her own words Silicon Valley is, "A boy's club, although women can join if they do it just right. This involves going to Stanford (MIT is also acceptable) and networking events and joining Angel List and having great recommendations on your LinkedIn profile... You are young and white and gorgeous" (Shevinsky 35). One of the reasons for Allen's homelessness is her doing unpaid work in the coding center. Although she finally had a break, this is not the common outcome for the ninety-three percent of unfunded female entrepreneurs in venture capital. Understandably, Allen is haunted by the analogy that Kate Heddleston made comparing women in technology to the "canary in the coal mine" (Shevinsky 39). According to Heddleston, replacing one dead canary with a new one doesn't solve the problem, because the reason the canary died was lack of oxygen in the mine, not too few canaries (39). Allen's story and Heddleston's allegory are both indicative of the tokenism practiced as a solution to gender discrimination by the chauvinistic male leadership of the industry. The miraculous survival of random canaries—in this case, Sunny Allen—is not a justification for the metaphorical death of many others in the poisonous to women and minorities environment in technology.

In the group of authors describing the exclusion and marginalizing of genderqueer and LGBT individuals, some are overlapping with race discrimination such as Deirdra Kiai, who is an independent game designer and of mixed racial origins. Deirdra Kiai, or her own choice of nickname Squinky, discusses the very important issue of being a misfit in her two essays, "Notes from a Game Industry Outcast," and "Making Games Is Easy, Belonging Is Hard." Squinky makes an astute observation that covers both discrimination of women and minorities and their exploitation: "The gaming industry is a business, first and foremost. As it turned out, gaming studios like Telltale games only wanted me insofar as my youth and passion helped them make money by providing them with cheap labor" (Shevinsky 87). Like author anne anthropy, who contends that "passion is the greatest weakness of anyone in games or tech," Squinky claims that passion makes it possible for the industry to exploit talent as "cheap labor." Squinky summarizes the neoliberal priority of making profit over human values and continues that, "When my passion extended towards a desire for positive social change that didn't directly further the ideals of marketers and producers, suddenly I became a liability" (87). Furthermore, Squinky explains that diversity isn't a human issue in the gaming industry, but a matter of either making or not making money. Similar to tokenism mentioned by many of the minority authors, Squinky shares her experience of being ignored because she was a genderqueer person of color, "Most people would rather pretend I don't exist than try to fit me into a category. My identity is a kind of invisibility cloak" (88). In her second essay, Squinky's leitmotif "Making games is easy, belonging is hard" is repeated four times, including the title. Her final paragraph repeats the first part for a fifth time and challenges the status quo: "Belonging is hard. But maybe it doesn't have to be" (96). The question of not belonging is addressed by every single author as both a concern and a reason to lean out. Exiting the industry is the commonly agreed upon strategy in the book.

Leanne Pittsford, an entrepreneur and the founder of *Lesbian Who Tech,* emphasizes the importance of the inclusion of minorities in one sentence: "Take for e.g. [sic] the name of this book *Lean Out;* it perfectly captures what *Lean In* missed. While the latter was an important step toward elevating the discussion of gender in tech, it primarily captured the straight woman's perspective. It's important for all women to be visible and heard, to share stories and experiences" (Shevinsky 166).

Pittsford addresses the glaring issue of economic inequality in technology regarding queer men compared to queer women—an issue that is doubled for lesbian couples with two low-paying incomes, and the pay gap deepens if they raise children (165). Equally important, Pittsford analyzes the different status of gay and lesbian couples in technology. For example, lesbians are underrepresented at LGBTQ events where 70 to 90 percent of the attendees are gay men and their male allies (167). Not surprisingly, the media's role in this matter is promoting disproportionally gay males in television, print, film, and online publications. After the realization that when asked to name high profile lesbians in technology, LGBTQ people were unable to identify any person even in other fields, Pittsford was motivated to found *Lesbians Who Tech* in 2014. The founder is currently working on growing the organization to the international level, and working toward a goal of a 50/50 percent split among women/men and adequate representation of people of color at the LGBTQ communities. As a result, there is an ongoing conversation between the chairman and CEO of Salesforce, Marc Benioff and Kara Swisher from *Lesbians Who Tech* about diversity in technology. *Lesbians Who Tech* issued their first award to former Chief Technology Officer Megan Smith for her relentless work for the rights of minorities and their inclusion in the industry. The activity and advocacy for lesbians in this particular case is leading to some positive results and to the creation of a welcoming environment for this kind of minority. The activity is congruent with Shevinsky's attempt to provide a solution to the hostile treatment of women and minorities in technology.

The next theme of racial exclusion features minority authors who are exposed to double discrimination—both gender and racial. They realize that they are token employees and are compelled to either succumb to the culture, or adjust while suppressing their real identities. Erica Joy, a senior engineering manager and a frequent writer for *Medium*, is outspoken about the psychological damage caused by her token status on her wellbeing throughout her career as a black female professional. In her essay, "The Other Side of Diversity," Joy argues on behalf of the discriminated minority that well intended diversity policies have detrimental effects on the token employees (Shevinsky 153-154). At times the only black person, and the only black woman on the entire floor, Joy was always a minority and made enormous efforts to fit in. In her own words, "I laughed at their terribly racist and sexist jokes, I co-opted their negative attitudes, I began to dress as they did" (155). In the course of thirteen years, Joy encountered constant stress caused by loneliness, alienation, and isolation that led to the need for psychiatric counseling and recovery. She changed multiple locations, from Atlanta, to NYC, to the Bay Area, in an attempt to find an environment that wasn't harmful to her social existence, and sometimes she was sent to different workplaces as a solution to her reporting discrimination on the job. Joy's story is congruent with the US Equal Employment Opportunity Committee report showing that over time more than 50 percent of women in technology are going to leave their jobs due to inhospitable work cultures, isolation, women's lack of advancement, and so on (2014). Joy's bravery and persistence along with her decision to speak out are helping other outsiders in technology because she sends them a message that they are not alone. Furthermore, Joy's writings reveal an enormous amount of emotional work that racism and sexism impose on her and all minority members. The harassment Joy encountered is not only pathological, but illegal, including jokes that her boyfriend and parents abuse her, and false assumptions that she is a single mother (Shevinsky 156). Joy's efforts to drink beer (which she didn't like) in order to be accepted as "normal" and fit in were also harmful to her (158). Joy's conclusion expressed in her last sentence is simple and profound, "My industry needs to change to make everyone feel included and accepted" (163). Joy's account of isolation, her hostile environment, and abusive interaction explains the scarce number of people of color in technology. At the time of Joy's essay, chief technology officer Megan Smith reported only two percent Black employees in high technology institutions such as Google, Facebook, and Apple (Kang). There are no available statistics for women of color in technology; however, mathematically speaking, if we consider the total of all women in tech at twenty percent, the number of women of color becomes almost non-existent at below one percent.

Entrepreneur and software engineer Katy Levinson explains in the chapter, "Sexism in Tech," a phenomenon called "avoidance" that exists as an effective silencing method in technology. In Levinson's words, "The culture of avoidance is very prevalent in tech. In the last three years, I was asked not to use the words 'sexism' or 'racism' when speaking on a diversity panel because it might make the audience uncomfortable" (Shevinsky 55-56). The method of silencing and obscuring the exposure of sexism and racism with ambiguous language is in fact supporting the bias. If the critic cannot identify the problem, it makes it harder, if not impossible, to solve it. Needless to say, the person making this request is an investor with significant financial stake at the institution Levinson works for. Again, the principle of accommodating the financially powerful and already dominating white males is perpetuating the problem of sexism. However, as shown by Levinson, the rampant sexism encourages further abuse in the form of sexual harassment, which was exposed recently for its epidemic occurrence. According to Levinson, the most dangerous consequence to women/men victims of sexual harassment who dare to complain, is being stigmatized as troublemakers, and therefore, risking their careers (56). Levinson compares the person who speaks out about sexual harassment to whistleblowers in other fields, "That shouldn't be too foreign of a concept: people we call whistleblowers, who outed the wrongs of government or industry, certainly aren't doing it for personal gain. In this way, sexual harassment whistleblowing is the same as any other kind of whistleblowing" (49). Defending an employee against sexual harassment in a safe way is not an option; therefore, it ensures further perpetuating of the problem. This notion is confirmed by recent *CNN Tech* reports in 2017. In a series of interviews conducted by journalist Laurie Segall, female employees reveal systemic sexual harassment in technology in a video publication titled "Money, Power, and Sexual Harassment" (O'Brien and Segall). The many women participating in the interviews explain the lack of financial and executive power of the victims, and the risk of publicizing the abuse. According to one of the interviewees, "When you talk about sexual harassment, it's like dropping a nuclear bomb on your career" (O'Brien and Segall). Most of the cases demonstrate abuse of power by the offenders, because the consequences for the victims are punitive—cutting off funds, firing, or labeling them as "difficult" (O'Brien and Segall).

In conclusion, the burden of unpaid or underpaid work in the digital industry carried by women and minorities is imposed on them by the patriarchal elites controlling new media. Because of their constant rejection, women and minorities are compelled to accept lower-paying jobs, or perform unpaid tasks hoping to improve their positions in technology. Moreover, these particularly marginalized groups are economically dependent on the wealthy minority who owns the digital networks and therefore is in a position to dictate policies of discrimination. Furthermore, although new media provide minorities and women with access to social forums, they implicitly promote the interest of their owners, exclusively white, wealthy and male, and overtly defend the corporations that generate profit through exploitation of marginalized, financially insecure women and minorities.

## The Professional Social Network: LinkedIn and the Dual Role of New Media

A specific example of the phenomenon of technology lagging behind other industries is the professional network LinkedIn, which I am using for the second case study in this chapter. I chose LinkedIn, because it represents the most successful and powerful business professionals, especially in the digital market, such as Bill Gates, Amanda Gates, Elon Musk, Jeff Bezos, Mark Zuckerberg, and so on. However, despite the fact that the network is open for everyone to join, LinkedIn is an organization with tendencies to treat women and minorities as inferior as I will demonstrate in the case study. My research is based on four years of studying the patterns, policies and rules of the site, its social groups and discussions, from 2014 to 2018, as well as my active membership for roughly the same time. Professional sites such as LinkedIn exemplify perfectly well Standing's theory about the feminization of labor. With only 21 percent female employees, 1 percent Blacks, and 3 percent Hispanic, LinkedIn, which is owned by Microsoft, epitomizes the standard policy of exclusion of women and minorities (2017 LinkedIn WDR).

Some important statistics about LinkedIn are necessary to illustrate the functions of the site and the demographics of its members. As of April 2017, LinkedIn has 500 million users and is considered the largest professional network in the world. According to *BI Intelligence* survey, LinkedIn is the most trusted digital social media outlet with 48 percent participants considering it credible in comparison with 24 percent giving credibility to Facebook, 19 percent to Twitter, and 4 percent to You Tube (*BI Intel*). Since LinkedIn was bought by Microsoft as of June 2016, and generated 960 million in revenue in 2016, it is now part of one of the largest corporations in the world (*BI Intel*). This purchasing transaction is consistent with the neoliberal policy of concentration of capital, globalization, and corporate lobbying. For example, in five years, between 2012 and 2017, Microsoft spent anywhere between 8 and 10 million each year for lobbying as reported by Center for Responsive Politics (*Open Secrets*). According to the same source, the closest lobbyists in technology are Amazon and Facebook, who spent slightly under $7 million each in 2017. This orientation towards big business, huge profit, and corporate mentality affects inequality and exploitation by widening class, racial, and gender gaps. Most affected by the resulting social stratification are women and minorities, as demonstrated by the demographics of the network's employees. Further research on LinkedIn's users' demographics shows that of all users 56 percent are male, 44 percent are female (Duggan et al.). More importantly, 44 percent earn more than $75,000 a year, and only 15 percent earn below $30,000 a year (Duggan et al.). In relation to age, 13 percent are millennials, and 51 percent, or more than half of all members, are over 50 years old. Therefore, from the Pew Research results could be concluded that the predominant users of LinkedIn are older, wealthy men. Not surprisingly, the network is more concerned with the unhinged pursuit of profit than with the quest for egalitarian society, or safe environment—topics that are not seen often on the newsfeed of the site. This case study examines the general sentiment towards social justice by focusing on five articles on gender equality, four of which are written by female authors. The articles are chosen based on their topics, popularity, and response from the audience, which is analyzed in detail later in this chapter.

All activities performed on LinkedIn qualify for free labor. From the countless hours of reading and writing articles on LinkedIn to responding to comments to participating in discussions to supporting or refuting different opinions, these various activities yield an intangible reward expressed symbolically in likes and shares, popularity and moral satisfaction. Based on the publications and activities of several members examined in this chapter, it appears that they are invested in time and free digital labor to various degrees. The forfeiting of the financial reward for hard intellectual labor has many underlying reasons. For a professional network such as LinkedIn, it is an investment in future employment. In addition, for LinkedIn and other social networks such as Facebook, Twitter, and Instagram, participation is propelled by anxiety—a prevalent symptom of the current generation. Journalist Jia Tolentino offers her colleague Harris's interpretation of the symptom, which is a result of the precarious status of the majority of the generation. Tolentino explains that according to Harris, "Anxiety, Harris argues, isn't just an unfortunate by-product of an era when wages are low and job security is scarce. It's useful: a constant state of adrenalized agitation can make it hard to stop working and encourage you to think of other aspects of your life—health, leisure, online interaction—as work. Social media provides both an immediate release for that anxiety and a replenishment of it, so that users keep coming back" (Tolentino). Because job insecurity and online threats affect more women and minorities, a female or minority active member spends exponentially more time than the average 17 minutes monthly for users (Aslam). Scrutinizing the market for jobs, asking for endorsements and endorsing connections, and applying for positions is a frequent routine that could consume several hours a day. Although these activities are not necessarily linked to gender, they are, nevertheless, disproportionally more time consuming for women and minorities given their significantly poorer chances of employment. Lower chances of being hired require an increased amount of applicants' activities leading to jobs, which results in an increased time spent in free labor on the Internet. Furthermore, anxiety associated with financial and job insecurity that is referred to as good for the economy by the ruling class, is finding its relief in the social networks. The influence of social networks on the public is designed not only to secure their return through perpetuating their anxiety, but to prepare them for their precarious professional and economic status, which is becoming the norm in modern economy.

For women and minorities, anxiety is amplified by personal attacks that are misogynist, racist, and homophobic, among others. As discussed previously, the threats and violence against women and minorities are real, with statistics showing that chances to be raped for women are one in five, compared to one in seventy-one for men (Chemaly). Moreover, technology is used to inflict fear and terror. For example, Erica Olsen, deputy director of a program created by National Network to End Domestic Violence, shares with the press: "In a 2012 survey, 89 percent of local domestic violence programs reported that victims were experiencing intimidation and threats by abusers via technology, including through cell phones, texts, and email" (Chemaly). These statistics explain the higher level of anxiety that women experience on social networks in comparison with men. The overt sexism, which dominates the digital world, is keenly reflected by journalist and activist Laurie Penny: "Although the technology is new, the language of shame and sin around women's use of the Internet is very, very old… Don't go into those new, exciting worlds: wait for the men to get there first and make it safe for you, and if that doesn't happen, stay home and read a book" (Penny 164). Since the inception of the Internet, female anxiety could be explained with the statistics showing higher probability of assault on women than men; moreover, scare tactics often are used as a tool for silencing women both online and offline.

Curiously, anxiety is described by Standing in a specifically gendered allegory in the image of a "bag lady" as opposed to "modest dignity" (Standing 23). According to Standing, "The precariat lives with anxiety—chronic insecurity associated not only with teetering on the edge, knowing that one mistake or one piece of bad luck could tip the balance between modest dignity and being a bag lady, but also with a fear of losing what they possess even while feeling cheated by not having more" (23). Standing explains further the phenomenon called "bag lady syndrome" with the results from a survey conducted by a life insurance company in 2006, showing that 90 percent of American women felt financially insecure, and close to half of them had "tremendous fear of becoming a bag lady" (73). Thus the majority of women are compelled to live lives of anxiety even if they never join the ranks of the precariat. The high number of women showing anxiety and fear for their future is an indication of their precarious social and economic status.

As journalist Harris emphasizes, anxiety is both released and replenished by social networks in order to assure the members' perpetual return to the sites. LinkedIn, which is considered the largest and most prestigious network, is mandatory for finding digital jobs. Sunny Allen, one of the authors in Shevinsky's anthology, describes LinkedIn as a necessary prerequisite to enter the race in Silicon Valley, especially for women and minorities. Allen presents Silicon Valley as an upward race toward a mountain; however, there are strict rules for participation that involve networking "and having great recommendations on [the applicant's] LinkedIn profile" (Shevinsky 35). To elaborate on Allen's brief reference, LinkedIn requires plenty more. In addition to the regular work experience and education, there are skills listed in members' profiles that require endorsement by connections. To be taken seriously, a professional member should have 99+ endorsements on up to 50 skills. Furthermore, the member is allowed to join any of the 1.5 million LinkedIn groups, some of which are professional and require background checks. For example, an Ivy League alumni group needs proof that the member attended one of the eight Ivy League universities, and some groups require publications or other activities. The group membership presents possibilities for posting materials and discussions. After reaching a certain level of activity, the member is allowed to publish articles on LinkedIn. If the articles generate massive response, the LinkedIn member becomes an Influencer—a title that requires multiple thousands of reads. A full profile titled "All Star" requires fulfilling the above listed requirements and meeting more, which include volunteer experience, publications, languages, honors and awards, membership in professional organizations, certifications, patents, test scores, projects, interests, and recommendations—given as well as received. Furthermore, the site is keeping a score of its members' profile views, reads of their posts, publications of articles, search appearance, and all other activities. Every comment, every like, every mentioning of a member's name is recorded and the member is notified. In addition, there are online sessions, classes and seminars that are offered to active members, most of them for purchase. Regarding these particulars on the site, there are no indications of differences among gender, race or other demographics that could affect the stage or quality of individual's profile. However, there are specifics in members' profiles such as names, geographical locations, photographs, and so on that could be used to identify people's ethnicities, gender and race.

From the very limited choice of articles with feminist ideas published on LinkedIn, I am using several pieces that have appeared in the last four years. I am analyzing in detail the first three of the articles written by Influencers and comparing them to the last two written by unknown authors. For example, some of the most popular articles on LinkedIn that promote gender equality are Gerald Karsenti's "It's Time For Women" from November 2016, Ann Crady Weiss's "Why Paid Maternity Leave Is the Most Important Issue" from May 2016, and Sallie Krawchek's article "A Letter to Young Women, A Year Into the Trump-nado" from December 2017. I will compare them to two controversial articles on the same topic, Miki Ding's "Ayesha Curry Doesn't Need to Stop Tweeting—You Are Sexist" from June 2016, and my own article, "The Double Bind Paradox: Why Women Cannot Have It All" from July 2014. Interestingly, such articles provoke mixed reactions varying from intense polemics containing both opposition and support, to elaborate comments to numerous likes and shares. Although the support is encouraging and sometimes overwhelming, the opposition could be punitive or derisive. Nevertheless, there are different reactions to these articles depending on the authors' class, race and gender. The first three articles are by prominent authors, Gerald Karsenti, Ann Crady Weiss, and Sallie Krawchek, who are high-status professionals with great numbers of publications and significant enough to acquire profiles on Wikipedia. The popularity of the authors is proportional to their visibility, and a profile featured on an established media outlet automatically attracts more views, sometimes by virtue of its well-known name or brand. I chose these particular articles based on their feminist topics and the popularity of their authors. For example, the first one by Gerald Karsenti generated more than 6,400 likes; the second article by Ann Crady Weiss—more than 3,200 likes; and the third article by Sallie Krawchek accumulated more than 1,500 likes. The first and the third authors are Influencers at LinkedIn, while the second author is a successful entrepreneur and a star from a TV reality show *Shark Tank* with 1,830 followers on LinkedIn. All of the examined authors generated large numbers of views, as well as initiated vigorous discussions.

Curiously, the member with the largest number of followers and author of the first article, "It's Time for Women," is male and foreign, Gerald Karsenti from France. Karsenti is Managing Director at Oracle, and affiliated Professor at business school HEC in Paris with 86,413 followers. Karsenti is a prominent writer with 27 articles published on LinkedIn. The examined article by Karsenti is widely supported with 1,250 shares and 215 comments (Karsenti). The article is an excerpt from Karsenti's book, *Leaders of the Third Kind.* According to Karsenti, "Today's world has been designed by men for men. Taking into account women's issues has scarcely been touched on. Every year, men make a few concessions as a token of goodwill, but without giving in on the most important: power. They let women organize their dissatisfaction—in the form of discussions and conferences—and then throw them a few crumbs. In other words, they play for time. In reality, there is an abyss between the words and the actions" (Karsenti). The author describes the current situation with candor and accuracy that are impressive. He emphasizes correctly the tokenism and the artificial gestures made routinely without substantial changes.

Interestingly, from the 215 comments, only 39 are negative and opposing the idea of gender equality, or 18 percent. Among the remaining 176 comments, the majority is positive and supportive—162, or 75 percent; only 14 are neutral, or 7 percent. It could be speculated that Karsenti is an Influencer on LinkedIn, a figure of authority and high professional position; therefore, he gets more support. Among the negative responses, the strongest is a long entry lecturing Karsenti about the US and its lack of gender discrimination. According to the commentator, "Americans are being told that they are racist, sexist, misogynistic, and worse—that those presenting these characteristics are doing so 'unconsciously.' Women are being told that that [sic] cannot achieve or attain because of sexism. Men of certain pigmentation are being told that they cannot empathize because they are privileged" (Karsenti). It continues with a few more paragraphs maintaining that Judeo-Christian values should be credited with dismantling slavery, inequalities and other social issues. Finally, the commentator is advising Karsenti on security for women in his native country, France: "Gerald, You should focus your energy on making France a safer place for women to exist. Your country still has a fighting chance, but that window is rapidly closing. America? We've got this" (Karsenti). The commentator claimed falsely (among other claims) that women are safe in America, which contradicts directly the statistics issued by the American Medical Association about domestic violence causing more female deaths than all other causes combined (Solnit 128). Similarly, there is one comment suggesting that Karsenti is pandering to potential female buyers of his book. Most commonly, the opposing comments maintained that there is no gender problem, because the stratification is a result of meritocracy. For example, there are a couple of personal challenges to the author, asking him to reveal his own demographics of his brunch of Oracle in France, and a suggestion by another commentator that Karsenti should "Lead the way. Give your job to a woman. Walk your talk" (Karsenti). However, the tone is respectful and no personal offensive remarks are made. Among the positive comments, many suggest that it has been time for women for the last century, or throughout history, and the article is relevant. Others are giving examples of their own companies that do not discriminate against women and minorities, praising Karsenti and appealing to more men to join the movement for equality. Overall, the article is widely supported and generates positive comments. For example, some of the supporting comments read: "Excellent we just have to believe that WE CAN!!" "Great post!" "Indeed, 'Women have qualities that men do not have and vice versa. The two sexes are perfectly complimentary.'" "Thanks for the thought," and so on (Karsenti). Therefore, the response is positive in general, with a few mildly critical comments.

The second author, Anna Crady Weiss, is a former Yahoo executive, and currently CEO and founder of Hatch Baby, a smart parenting device firm in San Francisco. Her article, "Why Maternity Leave Is the Most Important Issue," published on May 9, 2016, is popular on LinkedIn as it accumulated 3,275 likes, 387 shares and 141 comments (Weiss). The first paragraph of the article starts with a blunt demand of the audience: "Stop penalizing new parents. Stop making them feel guilty for not being back at work in a matter of weeks. Stop adding to the most stressful time in their lives by adding to their financial burden. . . . I've seen thousands of parents go through the same struggle. It's time to make a change" (Weiss). Weiss confronts the problem directly and demands changes in the system. Furthermore, she makes a compelling argument in favor of the idea citing the results of California's passing of the first national comprehensive paid family leave in 2002. According to a survey conducted in 2009, including more than 250 businesses and 500 individuals, nearly 90 percent of them report that the law had either positive or neutral effect on productivity, profitability, turnover and morale (Appelbaum and Milkman). The argument is made based on practice, not rhetoric, therefore, is more persuasive than theoretical speculations. Weiss gives examples and statistics from the experience of real companies and their employees, instead of just analyzing hypothetical situations. Arguably for that reason, the article accumulated more than three thousand likes, almost four hundred shares and nearly half of all comments support the idea of paid maternity leave.

The article leads to some intriguing results. Of the 141 comments, 69 are positive, 46 are negative and 26 are neutral. The dissonance between the "likes" and the verbal support deserves some exploration. Since the article is in support of the idea of paid maternity leave, 69 of the commentators are in favor of the idea, or 49 percent. From the remaining comments, the negative are 33 percent and the neutral commentators are 18 percent. Interestingly, 14 of the 46 negative responses belonged to one person, which lowers the numbers of opposition to 24 percent. Regardless of the slightly fewer than fifty percent positive comments, the over 3,000 people who liked the article indicate an overwhelming support. In analyzing the comments, there are certain patterns and demographics that could be useful for this analysis. For example, while the negative comments are exclusively from US readers, many of the positive comments came from foreign members such as the UK, Canada, Austria, Spain, France, and Australia, among others. For example, a French reader noted that: "In France, we also pay for unemployed lads unlikely to find a real job. Why wouldn't we pay also for those who are doing something as useful as raising kids?" (Weiss). Similarly, a British commentator stated: "I can't believe this is even still a debate in 2016. In the UK this is so normalised now that there's no question as to whether people should get a certain amount of time off as paid leave" (Weiss). Likewise, Weiss' article cites the positive results of implementing paid maternity leave in California. Inversely, the most repeated argument against paid maternal leave is that it is an entitlement, a personal choice and society should not have to pay for it. For example, a reader commented, "since you feel so entitled to this sort of 'benefit,' maybe you'd be willing to work an extra eight hours a day for free so the proceeds could be used to make restitution to all those who came before you and managed to get by without such 'entitlements'" (Weiss). Other arguments include the concern that small companies cannot afford it, and that it is only applicable to small countries with homogenous populations unlike the US. For example, one commentator opined: "Maybe it depends with what type of company it is. Some small companies just cannot afford that. But I like what you are pointing out there. There should be other ways." Another noted, "Please, make sure that the financial burden of paid maternity leave is state-financed" (Weiss). Curiously, the person actively opposing paid maternity leave who entered 14 comments, is a male LinkedIn member with a title MS, MBA, PMP, Assistant Provost for Research and Director. The opponent takes upon himself to confront nearly every supporter of the article. Here are some of his answers directed to the author or other commentators: "Why should other people pay for someone's choice to have a child?" "This is a matter for the free market to decide;" "No, government does not need to be your nanny. Stop depending on government to solve all your problems;" "It's not deserved. You are not entitled to have others subsidize your lifestyle choices. Nothing but a burden in that case. Regardless, YOUR child, YOUR problem. Quit reaching into my wallet expecting a handout to subsidize YOUR choices" (Weiss). It is interesting to note that one of the supporters of paid maternity leave addressed the opponent and expressed her surprise that a person with a title MBA should make political/moral remarks instead of arguing from economic/business point of view (Weiss). Another commentator expressed her hesitation to support the issue, because she was actively looking for a job, and was afraid that a supportive opinion of maternity leave would affect negatively her search for employment (Weiss). The fear of expressing one's opinion because of the person's vulnerability is very common on the site and supports my idea that reprimanding persons or groups who do not yield economic or executive power is a sign of class discrimination. Upon examining the titles of the members who opposed paid maternity leave, it could be predicted that they wouldn't hire supporters of paid leave for fear of their future demands for benefits, or even for being outspoken on the subject. Thus the result of this imbalance of power is a censorship imposed by the economic structure, and even self-censorship born of necessity to be marketable. Furthermore, although there were male supporters of the paid maternity leave, the opposition consisted predominately of men with power such as the member with a title MS, MBA and PMP, who participated with multiple comments, among other men. One reader noticed this demographic division and commented: "It's sad to see that a majority of the negative comments are coming from males. This is why our stance on paid maternity leave is so far behind other countries, because our patriarchal society cant think past the profit margin and begin to think of the benefits to society as a whole" (Weiss). Given that the media purport the idea that the population opposes any federal subsidies for healthcare, the social response to paid maternity leave debunks this false premise. However, articles such as Ann C. Weiss' are rare on LinkedIn because of the demographics of the members of LinkedIn, showing predominately wealthy older businessmen, and fewer women or young people who are concerned with parenthood. Even for members with interests in equality, gender, and social justice, the newsfeed on LinkedIn, supposedly personally tailored based on activity, contains predominately information about making money, acquiring leadership positions, influencing people for profit, and so on.

The third analyzed author is Sallie Krawchek, a former CEO of Bank of America, currently a co-founder of a startup company, Elevest, and an Influencer at LinkedIn with over two million followers. She elaborates on the extreme discrimination of women and minorities in her article, "A Letter to Young Women, A Year Into the Trump-nado," published on December 12, 2017 (Krawchek). The author has 161 articles published on LinkedIn, and writes for *Huffington Post* and *Reuters*. As a continuation of her previous advice to young women, Krawchek warns against the brainwashing propaganda of the media, "A point in fact: we've been under such a spell that we've actually been calling industries with 85% - 95% men 'meritocracies' with straight faces. They would be more accurately labeled 'man-tocracies' (Krawchek). As a corporation, LinkedIn is no different than Google, Facebook and Twitter, which have similar ratio of employees: all three have 1 to 2 percent Blacks, 3 percent Latinos, and women are 10 to 20 percent (US EEOC 2017). It is important to emphasize that we as a society have accepted the self-promoting deception of meritocracy advertised by the paid agents of the white male plutocracy. Ironically, one of the first responses to Krawchek's article is a male member's slogan, "Trump 2020." On the positive side, there was not much opposition on the first day of its publication with 49 comments. The next day, with 73 comments, criticism expanded to, "You know what? Enough already. The pile-on of men in America continues. I really wish we could have an intelligent discussion about such a serious topic without the usual man-hating that accompanies it. The victimization syndrome has become incredibly normalized and all of the 'it's all their fault' dismisses the real conversation we should be having. And BTW, if you think the Obama's didn't know what Weinstein was all about then I have a bridge I can sell you" (Krawchek). This comment summarizes successfully the chauvinistic mantra that encompasses clichés such as "victimization syndrome" "man-hating," and so on. Using purposely these phrases, the defenders of sexist policies imply that there is no such thing as female victims, and the entire campaign for human rights is simply a men-hating exercise. Such rhetoric undermines the egalitarian efforts of advocates for human rights who publish on LinkedIn and portrays them as unreasonable and obstructing "the real conversation" we are supposed to have. By real conversation, the commentator supposedly means that harassment and sexism should be regarded as normal, while resisting them—defined as abnormal; thus, his complaint about "incredibly normalized" accusations of sexism and harassment. This appears to be the lament of this commentator as well as his irritation about the annoying changes that disrupt the patriarchal balance of power. Moreover, regardless of the opposition described above, Krawchek's article received 1,545 likes, 211 shares, and 110 comments, thus proving the popularity of this kind of gender rights promotion. Considering that there are 100 thousand articles published weekly on LinkedIn, the response is also contingent on the popularity of the author to a certain degree (Smith). Among the total of 110 comments, a surprisingly low number are negative, only 9, and three are by the same commentator. One of his remarks contains a complaint about a coworker—a female electrician, who couldn't climb a ladder or bend a wire, but was kept on the job as a woman. His second entry is a demand that women be lovers, not haters, declaring that he sees the article as hateful and the commentators as a group of haters. As noted earlier, the first one was "Trump 2020." Another negative comment is by a woman who criticizes the female employees for not dressing professionally, implying that they are responsible for the lack of respect toward women in the work place. Regarding the scarce negative comments, I can speculate that because the title of the article contains the name Trump, perhaps it might be considered bait and therefore, avoided by readers who usually oppose gender equality. In any event, the number of oppositional responses is extraordinarily low, only bellow one percent, thus the article could be considered largely supported. However, for a LinkedIn author with over two million followers, 1,545 likes is a proportionally low number, also below one percent. Moreover, the number of likes is only half of the number of likes for the next author, Miki Ding, who is a student at Berkeley, and not necessarily a prominent figure.

Nevertheless, unlike the comments for the next two articles, the tone in the first three publications is respectful and there are no personal attacks. Similarly to the example of self-censorship in a power structure, which grants leadership positions to wealthy white males, the discrimination of women and minorities is evident in the statistics from the 2017's *LinkedIn Workplace Diversity Report.* According to the report, only 1 percent of the employees are black, 4 percent Latino, and 21 percent are female (LinkedIn). Moreover, 83 percent of all professionals in the world are members of the site, and as reported by *Foundation,* LinkedIn is the most used network by the CEOs in the *Forbes* 500 companies (Gallant). Consequently, this ratio in favor of wealthy white male professionals perpetuates the exploitation of women and pushes them further in the margins. The misbalance also explains the great degree of intolerance and condescending attitude towards active female LinkedIn authors that are either minorities, or are not in positions of power.

As a result, despite the supportive comments, the reaction to published articles promoting egalitarian society is frequently opposition. Inevitably, there are some aggressive commentators attacking the authors or commentators who support such efforts. Sometimes, they write derogatory and condescending remarks. Alerted by a LinkedIn member, Ann Marie Lynch, who posted a comment complaining that there are always the same men who oppose feminist writings, I conducted brief research and went three years back to my feminist article from 2014, "The Double Bind Paradox: Why Women Cannot Have It All." Surprisingly, I found three commentators with titles MBA, CPA, and CEO who opposed my article back in 2014, and were opposing feminist ideas three years later. One of them opposed Ann C. Weiss' article about maternity leave in 2016, and two confronted the author of the next examined article from 2016, Miki Ding, with multiple comments in response to her article "Ayesha Curry Doesn't Need to Stop Tweeting—You Are Sexist" (Ding). Miki Ding is a student at the University of California, Berkeley, specializing in Psychology and Public Policy with 1,784 followers. In her piece, Ding makes a point that even though she disagrees with Curry, the author is defending Curry's right to express her opinion on Twitter and not to be silenced because of her gender. I would like to compare the reaction to the next two articles with the response to the three articles discussed previously. Besides being controversial in her analyzing a black woman's public commentaries on Twitter, Miki Ding is also a minority (Asian American). Regardless, the author accumulates wide public support and her article generated 3,100 likes in 2017, more than double the number of likes for the third article written by an Influencer, Krawchek. The second article, "The Double Bind Paradox" from 2014, generated more than 10,500 reads, 120 comments, and over 200 likes; both articles initiated vigorous polemics. Ding's article of 2016 prompted 487 comments, and 220 shares. A close analysis of the comments shows that 96 are author's responses to commentators, and the remaining 391 comments comprise 268 positive, 99 negative and 24 neutral, or 68 percent positive versus 25 percent negative. Similarly, the "Double Bind Paradox" shows 62 percent positive comments versus 26 percent negative, drawn from 75 positive, 31 negative and 14 neutral (Hammond). However, I believe that the negative comments are more unrestricted and demeaning when the authors are less known or less powerful such as a student at Berkeley or a graduate student at the University of Utah. Moreover, the language becomes bolder and more patronizing when the authors are female, and escalates when they are minorities. For example, among the 99 negative comments to Ding's article, there are pure insults such as "Trash," "Garbage," "Shut up," and "B.S." (Ding). Moreover, the first commentator who is on record since 2014 replying to feminist material, responded similarly to Ding's article: "Let's be honest here. The entire point of this 'article' was to allow the author to shout 'YOU SEXISTS!' as she has been indoctrinated to do by the Feminist-Industrial-Victimhood-Complex. There is nothing else to it" (Ding). Obviously, the member does not read such articles, he just reacts to any post that includes trigger words such as "women," "feminism," "gender equality," and so on; then attacks the author or her supporters with clichés. This is evident in the commentator's repeated phrase in capital letters, copied and pasted, which does not address anything in the article other than its subject. "The entire point of the article was to let her shout 'YOU SEXISTS!' That's it and she did it in the title! Wheeeeee!" (Ding). The next step in such behavior is to attack a supporter; in this case, the commentator writes about a person who favors the article and alerts the audience about specific personal attacks. The opponent assaulted her by name, "Ann Marie Lynch is the face of modern Western feminism. *shudder*" This personal, offensive remark provoked Lynch's, response: "Did anyone notice that the article is about how men demean and harass women online and the men then come to the comments section to wave their magical misogynist tongue at the females who comment here? Are you sick of this ladies? I am, it's the same freaks every time. You can sue them and you can contact their work about their online activity. It is very important that there be ramifications on these men who have a deep need to abuse women. . . . Also notice that the age of the males berating and insulting me are from the age group that is identified as severely misogynistic" (Ding). Eventually in response to this remark, or for other reasons, the commentator deleted his comments in 2018. However, Lynch alerted me about the phenomenon of the same LinkedIn members repeatedly disparaging feminist authors on the site. It prompted me to search back the responses to my feminist writings in 2014. It also possibly prompted the commentator to delete his aggressive remarks or perhaps compelled LinkedIn to take actions. It is also possible that other female authors complained about this individual. Although this person's comments were deleted, some responses to his entries are still there referring to him by name, indicating that he had previously replied to other polemists. The same person wrote in response to Ding's article in 2017, "Feel free to take your 'article' and all its nonsense and put it on your personal blog." To my article from 2014, the same commentator wrote many oppositional comments, but the shortest is, "Don't rely on BS feminist 'data'" in regard to Larry Summers' notorious comment in 2005 claiming that women have inferior aptitude in science and math. The commentator then continued to deny Summers' remark, "I think we both know it's not true;" however, "The radfems then went crazy, twisted his words, and created a jihad which ultimately got him fired" (Hammond). Despite the denial of facts, sometimes the writers feel compelled to address the opposition with more facts and clarifications. Regarding the same article, the second commentator wrote back in 2014, "As soon as I read 'the women earn 77 cents for every dollar men earn' BS, I knew that this was just another in a long line of slanted, nonsense opinion pieces which I am sorry I wasted even a moment in reading. What rubbish" (Hammond). Even in the event of replying only to reasonable arguments while ignoring the mere insults, it always takes considerable amount of time to respond to criticism and to make available more accurate statistics. As of February 2018, the earlier cited negative comments since 2014 by the first LinkedIn commentator have been deleted along with the comments on Miki Ding's and Ann Crady Weiss' articles of 2016. The individual's personal account had been closed as well; however, it took almost four years of such activity before it happened, and the other two commentators are still present on the site. Most important, Lynch, the commentator who complained about such verbal harassment, indicated in 2016 that despite her complaint and reporting the individual's abusive behavior to LinkedIn's management, according to Lynch, "they have done nothing" (Ding).Therefore, Lynch confronted the commentator personally in 2016 in one of her comments, and threatened him with a lawsuit (Ding).

LinkedIn's indifference to such complaints is confirmed by journalist Nicholas Wapshott in his article published in *Newsweek* in August 2017. The article, titled "Hate Speech? Racism? Expletives? LinkedIn Doesn't Care a F***," details LinkedIn management's inefficiency regarding the protection of its members from abuse (Wapshott). After Wapshott published on LinkedIn an article by historian Vanessa Williamson, explaining the background of slavery in Virginia and its connection to modern racism, he received racist profane remarks and attacks addressing his advocacy for the "wrong" race as a "white Briton." According to Wapshott, when he officially complained to LinkedIn's management about the person calling him a "f*king liberal" in addition to racial slurs, the reaction was a series of automated responses leading to nowhere. As a result, the journalist decided to discover what LinkedIn's policy is "about such plainly racist and expletive-ridden members." Wapshott reveals more facts about the unhinged racism on the network, lack of transparency, and inefficiency in restricting personal attacks and even profane language. Wapshott's futile attempts to contact LinkedIn, and the obstacles he met dealing with LinkedIn's communication manager are described in detail in the article published in *Newsweek* (Wapshott). Most important, the journalist discloses that LinkedIn's investigation concluded that the flagged person and his profane racist language are considered "to not be in breach of the LinkedIn's terms of service" (Wapshott). The fact that racist and sexist language are not considered a problem on the site makes most acts of discrimination acceptable and facilitates the abuse of minorities as they are officially without protection on LinkedIn. As a consequence, the discriminated groups are conditioned to lower their expectations and are prepared to accept low-ranked, low-paying jobs as their only option. Furthermore, LinkedIn's manager refused to answer Wapshott's questions regarding the number of complaints they receive regularly and how many employees are in charge of online abusers. Wapshott discovered that the only protection against verbal abuse on LinkedIn is members' signatures when joining the network, and promising not to engage in such activity. Wapshott's conclusion is that unless these policies change, "LinkedIn will be a safe place for those who enjoy posting hate speech, racist language and misogynist threats" (Wapshott). *Newsweek* journalist's experience with LinkedIn expands the scope of written attacks to white males who promote civil rights and publish such material. In addition to this case of inappropriate behavior, the information about the three men who appear throughout the years with offensive comments on various articles promoting gender equality is important for several reasons. The most impactful consequence is that the professional site is allowing and maintaining an abusive environment by being indifferent or un-responding to such conduct. Furthermore, the discrimination is helping conditioning the female and non-white precariat to accept their inferior status in the digital world. Moreover, the opponents of equal rights seem to be more aggressive in their comments toward more vulnerable authors without economic power, such as female students, minorities, members looking for jobs, and so on, with the exception of authors who do not belong to these categories and instead express support for such marginalized groups. Finally, after properly filed complaints from members, namely Lynch and Wapshott, LinkedIn's management refuses to act accordingly.

This is a general illustration of typical activities on a professional site such as LinkedIn displaying reactionary behavior against published material concerning civil rights and promotion of egalitarian society. It is imperative to note that the tone, the language, and the attitude escalate if the person is female, minority, or wields no executive or financial power. Since LinkedIn is a professional site, the bias against the financially weaker women and minorities affects them negatively in their negotiations for jobs and preconditions them to believe that they have no alternative to being precariat. Sometimes, as in the case of the white male British journalist, the attacks are not restricted to women and minorities, but include their defenders of any race or gender. This is just an example of the daily attacks that authors who are in favor of equal rights for women and minorities are compelled to endure. I have to emphasize that this site is relatively civil, because most of its members are there to look for jobs, to recruit employees, or to advance specialized knowledge in different fields such as business, history, finances, science, philosophy, arts, music, film, and so on. In this way, it is different from solely social networks, blogs, and entertainment sites. However, on LinkedIn, the opponents of equal rights are usually professionals, with titles such as MBA, CPA, CEO, and other positions of financial power as indicated in the analyses of the articles. Given the demographics of LinkedIn, which show that the majority of the members are older, male, and wealthy, the predominant discourse on the site is in favor of male plutocracy and against equal rights. Consequently, members who do not fall in this category but dare to defend women and minorities are subjected to verbal attacks, and treated disrespectfully by some. More importantly, LinkedIn shows a high degree of tolerance to hate speech, which is unacceptable for any professional site.

The activities described above qualify for free digital labor as it takes time and efforts to maintain an active status on the social network. Moreover, authors with a relatively high reciprocity have to engage in answering questions, responding to challenges, or acknowledging the comments on their posts. Some authors respond or thank personally to every commentator, as is the case with Ding. This requires a significant amount of time performing unpaid work. In the process, new media facilitate both voices for equal rights and their opposition. When studying such polemics, it becomes evident that female and minority voices are regarded differently and are disproportionally subjected to marginalization. The examples of Ayesha Curry speaking on social media and being swarmed with derogatory attacks on Twitter, Ding's article in her defense and the following condescending remarks, as well as the British journalist who condemns racism and is insulted for it, demonstrate LinkedIn's tacit support for racial and gender discrimination. Furthermore, individuals with persistent chauvinistic remarks, usually white powerful men, prove that social websites are actively practicing discrimination. Moreover, LinkedIn management's inability to defend members who are subjected to derogatory remarks and even profanity is indicative of maintaining a bigoted culture. A look at the demographics of LinkedIn employees is enough to find out that according to LinkedIn's 2017 diversity report, Blacks are 1 percent, and Latinos are 3 percent (Durruthy). Moreover, female employees are only one fifth of all workers while poor female LinkedIn members are fewer than high income members. Finally, young members belonging to the millennial generation are only 13 percent. This ratio subtly sets the general tone of exclusion in all discussions, newsfeed, and articles published and circulated on the site. The inefficient response to complaints about racial and gender slurs shows indifference that could be interpreted by LinkedIn members as encouragement of such offensive conduct.

## Conclusion

This chapter investigates the use of free digital labor on the Internet in relation to gender, race, class, and sexual orientation among other aspects of intersectional feminism. Based on Guy Standing's identification of an emerging new class, the precariat, my focus is on the most vulnerable subgroups of this new social group, women and minorities. I build up on scholarly work of authors such as Tiziana Terranova, Maurizio Lazzarato, and Trebor Scholz, among others who explore the digital market and its relation to class and exploitation. Furthermore, I investigate the impact of these relations with specific focus on the female precariat in the field of technology, beyond the work of contemporary feminist authors such as bell hooks, Rebecca Solnit, Dawn Foster, Brook Erin Duffy, Dorothy Sue Cobble, and Linda Gordon, among others. In applying intersectional feminist theories to new media of the 21st century and shedding light on a specific social stratum, the female precariat in the digital market, my intention is to contribute to filling the current gap in scholar analyses regarding this multifaceted underrepresented social group. For this purpose, I analyze two case studies based on individual authors using different media. The first case study exemplifies Shevinsky's anthology *Lean Out*, and the second utilizes a professional social network, LinkedIn. In both cases it could be deduced that as a result of exclusion and discrimination, women and minorities are compelled to perform free labor on the Internet for various reasons. In the first case, women and minorities refuse to lean in and opt to boycott the neoliberal system of exploitation through crowdsourcing and concentrated private ownership of the digital networks. A collection of authors-entrepreneurs share their experience and suggest leaning out of an industry that is exploitive to them. The focus is on the representation of the points of view of marginalized social groups such as women of color, LGBTQ communities, and other minorities in technology. As underlined earlier, in comparison with all other industries, digital companies hire more than eighteen percent fewer women and almost fifty percent fewer minorities (US EEOC 2017). In the second case, LinkedIn, women are spontaneously given digital forums for expression and discriminated against in the same social networks. For instance, in order to acquire jobs, women and minorities are utilizing their access to digital networks to situate themselves against this bias. In addition, these particularly marginalized groups are economically dependent on the wealthy minority who owns the digital networks and therefore, is in a position to dictate policies of discrimination. More specifically, digital companies in general and LinkedIn in particular, maintain a very low percent of women and minorities at high-paying technical positions without being held responsible. In both cases, the research is congruous with the statistics of the US Equal Employment Opportunity Committee, showing significantly lower participation of women and minorities compared with all other private industries in the nation. This ratio leaves women and minorities only with opportunities for underpaid or unpaid work by virtue of their exclusion from the lucrative jobs in the digital industry. The multiple use of media for illustrating different aspects of digital work and female participation in the market in its complicated relation to financial and executive power leads to several additional conclusions. The increased blurring of the borders of paid and unpaid digital work, affecting women and minorities more and resulting in lowering their remuneration is evident in the statistics, interviews, social networks' discussions, and popular literature used in the chapter. In this process, characterized by Andrew Ross as feminization of digital work, new media play a twofold role. On the one hand, digital networks provide minorities and women with access to social forums; on the other, they overtly defend corporative profit accumulated through discrimination and exploitation of the same social groups in technology.

## Works Cited

Adichie, Chimamanda. *Americanah,* New York: Anchor Books, 2014.

Angel Au-Yeung. "The World's Six Richest Women in Tech in 2017." *Forbes* 23 August 2017. Web. 21 Jan. 2018.

Appelbaum, Eileen and Ruth Milkman. "Leaves That Pay: Employer and Worker Experience with Paid Family Leave in California." *Center for Economic and Policy Research.* January 2011. Web. 2 April 2018.

Aslam, Salman. "LinkedIn by the Numbers: Stats, Demographics, and Fun Facts." *Omnicore.* Web. 3 Jan. 2018.

*BI Intelligence's* Digital trust survey, (n=1740), April 2017. http://www.businessinsider.com/the-digital-trust-report-insight-into-user-confidence-in-top-social-platforms-enterprise-2017-5

Chemaly, Soraya. "There Is No Comparing Male and Female Harassment Online." *Time* 9 September 2014. Web. 19 May 2018.

Chomsky, Noam. *Requiem for the American Dream.* New York, Oakland, and London: Seven Stories Press, 2017.

Cobble, Dorothy Sue. *The Sex of Class: Women Transforming American Labor,* Ithaca and London: Cornell UP, 2007.

Cobble, Dorothy Sue, Linda Gordon, and Henry Astrid. *Feminism Unfinished: A Short, Surprising History of American Women's Movements.* New York and London: Liveright, 2014.

CWA Press Release, "Big Gains for Striking Workers in New Agreement." 29 May 2016. Web. 12 Sept. 2017.

Ding, Miki. "Ayesha Curry Doesn't Need to Stop Tweeting—You Are Sexist." *LinkedIn.* 28 June 2016. https://www.linkedin.com/pulse/ayesha-curry-doesnt-need-stop-tweeting-youre-just-sexist-miki-ding/?deepLinkCommentId=6153966330274922497&anchorTime=1467219908312&trk=hb_ntf_MEGAPHONE_LIKE_TOP_LEVEL_COMMENT

Donnelly, Grace. "Google's 2017 Diversity Report Shows Progress Hiring Women, Little Change for Minority Workers." *Fortune 29* June 2017. Web. 1 Feb. 2018.

Duffy, Brooke Erin. *(Not) Getting Paid to Do What You Love: Gender, Social Media and Aspirational Work.* New Haven and London: Yale UP. 2017.

Durruthy, Rosanna. "Our Commitment to Diversity, Inclusion and Belonging."https://careers.linkedin.com/content/dam/me/careers/diversity-page/workforce-report/2017-LinkedIn-Workforce-Diversity-Report.pdf

*Facebook.* "Managing Bias." Videoclip. https://managingbias.fb.com/

Fancher, Lou. "Shevinsky's 'lean Out' Builds upon Sheryl Sandberg's Message." *The Mercury News* 29 September 2015. Web. 12 Dec. 2017.

Fang, Lee. "The CIA Is Investing in Firms that Mine Your Tweets and Instagram Photos." *The Intercept* 14 April 2016. Web. 3 Oct. 2017.

Foster, Dawn. *Lean Out.* London: Repeater Books, 2015.

Gallant, Josh. "45 Eye-Opening LinkedIn Stats Every B2B Marketer Needs to Know." *Foundation* 28 June 2018. Web. 8 August 2018.

Google Diversity. https://diversity.google/

Greenwald, Glenn. *No Place to Hide.* London: Hamish Hamilton, 2014.

Hammond, Tamara. "The Double Bind Paradox: Why Women Cannot Have it All." *LinkedIn.* 6 July 2014. https://www.linkedin.com/pulse/20140706173807-108446891-the-double-bind-paradox-why-women-cannot-have-it-all/

Hooks, bell. *Where We Stand.* New York and London: Routledge, 2000.

Intern Bridge Report, 2010. http://www.ceri.msu.edu/wp-content/uploads/2010/01/Intern-Bridge-Unpaid-CollegeInternship-Report-FINAL.pdf

Kang, Cecilia. "Obama's Top Tech Adviser Takes Fight for Silicon Valley Diversity to Washington." *The Washington Post,* The Switch, 9 July 2015. Web. 12 Dec. 2017. .https://www.washingtonpost.com/news/the-switch/wp/2015/07/09/obamas-top-tech-adviser-explains-why-silicon-valley-is-so-bad-at-diversity/?utm_term=.9de85ef3245f

Karsenti, Gerald. "It's Time for Women." *LinkedIn.* 22 November 2016. https://www.linkedin.com/pulse/its-time-women-g%C3%A9rald-karsenti/

Krawchek, Sallie. "A Letter to Young Women, A Year into the Trump-nado." *LinkedIn.* 11 December 2017. https://www.linkedin.com/pulse/letter-young-women-year-later-sallie-krawcheck/?trackingId=rzLn9M3pEASe3o2gld6szw%3D%3D

Lazzarato, Maurizio. "Immaterial Labor." *Radical Thought in Italy: A Potential Politics,* 7. Eds. Paolo Virno, and Michael Hardt. Trans. Paul Colilli and Ed Emory. University of Minnesota P, 1996. 133-148.

Losse, Kate. "Sex and the Startup: Men, Women, and Work." *Model View Culture.* 17 March 2014. Web. 2 Dec. 2017.

Louis, Gregory "How Blizzard Increased its number of Interns by 166% in One Year." *LinkedIn.* 13 July 2017. Web. 3 Dec. 2017.

O'Brien, Sarah and Laurie Segall, "Sexual Harassment in Tech: Women Tell Their Stories." *CNN Tech,* 2017. http://money.cnn.com/technology/sexual-harassment-tech/

*Open Secrets Organization* https://www.opensecrets.org/lobby/clientsum.php?id=D000000115

Penny, Laurie. *Unspeakable Things: Sex, Lies, and Revolution.* New York and London: Bloomsbury, 2014.

Duggan, Maeve, et al. "Demographics of Key Social Networking Platforms." Pew Research Center, Internet & Technology. 9 January 2015.http://www.pewinternet.org/2015/01/09/demographics-of-key-social-networking-platforms-2/

Rader, Emilee and Rebecca Gray. "Understanding Users Beliefs about Algorithmic Curation in the Facebook Newsfeed." New York: Association of Computing Machinery, 2015. Web. 13 Nov. 2017.

Rosen, Rebecca J. "Don't Call me the Mother of the Internet." *The Atlantic* 3 March 2014. Web. 5 Aug. 2018.

Ross, Andrew. "In Search of the Lost Paycheck." *Digital Labor: The Internet as Playground and Factory.* Ed. Trebor Scholz. New York and London: Routledge, 2013. 13-32.

Sandberg, Sheryl. *Lean In: Women, Work, and the Will to Lead.* New York: Alfred Knopf, 2013.

Scholz Trevor, ed. *Digital Labor: The Internet As Playground and Factory.* New York and London: Routledge, 2013.

Shevinsky, Elissa. *Lean Out: The Struggle for Gender Equality in Tech and Start-Up Culture.* New York and London: OR Books, 2015. Print.

Smith, Craig "220 Amazing LinkedIn Statistics and Facts." Digital Media Report, December 2017. https://expandedramblings.com/index.php/by-the-numbers-a-few-important-linkedin-stats/

Solnit, Rebecca. *Men Explain Things to Me.* Chicago: Haymarket Books, 2014.

Standing Guy. *The Precariat: The New Dangerous Class.* London: Bloomsbury, 2016 [2011].

*Tech Target,* http://searchnetworking.techtarget.com/definition/protocol

Terranova, Tiziana. "Free Labor: Producing Culture for the Digital Economy." *Social Text* 18: 2 (Summer 2000), 33-58.

Thomas, Rachel. "If You Think Women in Tech Is Just a Pipeline Problem, You Haven't Been Paying Attention." *Medium.* 27 July 2015. https://medium.com/tech-diversity-files/if-you-think-women-in-tech-is-just-a-pipeline-problem-you-haven-t-been-paying-attention-cb7a2073b996#.sbufxt6ft

Tiku, Nitasha. "The Hard Consequences of Google's Soft Power." *Wired.* 1 September 2017. Web. 20 Dec. 2017.

Tolentino, Jia. "Where Millennials Come Form." *The New Yorker.* 4 Decembe 2014. Web. 3 Aug.. 2018.

US Equal Employment Opportunity Committee. "Diversity in High Tech." Report for 2017. Web. 13 Dec. 2017.

________." Executive Summary for 2014. Web. 12 Dec 2017.

Wapshott, Nicholas. "Hate Speech? Racism? Expletives? LinkedIn Doesn't Care a F***." *Newsweek* 26 August 2017. http://www.newsweek.com/hate-speech-racism-expletives-linkedin-doesnt-care-f-655321

Weiss, Anne Crady. "Why Maternity Leave Is the Most Important Issue You Should Think Today." *LinkedIn.* 9 May 2017. https://www.linkedin.com/pulse/why-paid-leave-most-important-issue-you-should-think-today-weiss/

Williams, Maxine. "Facebook Diversity Update: Building a More Diverse, Inclusive Workforce." *Facebook Newsroom.* 2 August 2017. https://newsroom.fb.com/news/2017/08/facebook-diversity-update-building-a-more-diverse-inclusive-workforce/

# Notes

[1] In her essay, Terranova credits the term to Italian autonomists such as Toni Negri from whose *Politics of Subversion* she quotes, as well as Paolo Virno and Michael Hardt (92).

[2] After the conference in 2009, Scholz edited and published a collection of essays under the title *Digital Labor: The Internet as Playground and Factory* in 2013.

[3] Coined by Guy Standing, this neologism is formed by the combination of "precarious" and "proletariat."

[4] In this interview Perlman contends that "The Internet was not invented by any individual. There are lots of people who like to take credit for it, and it drives them crazy when anyone other than them seems to want credit, so it seems best to just stay out of their way."

[5] Tech Target, http://searchnetworking.techtarget.com/definition/protocol Transmission Control Protocol/Internet Protocol. (Protocols are a special set of rules that ends points in a telecommunication connection use when they communicate. Protocols specify interaction between the communicating entities.)

[6] Spanning Tree Protocol: Where two bridges are used to interconnect the same two computer network segments, spanning tree is a protocol that allows the bridges to exchange information so that only one of them will handle a given message that is being sent between two computers within the network. The spanning tree protocol prevents the condition known as a bridge loop.

[7] The women are Judy Faulkner, a founder of a 39-year-old health records software company, and Meg Whitman, known for her decade of serving as a CEO of eBay; with an average wealth at $4.6 billion, significantly below the average of $8.7 billion for the list as a whole, and not even close to the over $100 billion of Amazon's founder Bezos, number one on the list.

[8] *Forbes* magazine features annually a list of 30 creative young stars in 20 industries that are under 30 years old.

[9] Heddleston made this analogy while criticizing Sandberg's message in *Lean In*.

[10] Noam Chomsky reveals in his book, *Requiem for the American Dream*, that Alan Greenspan, chairman of the Federal Reserve at the time, reported to Congress in 1997 that his success in running the economy was due to creating a "greater worker insecurity," which compels workers to accept lower wages in exchange for job security (40).

[11] According to Wikipedia's own site, the criteria for inclusion require the person to be featured in five credible independent sources such as newspapers, magazines, TV, and academic journals.

[12] Season 7, episode 14, Jan 15, 2016.

[13] LinkedIn's policy of news feed: "While we welcome your feedback on recommended content and continue our efforts to optimize your content experience, please note that we generally can't accommodate requests to change the content labels associated with specified content, or to remove specified content based on such labels. Learn more about sending feedback to LinkedIn." https://www.linkedin.com/help/linkedin/answer/72665

# Notes on the Authors

MARGIE BURNS is a professional writer with a Ph.D. in English literature who works as an adjunct at the University of Maryland, Baltimore County. For three years she has chaired the UMBC Adjunct Faculty Advisory Committee, elected by adjuncts. Publications include print and online journalism and refereed articles in *Shakespeare Studies*, *Persuasions: The Jane Austen Journal*, *Academe*, *Chronicle of Higher Education*, *Legal Times*, *National Law Journal*, Salon.com, *South Carolina Historical Magazine*, *Notes & Queries*, and elsewhere. She wrote the non-fiction book *Firearms Regulation in the Bill of Rights: Eighteenth-Century English Language and the U.S. Constitution* (2017). Her interests include Shakespeare, Jane Austen, the First Amendment, the public discourse, Early Modern English literature, and American literature and film. She is currently working on a book about Jane Austen's publishing history.

RACHELANN LOPP COPLAND is a humanities adjunct instructor at SUNY Morrisville and the University Success Advisor for the ONCAMPUS SUNY international student pathway program. Her research interests include instructional best practices, the deconstruction of discourses against the marginalized, the exclusionary notions of genre, and the development of the Western canon as a colonial pursuit of power. She has three young children, Malachi, Selah, and Sonnet, with her husband, Campbell.

TAMARA IONKOVA HAMMOND is currently a PhD candidate in the World Languages and Cultures Department of the University of Utah. She teaches Introduction to the Study of Literature and Culture, which includes various pieces of world literature with emphasis on non-canonical, contemporary dissident authors. Hammond's doctorate thesis isfocused on the digital labor market in the context of class, race, gender and ethnicity among other factors of intersectional feminism, with particular interest inthe dual role of new media evident in the split between the fourth and the fifth estate. Hammond's Master's is in Russian translation from Columbia University, and her Bachelor's is in history from Utah Valley University. She taught world history, both modern and ancient, in Utah Valley University from 2011 to 2013. Hammond has published recently at *The Projector*, a Journal of Film, Media, and Culture in January, 2019, and two lead articles, respectively in *Anamesa*, an interdisciplinary journal issued by New York University Graduate School of Arts, and in *Crescat Scientia*, a journal of history at UVU.

www.ingramcontent.com/pod-product-compliance
Lightning Source LLC
Chambersburg PA
CBHW061941220426
43662CB00012B/1988

* 9 7 8 1 9 8 8 9 6 3 0 7 5 *